Mao's People

Mao's People

Sixteen Portraits of Life in Revolutionary China

B. Michael Frolic

HARVARD UNIVERSITY PRESS
Cambridge, Massachusetts
London, England
1980

Library of Congress Cataloging in Publication Data

Frolic, B   Michael, 1937-
  Mao's people.

   1.   China—Social conditions—1949-1976—Case
studies.   2.   Chinese in Hongkong—Interviews.
I.   Title.
HN737.F76   309.1'51'05   79-23013
ISBN 0-674-54846-9

Designed by Mike Fender

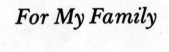
For My Family

Acknowledgments

THIS STUDY owes much to many people and institutions. I am grateful for the financial support and assistance of the Canada Council, the Joint Committee on Contemporary China of the Social Science Research Council, and the University of Toronto-York University Joint Center for East Asian Research. York University gave moral and material support during various stages of the research and writing. I was fortunate that the Universities Service Centre in Hong Kong provided such ideal facilities for conducting my research. The John K. Fairbank Center for East Asian Research at Harvard University generously supplied office space and access to their rich library facilities.

Several individuals contributed in an indispensable fashion to the manuscript, in particular my research assistant Hsu Hung-wen, without whose hard work and knowledge of China this book would never have been written. I was fortunate also to have the able assistance of Yeung Sai-Cheung and Leung Kei-kit in Hong Kong and later of Janet Lum and John Foster. At certain stages, the advice of several scholars was invaluable, in particular Victor C. Falkenheim, William L. Parish, Lucian Pye, and Martin K. Whyte. Special thanks go to Joyce Backman and Barbara Sindriglis for editing and typing. I am especially indebted to Thomas P. Bernstein and Ezra Vogel for their help and encouragement during the writing of the manuscript.

Acknowledgments

*Finally I would like to thank the many people inside and out-
side China with whom I have talked over the past few years. Although it is impossible to write a book that can include everyone's
views and thoughts on the complex nature of life and politics in
contemporary China, I hope they will be satisfied that the stories
and comments presented in this volume offer a reasonable portrait of a changing Chinese nation.*

B. M. F.
CAMBRIDGE, MASSACHUSETTS

*Note: The romanization system used in this book is pinyin, with the exception
of internationally accepted place names (such as Peking, Canton, Amoy). The
exchange rate between Chinese yuan and American dollars is calculated at 3:2.
For those not familiar with Chinese weights, 1 catty equals 1.1 pounds.*

Contents

Contents

Mao's People

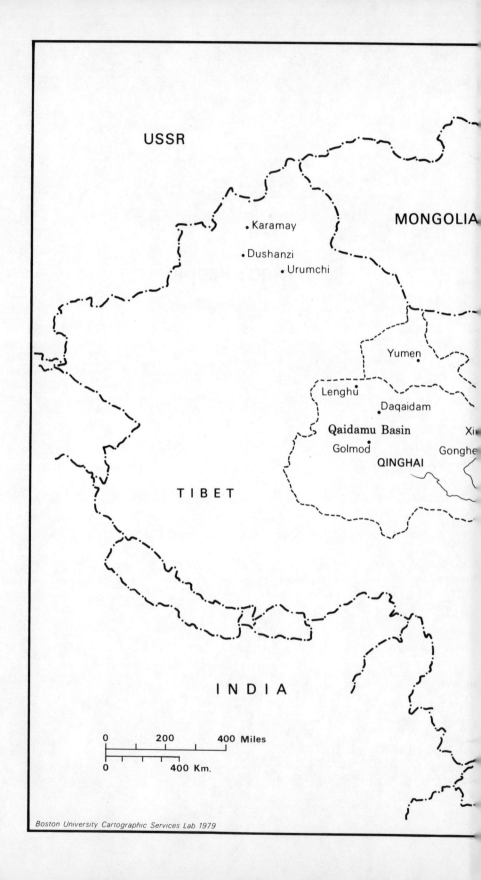

USSR

MONGOLIA

Karamay

Dushanzi

Urumchi

Yumen

Lenghu

Daqaidam

Qaidamu Basin

Xi

Golmod

Gonghe

QINGHAI

TIBET

INDIA

0   200   400 Miles

0   400 Km.

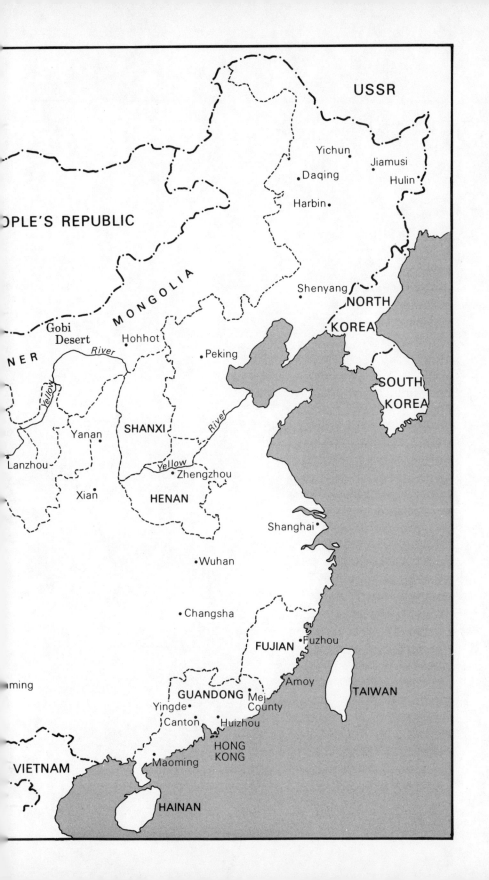

Introduction

FOR SEVERAL YEARS I have tried to "understand China" and the many changes that have occurred there. This search has taken me to China first in 1965 and again in 1971 for short trips. Later, in 1974-75, I served fifteen months in Peking as First Secretary in the Canadian Embassy. In between those visits I spent a year in Hong Kong interviewing people, collecting materials, and organizing my thoughts. Originally I intended to write a monograph on Chinese urban development. Then as I became more aware of the importance of China's countryside, I broadened my research to focus on rural-urban relationships and on how the Chinese "model" of development is bridging the rural-urban gap. Soon I realized that my real interest lay in understanding as much as possible of the totality of change in contemporary China and in communicating what I had learned to others.

Several factors propelled me in the direction of writing a book that looks at China more broadly. I was struck by the fact that most of the writing about China in the 1970s fails to present a balanced portrait of what happened during and after the Cultural Revolution. Too many people were returning from three-week trips to China, pen in hand, ready to tell the world what they had found. As a result, a spate of decidedly sympathetic accounts of Chinese life and politics emerged, the product of a "China fever" reminiscent of the similarly misguided pilgrimages made to the Soviet Union in the early 1930s. These instant China experts ignored the bad, focused only on the good, and repeatedly spoke of a developmental pattern that was unique

1

and, paradoxically, worthy of emulation. In the early seventies, Chinese hosts ensured that carefully selected visitors saw only what China wanted them to see. The few foreigners living in China found their movements circumscribed and informal relations with individual Chinese almost nonexistent. Official Chinese press accounts mirrored the rhetoric of the Cultural Revolution, as many of the changes apparently wrought by events of the sixties were paraded before us even as they were already being dismantled.

My reaction to this view of China was skepticism, born of residency in Peking and of previous long-term study of the nature of change in another socialist system, the Soviet Union. I began to consider writing my own view of what was happening, assessing its significance based on the results of my research and experience in China. The persistent lack of published materials and documentation for the narrower monographic study that I had envisaged, plus the unlikely prospect of doing serious field research in China in the near future, hastened the decision to write a somewhat different book than was originally intended.

Living in China also made me conscious of the value of ongoing Hong Kong research. From 1971 on, I had been interviewing former residents of China, to supplement my other information on rural-urban problems. Gradually I realized that the stories these refugees had to tell were richer and more vivid than any other data source. They produced a different picture of China than we were getting from travelers' accounts or from the Chinese press. Those who had left China spoke of a country that was complex, teeming with contradictions, and more "real" than what could be found in any other sources available at the time. Sitting in Peking and reading the transcripts of my Hong Kong interviews, I was struck by the fact that they were teaching me more about Chinese life and politics than I was learning in Peking. With that realization, I decided to base a book on the information about life and politics that I had uncovered through interviews with former residents of China. My research and China residency would provide the balance necessary for choosing, evaluating, and presenting their stories.

Is it acceptable, however, to rely upon the accounts of people who have deliberately left the system they are now describing? How can such apparently alienated individuals provide the objectivity we expect and require? Since they are refugees, won't they present a biased view of China? These are valid points, but past results of Hong Kong refugee interviewing, the nature of my own research method and sample, and the changes that are now taking place in China go a long way toward meeting those concerns. Some of the most important scholarship on contemporary China has relied extensively on refugee interviewing (Barnett, Bernstein, Bennett and Montaperto, Oksenberg, Parish, Solomon, Vogel, White and Whyte).[1] Over the past fifteen years scholars have refined their use of refugee data to minimize the political bias of respondents. Part of the solution is to avoid asking political questions, focusing more on descriptions of everyday life and on its various aspects. Another solution is to increase the size of the sample, made possible by the large influx of refugees to Hong Kong in the seventies. In 1979 several hundred thousand former citizens of China will have arrived in Hong Kong, adding to a pool of recent refugees that by 1980 could total as many as half a million. Finally, as we learn more about China and as more objective observers travel there for longer periods of time, researchers have learned to ask better and more detailed questions.

My own research followed these principles while building upon the studies and methods of others. I interviewed over two hundred refugees, between 1971 and 1977, with the help of research assistants. These refugees came from all parts of China; they were all ages and comprised a wide range of occupations. I administered a questionnaire at the outset, but when a respondent's story became interesting, I often abandoned the questionnaire, allowing the respondent to talk at his or her discretion. Sometimes an interview took only two or three hours; other times it went on for days. Sometimes a tape recorder was used; other times respondents did not feel at ease with a tape recorder, and handwritten notes were taken. Tape recordings and notes were transcribed, translated, and typed out as quickly as possible so that respondents could clarify and expand on points made during earlier sessions. Some respondents were called back and reinterviewed later, in order to clear up certain points. Gradually I accumulated a mass of material: the final data source for the sixteen stories appearing in this book totaled 1985 pages of typed manuscript.

The basic questionnaire that was pre-tested in 1971 contained over one hundred questions in the final version. At the beginning we scrupulously tried to elicit answers to all questions. Later we let respondents set the pace, sometimes ignoring the questionnaire in order to follow an interesting story. The stories selected for this book were judged on the following criteria: Did they present new and reliable information? Were they interesting? Did they fill the need for a particular type or category of information? The sixteen interview transcripts were then reviewed and respondents were reinterviewed where necessary. To ensure the respondents' anonymity, some names and places were altered and in some cases we avoided reference to their manner of exit from China.

Despite the security of a large "sample" and scholarly acceptance of the principle of controlled refugee interviewing, I hesitated to base this book on refugee accounts because their view of China was often different from the official Chinese view, or from the picture given by travelers just returned from China. In the past three years, however, China has changed markedly,* and the Chinese have become more open and self-critical. Many of the criticisms made by refugees have now been openly echoed by official Chinese sources or were posted on Peking's short-lived Xidan Democracy Wall. Thus, refugees in the past complained about elitism, lack of responsiveness to mass needs, inept policies, overpoliticization, unnecessary political purges, harsh life in forced labor camps, and so on. These complaints were often dismissed as sour grapes and made us question the credibility of such accounts. Now that the refugees' total view of China corresponds so closely with the official Chinese view, those of us who relied upon refugees in our research are justifiably more confident in that choice.

There could easily have been thirty or forty narratives in this book because each individual has a unique story to tell. The sixteen here represent a combination that in my opinion best pro-

---

*Right after Mao's death in 1976, the so-called Gang of Four—Jiang Qing (Mao's wife), Wang Hongwen, Yao Wenyuan, and Zhang Chunqiao—was purged from the leadership and placed under arrest. This signaled a move to more moderate, less radicalized policies under the leadership of Deng Xiaoping and Hua Guofeng. Past failures and shortcomings have been blamed on the Gang of Four, and many of the policies of the Cultural Revolution have been called into question. Even some of Mao's own actions and decisions have been implicitly and explicitly criticized in the official press.

vides a picture of China in transition. Some stories focus on an individual's entire life, such as the Oil Man's twenty years in China. Others deal with only one event in a life, as in "Little Brother's Wedding." I have tried to select a cross-section of people and narratives that best typify China. These are not stereotypes, and yet I deliberately chose individuals from specific occupations and age groups: peasants, workers, intellectuals, youth, soldiers, women, old people, cadres, dissenters, and even criminals. The people in this book lived and worked all over China — as far west as Xinjiang province, to the Soviet border in the northeast and down to Hainan Island in the south. The range of time is from the mid-fifties to 1976, although the focus lies in the period between 1966 and 1974. The stories are edited and, in some cases, paraphrased versions of original interviews.

In their totality the narratives paint a picture of a nation struggling to modernize and facing major obstacles along that path. Tradition is still firmly rooted in rural China and is a bar to rapid change. In "A Foot of Mud and a Pile of Shit" we see how positive change occurs in a village, but we also observe how many obstacles still lie ahead. In other stories we are made aware of the strong tendencies toward elitism that remain and how in the final analysis the Cultural Revolution may have only barely narrowed the formidable gap between leaders and led. In "Eating Pears in Fuzhou," the narrator criticizes the privileges of this elite, in particular the army that was abusing its recently gained privileges. In "Flying Kites on White Cloud Mountain," young demonstrators ask why so little has changed despite the Cultural Revolution, hoping that their protest will bring some of the benefits promised several years earlier. The gap between countryside and city remains large despite a decade of policies designed to reduce these differences, and several of the stories deal with this theme. Urban youth dislike being sent down to live and work with peasants, and Chairman Mao himself tries to ease their condition in "Chairman Mao's Letter to Li." In "Little Brother's Wedding" and again in "My Neighborhood," we see that women still lag significantly behind men, even though women have made impressive gains since 1949.

In terms of recent policy changes in China, the Oil Man's emphasis on making China self-sufficient in oil is especially relevant. In "The Apprentice" we see that in the struggle between production and politics, workers clearly preferred the former, and today that is the direction China has once more chosen by giving workers more material incentives and bonuses. In "The One Whose Girlfriend Turned Him In" the narrator laments the unjust treatment he received because of one political mistake: now China is rehabilitating victims of the campaigns of the fifties and the Cultural Revolution, although, as the narrator in "Kill the Chickens To Scare the Monkeys" observes, people don't easily forget what is buried in their hearts. China has reestablished a specialist-elitist system, and in this context the narrator's metamorphosis in "Down with Stinking Intellectuals" from radical student to "stinking intellectual" is a most appropriate lesson to remember. Finally, the events described in "Flying Kites on White Cloud Mountain" and the criticisms made in 1974 by Li Yizhe and others are now being voiced publicly in discussions concerning the nature of socialist democracy and the future form of socialist legality in China.

Returning to the broader theme of "understanding China," the sixteen stories combine to permit a number of generalizations. Daily life goes on, regardless of the big political campaigns of the moment. Individuals have enough trouble coping with the small things of life, and they are weary of big solutions. Most individuals are more concerned with personal survival, both in political and in economic terms. Consequently, they externalize acceptance of the current line and political ideology, in order to remain politically "safe." Some unfortunately miscalculate and pay a heavy price, such as the loss of a career. The majority, however, display a veneer of ideology that gets them through most crises. Still, that veneer is thin and one suspects that it can easily be removed or altered if the line were again to shift. The system in general is slow to respond to change from the top, partly because tradition exerts a powerful hold on rural China and partly because, in physical terms, China is a large sum of many small scattered parts. The "center" is far away and often dimly perceived by those living in the countryside or in the interior, and this is the vast majority of Chinese. It took the narrator of "Frontier Town" two weeks to get to Qinghai, and most rural Chinese have never gone beyond 30 kilometers from home.

So modernization as it comes poses immense tasks. China's leaders may have the will to modernize based on a strong sense of being part of a special civilization. They may with the best of intentions earnestly strive to pull China into the next century— but desire alone may not be enough. China must generate capital and resources to finance rapid economic growth, if only to move beyond providing food for a population increasing by some 20 million every year. Can Chinese socialism provide these resources, and will the current changes affect the basic system described in this book? No one's understanding of China can permit him to answer that question today, although the stories in this book may provide a fuller insight into the remarkable scale of China's attempt to modernize as well as the enormous problems the nation faces in that task.

Thousand-Dollar Pig

IN THE FALL OF 1968 the Chinese set up the first May 7 Cadres Schools. By the early seventies there were several thousand of these schools scattered throughout China. Their stated purpose was to "reeducate" city cadres. (A cadre, or ganbu, *is a person performing any type of leadership role, from small rural team leader to head of one of Peking's vast bureaucracies. He may also be any salaried member of any state bureaucracy.) By working with their hands and learning from simple peasants, city people were supposed to "cleanse their hearts and minds of the bureaucratism they had acquired sitting behind desks in comfortable urban offices, ordering about subordinates." After an appropriate stay in the countryside they were to return to the city, reeducated and better able to apply Chairman Mao's Thought in practice.*

The May 7 Cadres School was an innovative attempt to solve a nagging problem of socialist development, that of the bureaucratization of the revolution and the tendency toward elitism historically associated with this process. Earlier attempts in the 1950s to solve this problem, by sending cadres in rotation to serve in the countryside, or in factories, had not been very successful. During the Cultural Revolution (1966-1971) Chairman Mao made his attack on bureaucrats one of the cornerstones of his "Maoist vision," and the May 7 Cadres Schools symbolized the anti-bureaucratic and anti-elitist nature of the Cultural Revolution. In fact, many cadres initially were sent to these schools for punitive reasons because, like the "Biggest Fish" in this story, they

9

*had been on the losing side in the Cultural Revolution. Their
reeducation came at the hands of cadres from the winning side
rather than from the local peasants. In more recent times the
Cadres Schools have become routinized versions of "summer
camps," where cadres have minimal contact with peasants
and stay for only a few months. It is conceivable that in the post-
Mao era these schools might be replaced by a less expensive system of cadres rotation, as has been suggested by recent Chinese
visitors and by articles in the Chinese press.*

*This story takes place in a May 7 Cadres School in Henan
province between 1970 and 1973. The focus on pigs is well
founded in Chairman Mao's policies and maxims of that time.
Every rural household was urged to raise pigs because "every pig
is a miniature fertilizer factory." The goal was to raise one pig per
person per year. Squad Leader Ho's earnest attempts to apply
Chairman Mao's theory of contradictions to pig raising are fully
in keeping with the spirit of the times, which stressed both the
raising of more pigs and the practical application of Chairman
Mao's Thought. However, the determination of the cadres to out-
perform the local peasants in pig production in order to prove
cadre superiority suggests that the cadres were not being reeducated quite in the manner that Mao had intended.*

W E DECIDED TO BUY the pig after the head of the military control commission visited our school and was
appalled by the condition of our pigs. He had heard the
local gossip: "Those city slickers at the May 7 Cadres School are
so dumb they can't even raise pigs." We were a local embarrassment, to be sure. Surrounded by sleek, fat, pink peasant pigs, our
scrawny pigs had lost face. The military representative scowled at
our pigs and remarked, "They're so skinny, they look like wooden
benches. You'd better get some decent pigs here fast, or your
Ministry will be a laughingstock!" After he left, we had an emergency meeting to discuss the situation. Director Lin said, "We
have poorly applied Chairman Mao's Thought to our work.
Skinny pigs are proof of that. Fat pigs are what we need to show
that we are completely devoted to Chairman Mao." The Party
secretary then asked the question, "How do we apply Chairman
Mao's Thought to get fat pigs?" Squad Leader Ho (who knew the

most about pigs) replied that, according to Chairman Mao, one must investigate the problem fully from all sides and then integrate practice and theory. Ho concluded that the reason for our skinny pigs had to be found in one of three areas: the relationship between the pigs and their natural environment (excluding man); the relationship between the cadres and the pigs; and the relationship among the pigs themselves. He went on to say: "I've investigated each of these three relationships. The principal contradiction is the relationship among the animals themselves, not in what they eat (pigs and their environment) or in how we cadres take care of them (pigs and man). Our pigs are skinny because their ancestors' ancestors were skinny pigs. We need a better breed of animals in order to get fatter ones. In the case of our present pigs, the internal factor (the pig itself) is the main contradiction, and external factors (the food they eat, the way we care for them) are only a secondary aspect."

After Ho sat down, both the Party secretary and Director Lin congratulated him for his brilliant application of Chairman Mao's theory of contradictions to the concrete problem of pigs. "In taking Chairman Mao's teaching to heart," said Director Lin, "you have clarified the problem for us. We need better pigs in order to produce better pigs. So let us find such animals at once. How many do we need?" Squad Leader Ho replied that in his opinion only one would be necessary but that it must be outstanding, one that could sire an entire new generation of pigs. One great pig would resolve the principal contradiction among our skinny pigs. Director Lin then asked: "If we agree with Squad Leader Ho's analysis, where will we find such an animal?" Several suggestions were made. "Why not send a team of cadres to scout the local market fairs?" "Ask the local peasants who has the best pigs." "Go to Zhengzhou and talk with provincial agricultural experts there." "Check with the Ministry since they will have to provide extra funds."

We sent a group of cadres to look at what was available in the market towns, and we also visited with the local peasants, casually bringing the discussion around to pigs. Squad Leader Ho and another cadre went to Zhengzhou. We also informed Peking that we planned to buy a great pig and asked for instructions. The cadres came back and reported that they hadn't found any exceptional local pigs and that the local peasants weren't very helpful. One peasant had told them: "The only sure way to get fat pigs is to get a fat mother-in-law—the rest is up to Heaven. Maybe Heaven will make an exception for fat cadres." Officials in Zhengzhou were evasive. "Why come to us?" they asked. "The State Experimental Farm doesn't sell its animals." Our cadres, led by Squad Leader Ho, said we needed only one pig just for a year or two. "We even could borrow it for a year or two and then return it if you don't want to sell it to us." But Zhengzhou didn't budge, replying, "This is an unusual request and we will have to study the matter carefully." Since we cadres were well acquainted with the jargon of officials, we knew that their answer was an effective no and that they would "study the matter" forever without ever giving us a single pig.

At this point the Ministry intervened. The head of the military control commission had returned to Peking and made his report. The ministry wanted immediate results. Director Lin was told that a large black pig would be shipped from the northeast within weeks and that we should stop running around Henan looking for pigs. "The animal we are sending you will be beyond your expectations. There is no other pig like it in Henan. We have made all arrangements and have authorized an expenditure of 1000 yuan to pay for the pig, plus transportation costs. It will be accompanied by an expert who will stay at your school for several weeks while the pig is getting used to his new surroundings. We expect regular reports on the pig's condition and progress."

The Thousand-Dollar Pig arrived six weeks later, in a wooden crate on the back of a truck. Sitting beside him was the expert from the northeast. Neither pig nor expert impressed us at first glance. The Thousand-Dollar Pig didn't look much different than any of the fatter local varieties. His piggish red eyes peered sullenly out at the cadres who came to look at him. He lay around weakly flicking at the flies crawling all over him. The expert, who stuttered and had a difficult accent, turned out to be a peasant from a state farm. I guess he knew his pigs, but the problem was that half the time we couldn't understand what he was saying. Even Squad Leader Ho had problems understanding his stutter. We nicknamed the expert Two-Time Li because he repeated everything twice. He stayed at our school for eight weeks and then was sent back to his pig farm. I guess it cost us several hundred yuan to pay his expenses and to cover the cost of transporting our pig a thousand kilometers. So that Thousand-Dollar Pig cost about 1400 yuan when you figure it all up. You could get a good local pig at the market, same weight and age, for about 300 yuan. It was quite a difference.

A few months later, my turn at the school was up and I returned to Peking. So my comments about the great pig's progress are partly second hand. It took that pig a long time to recover from his trip, but then he went to work with a vengeance and soon our piggery was bursting at the seams with uncommonly large litters of his squealing offspring. We had to expand the piggery, and even the local peasants were impressed by his prowess. But we soon realized that while we were now getting more pigs, they weren't any fatter. Our pigs still looked like long wooden benches—only now there were more of them.

We held another meeting to discuss the problem. Squad Leader Ho suggested that we breed our great pig to the best of the local sows, to raise the quality of his progeny. Director Lin wondered if we shouldn't bring Two-Time Li back to tell us what we were doing wrong. The Party secretary said that this wasn't necessary and that we didn't need to bring in local sows because we had achieved our purpose—we were producing more pork than ever before, and it didn't really matter if our pigs were still skinny. "We can tell Peking that we have increased our yield of pork by 20 percent. That's what really counts." Put in that perspective, I guess the Thousand-Dollar Pig was a success. But was it worth the overall cost? We spent over 1400 yuan to get that pig. The pig turned out all right, but we could never repay the investment.

Actually the Ministry wasn't upset. The May 7 School never was economically viable. It cost Peking about 200,000 yuan to subsidize the three hundred of us living in the Henan countryside. It would have been cheaper, for example, to buy all our food locally from the peasants instead of growing it ourselves, as we did. Officially, cadres were exhorted to be self-reliant, but in fact I can't think of any May 7 Cadres School that wasn't financed by substantial subsidies. How can you expect a bunch of city slickers to plant rice, grow corn, and raise pigs as if we were peasants with centuries of experience behind us? Some of us had never before in our lives held a hoe. None of us knew anything about farming methods. We didn't know about local weather conditions: when it was right to plant, to harvest, and so forth. Our May 7 School had been an uneconomical state farm before we took it over in 1969, and it was hardly likely that the soft hands of cadres could make a profit where the calloused fingers of peasants had failed. So there was no basis for objecting in principle to the subsidization of our May 7 School. However, the great pig fiasco was an embarrassment to our school because it was such an obvious misuse of funds, and also because it was merely the latest in a long line of fiscal disasters at the school. For example, we actually trucked in fertilizer from hundreds of kilometers away because the school's leadership figured that this would lead to bumper harvests that would pay us back handsomely, but we must have used the wrong fertilizer because our crops remained 30 to 40 percent below those grown in the surrounding communes, even though we used all that expensive fertilizer. It cost us thousands of yuan while the local peasants used their own shit, or nothing.

Then there was our paddy rice experiment. The soil was laced with alkaline, so we decided to dilute it by diverting water from the Huai River. We ran the water pumps twenty-four hours a day. We did get a crop of rice, but it cost us three times more than the crop was worth, due to high electricity and diesel oil expenses. We had several tractors, combine harvesters, and sowing machines, but our harvest per man was much lower than that of the local peasants, who had almost no machines.

Still, the May 7 Cadres Schools were an important achievement, even if heavily subsidized. When all the joking about incompetent cadres trying to masquerade as peasants is put aside, the conclusion is that the May 7 Cadres Schools are a good thing. Take my case as an example. When I was sent down in 1970 I was unhappy and even angry. Who wanted to spend months or even years living like a peasant, away from one's family, job, and friends? Did anyone really expect to be "reformed through physical labor," especially if it was only for a short time? Wouldn't we serve the Party more by working harder at our regular jobs? Weren't many of us too old to be useful in the countryside? And so on. I must confess that when I jumped off the back of the truck and saw my new rural home, all my suspicions were confirmed. It looked grim—the crops were in bad shape, the housing and amenities were poor, and the peasants didn't exactly rush out to welcome us. I didn't relish the prospect of months and months of political reeducation and study, living together with many of the very same people I had been struggling against back in Peking. So there were many reasons why I approached my stay there with trepidation.

Yet in a few short weeks my negative feelings had changed. Those two years at the school turned out to be the best time of my life. Sure, life was simple and tough, but I came to enjoy it. I was toughened up physically from working in the fields — at the beginning I was so sore I couldn't squat. Compared with the neighboring peasants whose skin had been burned by the sun, at the outset we looked like real ghosts.[1] It wasn't long, however, before I too was sunburned black like a peasant. I had lost weight and felt good, even though the diet wasn't as rich as in Peking and all our cooks were amateurs. Actually, the flour was better in Henan and so our *mantou*[2] were of better quality. We couldn't help becoming physically fit, being outdoors all the time and doing physical labor. I began to feel like a young person once more. This also had a bearing on my attitude. Back in Peking I had been closely involved in the internal politics of our unit and in the "big politics" of the Center. But there in Henan, Peking was suddenly remote. The turmoil of past political struggles seemed inconsequential when one was trying to grow cabbages and grain. How easily you could wipe your mind clean of recent events! We were all in the same boat out in Henan and there was no point in reliving past quarrels. Furthermore, many of your former enemies were working right beside you, shoveling the same shit into the same piles. The person who just yesterday had screamed that you were a "dog's head that deserved to be beaten" or a "stinking son of a turtle's egg," today merely said "Comrade, pass the shit bucket," or something like that. So our frame of mind was different out there. You know, in Peking it always seemed as if a thousand things were happening at once, but in the countryside hardly anything ever happens that is surprising. In Peking, politics and bureaucracy are what counts, but in the countryside the weather is the key. It seemed as if all our petty lives and quarrels had been taken over by the four seasons of the year, by the certainty of rain and wind, sunshine and snow. The timeless pattern of nature took over our lives and brought me peace of mind.

Of course peace of mind and physical fitness were not what Chairman Mao had in mind when he set up the May 7 Schools. Their main purpose was to change our political thinking and we did spend a great deal of time in political study and reeducation. Look, don't get me wrong. I didn't mean to ignore that part of my life — I was telling you about the good things I remembered, not about everything. It's true that we devoted a large part of each day to politics and to political study, but I can't say I enjoyed that. It wasn't much different from what we had done in Peking, you know: "study Chairman Mao's works"; "apply the correct line to daily activities"; "fight against counterrevolutionaries and revisionist thinking"; "help those who have made political mistakes reform their thought"; "learn that through struggle one can remold one's way of thinking." That's what we had been doing in Peking. We used to stand in front of Chairman Mao's picture every day singing, "The East Is Red," clutching our little Red Book in our hands. We held an elaborate ceremony that involved "confessing" our daily sins to the Chairman and then reading a bunch of appropriate quotations. Well, it was the same at the May 7 School. We had a nice color picture of the Chairman surrounded by such sayings as "Dare To Make Revolution," "The Great Helmsman," "Ten Thousand Years Long Life," and so on (even the sayings were the same in both places). We'd also sing the song "Sailing the Seas Depends on the Great Helmsman," and there'd be a reading by one of the cadres from the Red Book. When you sang or looked at Mao's picture, or confessed, you always placed the Red Book on your heart. We had the same kind of meetings in Henan as in Peking. Our squad would discuss key editorials, documents, or quotations, and there would be long-drawn-out lessons, struggles, and confessions.

Mind you, there were some differences between political study in Peking and in Henan. Once we had been sent to the countryside, we knew what the issues were (finally) and could now relate ourselves more clearly to them. In Peking there was so much confusion one often didn't know how to respond. Moreover, once we arrived in Henan, our own political position had already been defined for us. We knew which faction had won, who the counterrevolutionaries were, and, most important, who was being accused of "ultraleftism," of being a member of the 516 conspiracy.* For us at the May 7 School the political uncertainties of the

Cultural Revolution and our own political position had been basically resolved prior to our arrival. In a sense "political re-education" meant rehearsing and learning our current and future political roles, rather than any startling transformation on our part. The exciting aspect of Cultural Revolution politics was over, and politics was, in effect, becoming routine again. True, we still were busy struggling against 516 elements, but this was done in a nonviolent way, without any of the name calling and ugliness of a year or two earlier. Most of the 516 ate and slept together with the rest of the cadres. Only the big fish were segregated from us. The "Biggest Fish," the 516 leader from our Peking unit, was confined to the school under guard and was fed separately. We took turns guarding him. Eventually, he realized that it was useless not to confess and then even this Biggest Fish was no longer above the rest of us.

Coming back to your question, I think it's too simple an explanation to say that the May 7 Cadres School's main purpose was political reeducation because there were other factors involved, making it a complex matter. When we were first asked to set up a school, the head of the military control commission didn't talk about political reeducation. Instead he talked about the Soviet danger, that in the interests of national defense cadres should leave Peking. He said, "We must decentralize to make sure that the Soviets cannot knock us off in one blow. It is only a matter of time." So at the beginning relocation to Henan was presented as part of a policy of decentralization of the large Peking ministries rather than as punishment or reeducation. The military control commission head remarked, "We will reduce Peking's population to two million by 1970."[3] At the beginning cadres were urged to go down with their families who could live in nearby communes if there was no space in the May 7 Schools. Practically no one volunteered on that basis because we were afraid that we might wind up there permanently. No one wanted that fate—not just being forced to give up one's precious Peking residence, but to be banished forever to the countryside. Even the most dedicated follow-

*The 516 group allegedly was organized an as ultraleftist conspiracy by younger radicals against the leaders of the Cultural Revolution. Later, high officials such as Chen Boda and Lin Biao were associated with this group. Now the Gang of Four (those at the very top during the Cultural Revolution) itself has been accused of being the real leaders of 516. (For more on 516, see "Kill the Chickens To Scare the Monkeys.")

er of Chairman Mao's revolutionary line found some way to avoid volunteering. Later, when cadres were being sent down for reasons other than decentralization, because they were ultraleftists or simply because a routine of cadres rotation had been set up—then cadres weren't afraid of being "left to die in Henan," because they knew they'd be back in Peking eventually.

At first we were sent down on an *ad hoc* basis, depending on the political campaign of the moment and on our instructions from above. Then we received a general instruction of "Three One Thirds," that is, one third had to remain in the office, one third was to be on assignment somewhere, and the remaining third was to be sent to the May 7 School. The section head in the Peking unit would have to juggle his personnel to maintain work output while so many were away. We held a section meeting and those who were leaving had to explain their work to others. We made sure the work was not seriously disrupted. It used to go like this: the section would hold a meeting and the head asked, "How many people can we spare?" We would decide, for example, "Ten can go. Let's ask for volunteers." Of course everybody asked to go. It was part of our political ritual; everybody wanted to have his name down as being the first to volunteer. But a list had already been drawn up by the section head, together with the higher unit Party organization or revolutionary committee. That list was divided into two groups: those from 516, who had been politically criticized, and those like myself, who were going down on a rotation basis. Those who were being politically criticized were going whether they volunteered or not, and the rest of us would be sent down if it suited the section and the unit involved.

Once we were "chosen" we underwent a long briefing session, as well as finding out through gossip what it was going to be like in Henan. Study meetings were held to help cadres learn how to act with peasants, what to say to peasants, and how to deal with various problems. We were told not to take too much along since fifteen of us would sleep in a large room and there wasn't much space for extras. Most of us took a few eating utensils, a bed roll, some clothes, and of course our well-thumbed little Red Books. Wives had to stay behind, unless they too were cadres at the school. In that case it was possible for husbands and wives to be sent together and to stay in married housing, but that was quite rare. I saw my wife and children for twenty-four days out of the eighteen months I was in Henan.

The three hundred of us lived in an area separated from the local peasants, who lived in nearby communes. There were no peasants at all at our school, but occasionally we consulted them or paid them visits. There was a small group of "service personnel" who were sent down from Peking to drive trucks and tractors. They were the only non-cadres at the school. We lived in barracks, fifteen to a room with a coal-burning stove in the middle of the room. Men and women were put into separate dorms. There were three men for every woman, and that became a problem. For the sake of harmony, better not to have any women than to have so few. There were some awkward moments because of the shortage of women. All the buildings were brick and tile, with earthen floors. The living conditions were sparse but adequate.

The school was divided on military lines into companies, platoons, and squads. The squad was the most important unit because jobs were rotated monthly, by squad. One month you might be a member of the cooking squad; the next month it might be the piggery squad; then the vegetable squad. We planted wheat, corn, sorghum (*gaoliang*), beans, and vegetables. We also had a tree farm, orchards, and of course our piggery. Squad leaders were appointed by the school's Party committee, in conjunction with the director and deputy director of the school. All squad leaders, as a matter of fact all cadres in responsible positions of leadership in the school, were Party members. I'd guess that over half the cadres at the school were Party members. The top leadership was also rotated and this was unfortunate because, just as you had some continuity in direction, the leadership would change. While I was there, Director Lin was replaced. He was a pretty good director, but he had been there for three years and it was time to go. Also, even though it was Peking's decision to buy and send the Thousand-Dollar Pig, he was later blamed for this "extravagance." This was during a campaign against waste of state resources, and he was criticized for authorizing such a wasteful expense.

There weren't any major organizational or administrative problems. Because of the school's small size, everybody participated in meetings and discussions. Since we all had come from the same original work unit we knew each other pretty well. As long as cadres knew they would return to Peking, there were no problems. However, when after the first year no word had come as to when the cadres would be replaced, we all became nervous and edgy. Cadres began to go back to Peking for their two-week holiday and refused to return to the school, staying on in Peking for weeks longer. One cadre stayed away for three and a half months and returned only after the leadership sent him three telegrams and threatened him. Cadres became openly unhappy, dropping such remarks as, "I'm going to be here so long that I'll have forgotten everything that I've learned," or "I'm going to work like a Taoist monk, beating the gong every day."* The leadership was aware of our unease, but could do little to get us rotated back to Peking. So they held frequent meetings, to remind us that we were in Henan to remold our world outlook and ought to be thinking as if we might have to stay in the countryside forever. They pointed out that a cadres school is not supposed to be a summer vacation or a camp holiday. They especially criticized those who acted like monks beating gongs. On balance, however, the group of unhappy cadres was a minority. After the first few years of uncertainty, cadres were rotated on a predictable basis, based on clearly defined terms. They knew how long they would be there, and they knew they would return to Peking when it was over. So this relieved the pressure and made their stay into something more finite, like a dose of medicine. Some thoroughly enjoyed their stay, although there are always those who don't like to take any medicine at all.

Before we left for Henan we were given careful instructions about relations with the local peasants. We were not to tell them about any of the internal affairs of our work unit. We were not to reveal our salaries (we continued to receive our comparatively huge Peking salaries even while we were in Henan). We were told not to eat or drink too much because the peasants had a much lower standard of living and it wouldn't be right for us to spend our high salaries on extra food. Not only would it make us look like what we really were (rich urban cadres), but we would be defeating the purpose of living the simple peasant life. We were told to be modest and not to show off, and we were instructed to listen to the peasants and not to tell them things. Of course, in receiving education from the poor and lower-middle peasants,

*This means living from day to day, caring about today and not tomorrow, because the (lazy) monk supposedly says, "Today I beat the gong, and tomorrow too." A similar Western aphorism might be "punching the clock" or "putting in time."

we were also supposed to be propagandists and advisers to them. Those were our main tasks, though I don't think we fulfilled them very well.

Actually we just didn't mix with the peasants. Only once in a while would we invite an old peasant to come and to tell us about the old days by "speaking bitterness," reminding us about his past sufferings. Few peasants ever came to the school, except when we needed advice concerning production. We didn't socialize with them at all, although there were occasional ritual short-term visits when we would go and be with a peasant family for a few days. We lived in two worlds and it was hard to penetrate the other world. I can't even recall any romance between a cadre and a peasant girl—that's how far apart we were. In spite of our instructions, the peasants knew all about us—who among us had been criticized, our high salaries, and other such information. They knew we secretly trucked in extra food and supplies to the school every few days, and that we were heavily subsidized from above. To the peasants we were a bunch of strangers thrust in their midst by Peking, for no sensible reason. They laughed at our mistakes and envied our wealth. Somehow I don't think we ever educated those poor and lower-middle peasants in the way that Peking had intended. We used to buy their vegetables and chickens on the side, even though we were forbidden to do this by the school leadership. But practically every cadre did it, and you could see illegal chickens running all over the compound. When any outsiders remarked about this, we always replied, "Oh, those chickens belong to the neighboring commune, they must have strayed over here." The peasants knew about such practices, so they only listened with one ear when we tried to propagandize them or advise them politically.

I would say that by and large all May 7 Schools are like ours. Some are larger, and some may be more economically viable. Some, like Nanniwan, are more effective politically although I think we did a good job at our school in the area of political education. As for relations with the peasants, I think ours are probably typical, although I have heard that in a number of schools peasants actually live and work in the school itself. We never had peasants living on our farm,[4] and I personally think we should have because not only did we never get to know and learn from them, but we also didn't take advantage of their expertise, as in the matter of buying our great pig. If we had been more willing to work with the peasants instead of trying to impress them, I think we would have been doing what Chairman Mao thought could happen. But we didn't and it never happened.

Like all long stories, there isn't much of an ending to this one. The pig did upgrade the quality of our pork production, although nowhere near the grandiose level we originally had envisaged. Since we consumed all the pork we produced, it only wound up in our own already overfed (by local standards) stomachs. We did get another benefit, an increase in pig shit, which ultimately improved the quality of our crops. Eventually the peasants came out of curiosity to see the great pig. Of course they knew the whole story—all the details—and they used to laugh uproariously at Peking's folly in bringing a pig so many kilometers for so much money. Squad Leader Ho bore a large share of the criticism, but he soon was rotated back to Peking, along with the party secretary. After Director Lin was recalled to Peking there wasn't any responsible cadre left to blame for the affair.

The pig became a celebrity at our school because he outlived several sets of cadres over a number of years. Eventually, back in Peking, when we were assigning cadres on rotation to go to Henan, we didn't say they were going to Henan May 7 Cadres School, but that they were being assigned "to the Land of the Thousand-Dollar Pig." Informally, the name of the school was changed to "Great Pig Cadres School" (*dazhu ganxiao*), and people jokingly used to say, "If you're lucky we'll send you there in a special compartment with your own escort, like the Great Pig!" From the time he returned to Peking ex-Director Lin was permanently saddled with the nickname "Old Thousand-Dollar Lin."

A Foot of Mud and a Pile of Shit

DESPITE A VENEER of industrialism, China is still a peasant society. Eighty percent of its population lives in the countryside, almost all in villages in which the basic unit is the family house-hold and where traditional customs and habits play a major role in everyday life. But change is taking place, through collective organization of labor, mechanization, and improved agricultural techniques. An example of such change was the Dazhai production brigade, which in the past decade served as the model of socialist rural organization. Dazhai emphasized the virtues of hard work and a correct political line that stressed collective values. Here private plots were eliminated; peasants received housing from the brigade for a nominal rent; and private sideline industry did not exist.

Dazhai was a model, however, and the vast majority of China's five million production teams, the basic economic and administrative unit in China's agriculture, could not hope to duplicate its achievements. Some teams lack political cohesiveness and will; others are hampered by inadequate economic resources; and some find it difficult to respond to change because of the persistence of old social norms and structures. In the post-Mao era, peasants have been encouraged to develop their private plots to expand sideline production, and the Dazhai model has been set aside for the indefinite future.

The team described in this story is fairly typical of rural life and organization in central and northern China. It is an ordinary team that responds grudgingly to change because of traditional

23

values. At times personal rivalries and village customs appear to override the Party's will. These peasants view any kind of change with the suspicion born of centuries of life in the village (this is the way it has always been done—why change now?). Every proposal is carefully weighed in economic terms: for instance, Pigeon Turd's main concern is "How much more will I get if we agree?" Self-interest remains the critical element in persuading peasants to adopt new policies. Peasants cooperate if convinced that they will have more money in their pockets.

The story also shows that much has changed in thirty years, despite the layers of the past and the peasants' reluctance to try new things. Peasants now have a larger voice in the decisions affecting their daily lives; the Party does not always force policies upon them, but spends a great deal of time in persuasion and bargaining; the peasants seem to agree that a mixture of collective organization and individual enterprise has improved their lives over the years. In the context of China's massive task of modernizing its agriculture, these are significant achievements, and they provide a favorable basis for the further changes that undoubtedly will occur in the Chinese countryside in the next decades.

I'VE BEEN A PEASANT all my life and I'm proud of that. Many people think that the countryside is backward and that peasants are stupid. When city folk were sent to my village I could see those feelings in their eyes, even though they pretended to want to learn from the poor and lower-middle peasants. We knew better. We felt inferior, and who didn't hope for a son who would be lucky enough to be admitted into the army or become a worker? I myself was guilty of using influence to get my eldest son a job in a tractor factory in Zhengzhou. Am I ashamed of having done that? I don't know—is it wrong to hope for a better life for your children? We've been told for centuries that there's nothing worse than being a poor peasant, so it's difficult to change our whole world in just one or two generations. You know, we have a saying that peasants are nothing more than a foot of mud and a pile of shit. In the spring, when the land turns to oozing mud and it's raining, windy and cold right through your skin, it's easy to feel that way. Life is hard in the villages and our world really is full of mud and shit. But you need mud and shit to grow the crops, and where would China be without the grain that we deliver to the state each year?

I'm over sixty years old and have seen many things in my lifetime. I was twenty-seven when the Japanese invaded China, and at the time of Liberation I already had two sons. They made me a team leader in 1961 and I did that for over ten years. There have been good times and hard times—life hasn't been easy, but I want to say that it has been much better for me since Liberation. I don't want to "recall bitterness" (*yi jiu shehuide ku*) because you know how it was under the Kuomintang, but I got this scar on my face from a landlord's whip. In those days you couldn't escape the clutches of the landlords. Once poor, you were doomed to eternal poverty. You were beaten, starved, and practically left for dead. Children were bought and sold like cattle, and lives were as fragile as rice paper. We watered the plains of Henan with our tears. Such misery! The times when we had to eat tree bark and boil leaves in order to wait out the many weeks before the summer harvest! The shame of burying dead children and parents without a coffin! I could go on telling you how bad it was then. I have many bitter memories.

After Liberation, my life improved. It wasn't easy and there were setbacks. We had problems in the late fifties during the creation of people's communes and then there was a time when again we ate leaves and bark, during the Three Difficult Years [1959-1961]. But for every setback there were ten thousand gains: more food, a better life, education, a strong future for our children. In my village we prospered under the policies of Chairman Mao and the Communist Party. Maybe it isn't always clear to outsiders how much the countryside has changed. I feel it because I'm a peasant whose working life spans a half century in the fields. In 1975 there is food in our bellies and we don't worry about natural disasters. We're secure. We have more free time for ourselves and our families. We take a greater responsibility for our own lives. We make decisions that used to be made by landlords, clans, or secret societies, and the peasants do a far better job. We have more respect for ourselves now, although I know that the countryside is still inferior to the towns and cities. You see, we have much catching up to do. That's why many peasants still think of themselves as so much mud and shit. Everything takes time.

Changes can take place, however, often without people real-

izing what has happened. Let me tell you a story about my village
and how it changed in a quiet way, how peasants can develop
their consciousness slowly as they fight against feudal ideas and
bad thoughts. It has to do with the merging of two teams in my
village. Nothing on a grand scale really. Only thirty households
were involved, but because of clan rivalries and lack of understanding almost all of the one hundred and fifty people involved
initially opposed the merger. Seven years earlier a similar merger
had been tried and discarded after only a year — the members of
both teams were simply unable to cooperate. In 1971 it was tried
again, while I was the leader of one of the teams involved, the
No. 2 team of East Liu Wei production brigade, in Liu Wei village.

It was around the end of October after *shuang jiang* (the
descent of the hoarfrost)[1] that I first heard of the plan to merge
our team with the No. 4 team of the East Liu Wei brigade. I was
at a brigade cadres meeting one evening and the second secretary
took me and the No. 4 team leader aside for a heart-to-heart talk.
He said the brigade was in the midst of settling year-end accounts
and this was a good time to think again about joining our two
teams. "The No. 2 and No. 4 teams are the smallest of all the
teams in the whole commune. They should have been merged
years ago. It makes economic sense. Now's the time to do it, after
a good harvest, in the slack season. We will announce the leadership's intentions at the next mass meeting of the brigade. Then
we'll try to work out all the details of the merger so that when the
New Year comes we will have settled the issue." I had mixed feelings about the merger because I wasn't sure that I could persuade
my team to agree. Nor was it likely that the No. 4 team leader
would have any better luck in convincing his team members, even
though I knew he was more eager for the merger than I. Hatreds
between the two teams had prevented us from joining once before
in 1964 and, as far as I could tell, those hatreds still existed seven
years later.

The public announcement of the proposed merger took
place at a mass meeting of all brigade members about a week
later. You know how these meetings are organized. The night
before, when villagers were at home eating their cornflour por-
ridge and vegetables, the voice of the brigade Party secretary
crackled over the loudspeakers: "Attention, attention, all brigade

members. Tomorrow morning at 10:00 a.m. there will be an important mass meeting. We will relay the latest instructions from the higher levels to you, so everyone must attend and they must be punctual." No one really paid much attention to the announcement since we had those kinds of meetings once or twice a month. The main thing was we didn't have to work that morning, but still could collect work points. So some people planned to get a little extra sleep and others were going to do personal chores before the meeting. Most mass meetings never started on time — if it was called for 10:00, you could be sure that it would begin around noon. You could count on a whole free morning. Some peasants even got up early and spent the entire morning at the market 15 kilometers away, buying and selling food and other commodities.

The brigade cadres asked me to help prepare for the meeting, so I didn't get any free time. The podium had to be set up in the large space in the village center, and we brought over tables, chairs, and a microphone. At the back we hung a large picture of Chairman Mao on some poles, and across the front were posters that read: "In Agriculture, Learn from Dazhai"; "Long Live Chairman Mao"; "Long Live the Communist Party of China." We had made these posters a long time ago out of yellow paper pasted on red cloth and they were starting to get tattered, so we prayed a little to Heaven that there wouldn't be a strong wind. At 10:00 we were ready but no one had arrived. So the third Party secretary used the microphone to announce that the meeting was about to start. When still nobody came by 10:30, the ten team leaders were asked to go round up the team members. Gradually the place filled up with men, women, and children all milling around, making noise, running and talking. Finally the second secretary asked everyone to rise and sing "The East Is Red." Then we sat down and he said: "Take your precious Little Red Book, and we shall read a few quotations.[2] Turn to page 16. Our great leader Chairman Mao teaches us . . . " and we read several quotations in unison. Then he announced that the brigade first secretary would give his report.

The brigade first secretary always gave the same kind of report. First he would quote Chairman Mao, the Party line, and sprinkle this with quotations from the Red Book. Then he'd talk about the many achievements of our brigade and how we were contributing to the state and to the growth of socialism. That usually took thirty to forty minutes, and nobody listened to that part of his speech. Even I had memorized it by heart after hearing it so many times over the years. So while he was talking there was chaos. Children were running around and people were squatting in groups talking to one another. The women had brought their sewing, and they were working furiously making shoes and talking among themselves. No one seemed to be listening, but then the Party secretary paused and his tone changed: "While our achievements have been many, there have been shortcomings and problems that we must resolve." When he got to that point in his speech, the drowsy, buzzing crowd suddenly quieted down and began to listen carefully. The important part of the speech was about to begin, and brigade members were already speculating in their minds as to what it might be—a new campaign? further restrictions on private plots or on sideline industry? changes in work-point evaluation? Even I didn't know what the secretary was going to say, aside from the announcement of the proposed merger. I wasn't a Party member so I didn't know in advance what the Party's instructions would be.

First the secretary said that we would have to increase production by deep-digging our soil (*shen fan*), a method that had been tried elsewhere and could increase yields by 20 percent. So after New Year we were going to do this—it would take time away from other tasks, but supposedly would be worth it. Second, we must increase our use of fertilizer. He pointed out that Chairman Mao had said that each pig was a small fertilizer factory, and it was up to us to increase the production of pig manure. At this point you could see the crowd shifting uneasily. Every household raised pigs and sold the shit to the team. What did the Party have in mind? The secretary continued: "In order to get more manure, the first step is to pen up all pigs. From now on, all pigs must be kept fenced in. This way the manure will be in one place and easier to collect. Any pigs not penned up will be confiscated." The crowd was stunned and people were saying: "How can I feed my pigs if they're fenced up? Up till now I could let them forage around the village for whatever they could get. Where will I find the food to fatten up my sucklings if they're locked up? The leadership is clever—they talk about fertilizer but they really want to keep our pigs out of the collective fields. What a blow!" By the time the secretary came to the third item on his list—the proposed merger—no one was really listening. They heard his announcement with one ear: "Because of the small size of the No. 2 and No. 4 teams the leadership proposes that these teams join together in keeping with Chairman Mao's instructions to make agriculture more productive by increasing the size of the basic unit. The two teams should discuss the matter carefully and meet with brigade cadres to discuss the details and set up a timetable." That was all, and it really was an anticlimax. I could see that most of my team were thinking about their pigs and hadn't digested the news about the merger.

While everybody was still thinking about penning up their pigs, the secretary announced: "Everybody rise so we can close the meeting." He had to say it three times before the crowd grudgingly got up and then he said: "Ok, let's sing 'Sailing the Seas Depends on the Helmsman,' " which we did, and then the meeting was proclaimed adjourned and we all headed slowly to our homes for lunch.

You can imagine that when I rang the bell to call my team together for work that afternoon, no one's mind was on our assigned task, repairing the irrigation gate. People were upset about the pigs, but now they had thought about the more serious matter of merging with No. 4 team. Three-Fingers Li, an older peasant, said: "I speak with an open heart. I'm an old man and I have the right to speak my mind. I say that any merger with No. 4 team will turn out badly. We are two separate branches of a clan, and for as long as anyone can remember, we haven't got along. We don't intermarry, we don't even drink tea together if we can help it. We've lived in our separate parts of this village for so long that no one could imagine it otherwise. During the one year that we were joined, remember all the problems? People wouldn't speak to each other; no cooperation; each team was suspicious of the other. I say that we are two separate units— we are all called Li, but we are two separate families and people from separate families can't form one family. You can't wipe away the facts of the past—ancestral tablets can be destroyed, but they stay in our minds. A tree can grow a thousand feet high, but its leaves always fall near its roots and our two teams have separate roots. How can we join together if we have separate roots?"

Most of the others agreed with Three-Fingers Li. Another

old peasant said: "Why waste our time again with talk of a merger? It didn't work seven years ago and there's no reason to think it will succeed now. The members of No. 4 team haven't changed one bit. They still argue with us over every little piece of team land; we have to fight with them over who gets first rights to the water. When our melons are stolen from the fields we know in whose storehouse they've been hidden. Our team is richer and our average work-point value is higher. Why should we reduce our income? There's no reason at all to talk of merger. Better to worry about our pigs. That's the more serious problem right now." It was thus made clear to me that the majority of my team opposed the idea of merger and that it would take a great deal of discussion and preparation to carry it out. Later that evening I spoke with the leader of No. 4 team and he said that his team felt exactly the same as ours. He commented, "You know, feelings run deep between our teams, and I'm not sure that the wisdom of the Party or the correctness of Chairman Mao's Thought will help bridge this large gap between us."

Still there were some positive opinions about merger within my team. Two important team members, Da Dui (Brigade) Li and the Accountant, both were in favor; and so was I, although you will see that each of us was in good part motivated by selfish reasons rather than the good of the collective. Da Dui supported the merger because he thought it would advance his career. He was an ex-army man who had come back to Liu Wei after five years' service and got a matchmaker to find him a wife. But she had big teeth and was sloppy, so Da Dui took to chasing after other women and to hanging around brigade headquarters. That's why we called him "Da Dui" behind his back—it was obvious to everyone that he wanted to become a brigade cadre. Because he was a Party member, and an ex-army man, they made him head of the brigade militia platoon, but he wanted to become brigade secretary. Da Dui figured that if he worked hard on behalf of the merger, the brigade leadership would be impressed and this would count heavily in the future when they were looking for a new brigade secretary. Once he became a cadre, he would be ready to fulfill his ambitions. Then he could be somebody important in the village.

The Accountant was concerned about his future livelihood. He figured that when the merger took place there would be two former team accountants vying for the position of accountant on the new team. The Accountant, who had been our team accountant for eight years, wasn't worrying about losing his job because he was more skilled and older than the accountant in No. 4 team. The Accountant had other ideas. He knew that there was an upcoming vacancy for an accountant at the brigade level. His uncle had told him that in confidence. The Accountant figured he had a good chance at the job. "Why not?" he told me one night. "I'm as skilled in my profession as anyone in the brigade. When the two teams merge, they'll have a spare accountant (me). I've got good connections at the brigade level with my uncle there. The brigade needs my support to convince our team that we will improve our economic position through merger. I can explain why we will be better off financially; why our work-point cash values should increase; why we can increase productivity if we are a larger unit. I can tell them exactly what the other team's economic position is, what kinds of cash reserves they have, and whether they're lying to us — that's because through my uncle I've seen the No. 4 team's ledgers. Also I'm friendly enough with the No. 4 team's accountant to have a very good idea of their finances. He wants to be an accountant in the new team and he knows my plans. So I'm supporting the merger and you can count on my help."

My own feelings about the merger were mixed. I knew that it was in the collective interest to join the two teams. That was the most important reason for supporting the merger. The Party wanted it; it was in line with the Chairman's instructions to improve the organization of agriculture wherever possible; the brigade intended to push for the merger, and it was certain that the commune leadership was solidly behind the brigade's decision. Yet I had my doubts. Back in 1964 we had failed to make it work. I was leader of the merged team then, and it was a difficult time. Team rivalries were sharp, and I had been unable to overcome the great hatreds that existed between us; after a few short months it was impossible to continue as one unit. Maybe I lacked the correct political consciousness, and maybe I was too biased in favor of my team. Whatever the reason, I failed as leader of the joint team. This time, though, I figured they would find another leader, not just because of what happened in 1964 but because I was getting too old and I wasn't a Party member. It would be logical to choose the No. 4 team leader. He was only thirty-eight, and a Party member. He had been a brigade cadre once and the brigade thought highly of him. I was sure that he would be the brigade's choice and I felt it was a good choice, one that our team could eventually accept. For personal, selfish reasons, I hoped the merger would go through because then I could give up my position without losing face. You see, I was nearly sixty and had been team leader for a decade. Being team leader was a burden. I did all that extra work and received almost nothing in return. For a whole year of countless meetings and other demands on my time, I only got about 100 extra work points. I could make twice that much if I bought a handcart and did odd carrying work for the team or brigade, and I would have more time to fix up my house and just take life a little easier.

So I secretly welcomed the idea of merger because I figured it would let me retire without loss of face. Maybe it was a selfish reason, but you know I'm an old man and you have to think about your household affairs when you get over sixty. Also, it was time to give way to younger people. It wasn't good that our team should have such an old leader. Only the No. 9 team had a leader who was over forty—the rest were all younger; one was even in his late twenties. I think the brigade first secretary knew my innermost thoughts because we had known each other nearly all our lives; he expected that I wouldn't seriously oppose the brigade's decision to support the No. 4 team leader for the leadership of the merged team.

It got to be December and we still hadn't settled anything. There had been lots of talk and quite a few meetings, but we were a long way from getting the two teams together. People were suspicious of change, and both teams were convinced that one team would profit at the other's expense. I had a long talk one evening with my friend, old Pigeon Turd, the animal tender. We called him Pigeon Turd because he raised pigeons on the second floor of his house and sold the droppings to the team for manure. Old Pigeon Turd was a down-to-earth peasant who had no great ambitions and got along with everyone. "Forget about the clan rivalries and old jealousies," he said, sipping his *bai jiu*.[3] "You can't change what's in people's hearts. The real issue is economic—we all feel that after the merger we'll be worse off than before. Take me, for example. Why should I agree? A larger team means we'll want to buy a rubber-tire cart. That means we'll have to sell some of our animals to pay for the cart. We'll have to sell several work animals in any case because we won't need so many with only one team. And what will the expanded team do with two animal tenders? If the new team leader isn't from our team, I could lose my job. And I like it and don't want to give it up. Then, what about my pigeons? I make 70 yuan a year from selling pigeon shit to the team. Who's to say that it will be the same with a merged team? With a bigger team it will be easier to apply for a fertilizer loan from the commune credit cooperative. Maybe the new team will then decide to lower the price they will pay for pigeon shit. Maybe they'll cut down on sideline industry altogether. Look at that pig business. It's going to cost us all more now to raise pigs because there's no more free fodder if our pigs have to be penned up. They're always talking about emulating Dazhai—well, the first step is to make the basic unit larger and then they'll take away our sideline industry and give it to the team. I'll eat all my pigeons before I'll give my coop over to the team. You can see that I don't like it one bit. And they tell us our work-point value will rise if we merge. Why is that? Everyone knows we're a richer team. Seems to me that only No. 4 team's work points will rise. They say that 'bigger means better,' that a bigger team will do everything better and that production will rise. Who can say that is so? Sometimes it works out that way, but often it's the reverse."

My talk with Pigeon Turd convinced me that we needed an open meeting of the two teams, together with the brigade cadres, to clear the air. It was agreed, and one December afternoon we met inside brigade headquarters. There were over a hundred of us and we listened to the brigade cadres trying to explain why the merger would lead to higher household incomes for all of us. They pointed out that by pooling our livestock and equipment we could sell enough of the surplus livestock and tools to buy a rubber-tire cart. The rubber-tire cart would save hundreds of yuan per year on transportation costs and could be hired out to other brigades as well. So there would be extra profit for everybody. It would be more economical to work the fields. Some of the combined fields would be large enough to be plowed by a small tractor. The combined team would be big enough to qualify for a larger loan from the credit cooperative to finance increased mechanization and fertilization. The combined team would be the same size as all the other teams, and the work-point values of those teams were at least as high as, if not higher than, the 30 cents that No. 2 team got last year and the 28 cents that No. 4 team had received. Despite the local gossip, both teams were almost identical in economic capacity; they had roughly the same grain and cash reserves, the same land, and the same amount of labor power. The brigade cadres emphasized that the size of private plots would not be reduced and that there was no intention of eliminating private sideline industry by giving it over to the team. "This is not Dazhai," said the brigade first secretary. "We do what's best for Liu Wei village, in accordance with Chairman Mao's instructions. We have no desire to change anything in the private sphere. Except, of course, you must now remember to fence in your pigs, and the same rule applies to your chickens, by the way."

After the brigade cadres had spoken, there was a long silence. This was to be expected in a room full of people who didn't normally talk to each other and were also being confronted by a Party policy they didn't like. No one wanted to stick his neck out and speak against the merger in front of the brigade first secretary. In such a setting even Da Dui and the Accountant hesitated to speak in support of the policy. So there was silence until Pigeon Turd finally stood up and said: "We all know that the leadership wants us to join together. But we also remember what happened in the past. You say we will be better off and that our incomes will rise. You tell us that we have nothing to lose and everything to gain. You say that our work-point value will rise, and that's a big plus—we all want more income. Maybe so, but what if it doesn't? Then we're stuck with each other just like the last time." Pigeon Turd had expressed the feelings of most of us. You could see that for once members of both teams were in agreement, and they waited for a reply from the brigade.

The brigade cadres talked it over and then the first secretary stood up again. "We expected to settle this matter by the end of the year, but now this seems impossible. We wanted to start the fiscal year off with the new team. It makes it easier for accounting purposes. But it's stupid to force you, and we at the brigade level must think how best we can persuade you so that we can settle the issue by the New Year. Let me just say now that if the two teams merge, the brigade will guarantee that for the coming year you will get whatever loans you need from the credit cooperative for machinery and equipment. For the first year, also, the brigade will supply at its own expense a tractor driver to help you work the combined fields. This is a very generous offer and is worth hundreds of yuan when you think it all out. So go home, discuss the matter among yourselves, and then let's meet again."

Well, we went home and talked among ourselves, and I could see that we were making some progress. The majority of peasants still opposed the merger, but now even Pigeon Turd was a bit less critical. One evening, as we sat together smoking, he said: "I guess we don't have much choice in the matter. It's clear that the brigade will push for the merger to the bitter end. But the longer we wait, the better a deal we might get from them. In the short run, they'll help us out financially—you can see that from what they said about loans, fertilizer, and the tractor driver. Maybe we can get them to guarantee a higher work-point value in the first year or so. That will go a long way to convince a few old peasants like me, for example. Let's wait and see what happens between now and the New Year. This is the time of year we traditionally forgive past quarrels and settle our affairs. Let's hope the brigade will help us do that." Then, like all old peasants, he reached into his mouth, picked off some of the stuff stuck between his teeth, and used it to glue a new cigarette he was making. We smoked together quietly for a long time and then he said: "Maybe it will work out after all. Let's see what the New Year brings."

The New Year came suddenly upon us in a rush, and for two weeks life was completely focused on the celebrations. Everybody was busy making new clothes, buying and selling at the market, cleaning up the house and preparing food. The merger was pushed into the corners of our minds and replaced by red packets, firecrackers, and remembrance of ancestors. So there it was, mid-February, and still no merger. Soon the slack farming season would be over and it would be time for serious work in the fields, but we hadn't resolved the issue. We were more receptive now to the idea, but nothing concrete had happened and the brigade leadership was getting quite concerned. They called me and the No. 4 team leader together and told us bluntly to get our teams together to make final arrangements for the merger to start before Qing Ming, around the beginning of April. The first secretary waved his finger and actually shouted at us: "Too damn much talk and no action! Enough is enough. Get your teams together to elect a new team committee in the next week and then we'll discuss the final arrangements."

Selecting a merged team committee turned out to be a terrible task. The brigade by this time had made it clear that they wanted the No. 4 leader to be head of the new team. Secretly I was happy — it meant I could finally be relieved of my job — but it was a big blow to the rest of my team, who felt that if the No. 4 team leader ran the new team, then the old No. 4 team would always have an advantage. Three-Fingers Li said, "A team leader controls his team. He can assign the best jobs to his friends. He has the power to reward them and to make life miserable for those he dislikes." I argued that it wasn't so, that he had to consult with the team committee and that half of the cadres on that committee would come from our team. Furthermore, the new team leader was a Party member who had stronger loyalties to the brigade than to the No. 4 team. He had been a brigade cadre before and actually had been implanted [sent to live permanently] in the No. 4 team four years ago. He wasn't a Li, and I knew him to be a fair man.

"Maybe so," said old Pigeon Turd, "but you know that he was demoted in 1963 for corruption. He used his position as a brigade cadre to take large sums of money from the brigade accounts to engage in private speculation. Do we want someone like that entrusted with the key to our cash and grain reserves?" The Accountant replied, "Yes, it's true that he was guilty of corruption. But he paid back every cent. Besides, who among us wasn't guilty of such practices then? I think there are plenty of safeguards to protect us now, and he won't make the same mistake again." After long discussion, we finally agreed to accept the No. 4 team leader, provided that our team selected the deputy team leader and the warehouse keeper (who was in charge of all implements and animals). The Accountant had his sights set on bigger things and he didn't want to be selected as team accountant; and the only other important post to be selected was the work-point recorder. We agreed that the team leader ought to decide whom he wanted to record work points, even though this, too, was a job which could easily be abused — a work-point recorder and team leader could easily give their friends more work points each day than they actually deserved.

Still we thought it was a good compromise: they would get the team leader, accountant, and work-point recorder, and we would get the deputy team leader and the warehouse keeper. To even out the two teams' representation on the team committee, which had eight members altogether, we would get two of the three remaining posts. We felt it was a workable solution although the No. 4 team had an advantage. Yet when I spoke with the No. 4 team leader, he was visibly upset. He didn't want to have his deputy selected by someone else, he said: "I want someone I can trust." So he turned down our proposal and stayed in his house for several days, sulking. When the brigade first secretary found out about that, he angrily stormed down to his house and cursed him for being so stubborn. He said that if the No. 4 team leader didn't agree to the No. 2 team's proposal, the brigade would withdraw its recommendation that he be the new team leader. "Then you can rot forever in your house because you'll never get to be a brigade cadre as long as I'm in charge." (At least that's what the gossip was; I wasn't there and who knows what was said? But it sounds likely.)

The No. 4 team leader didn't want to lose face. He prized the job and he didn't want to lose his chances of being promoted in the future—but a way had to be found to let him accept our offer. So he agreed to try it our way until the end of the year, at which time we would agree to review the composition of the team leadership. If after eight months he could not work well with the deputy leader, then we would select a second deputy, one from his old team. The rest of the team cadre and committee positions would be adjusted accordingly, to make sure there was equitable representation from both sides.

Having agreed upon the new leadership, we now settled down to resolve the remaining issues. The brigade called another meeting of both teams, and the first secretary pointed out that we had shown the wisdom of the masses and of the Chairman's policy of integrating smaller units into larger ones. Now all that was left was to get formal approval by both teams. To help us in this direction, the first secretary announced that the merged team would be allowed to operate a sesame-oil press. This was a big concession. Only one other team in the brigade had a sesame-oil press, and that team not only got a substantial cash income from the sale of the oil but every household got extra sesame oil from what was conveniently "spilled" in the process. Having a sesame-oil press meant that we all would be able to squeeze out a bit of precious cooking oil for ourselves at the expense of the state. This was a real bonus. The first secretary paused to let this sink in, and then he added: "We think that the expanded team will increase its production considerably. I know some of you doubt that, but we are absolutely certain. If you work well together, your work-point values should rise by at least 10 percent. The brigade will guarantee half that rise in the first year only. That is, the combined work-point value of both teams is approximately 29 cents. We will guarantee a rise to 30.5 cents. So you have nothing to lose by joining. If you make more than that, it's all yours."

Well, those concessions settled the matter finally. Both teams were getting a good deal economically, and the sesame-oil press was a real bonus. We had settled the leadership question reasonably well. That, of course, left the same old clan rivalries and hatreds. The two teams had never got along in the past — would they do so now? Would they cooperate in working in the fields? It was up to the new team committee to organize the work so that the members of the old teams wouldn't have to work together right away on the same projects. The idea was to start the cooperation slowly, and then hope that in the fields the members of the two teams could eventually work as a single unit. But that would take time. No one knew how we would work together, but we had at least finally reached agreement that we would merge.

One of the new team's first decisions was to buy a rubber-tire cart. The cart would cost 1500 yuan, including the mule and two donkeys to pull it. The combined team had enough cash and grain reserve to pay for the cart, but we couldn't get permission to spend that money. The brigade made it clear that we must get the 1500 yuan by getting rid of our surplus oxen and by taking out a loan at the credit cooperative. We sold two older oxen at the market fair and received about 300 yuan. The third we took to be slaughtered at the commune abattoir. First, though, we took the head of the abattoir, a crafty old peasant, out for a big meal and lots of *bai jiu*. We tried to soften him up because it was up to him to decide how much the commune would pay for the carcass. He was a tough bargainer in spite of the friendly drinking, so we only got another 100 yuan for the hide and the meat that was still good. Actually we were lucky because there were quite a few sent-down cadres living in the area. They were crazy over beef (most of us didn't like to eat it, even if we could afford to) and would pay high prices to the commune for any fresh beef. They even liked to eat the tongue, liver, and tail, which we just threw away.

Anyway, altogether we scraped up about 400 yuan. Then we arranged with the credit cooperative to lend us the balance at 1.8 percent interest. We expected to pay off the loan in a year. The brigade made sure that the cooperative agreed to lend us the money. Once we had the money in hand, things went surprisingly well. The new team leader personally went out looking for a good cart, donkeys, and a mule. He took old Pigeon Turd with him because everyone knew that Pigeon Turd knew his animals. He even slept with them every night to be sure they were properly cared for and fed! Anyway, the two of them went off to the market fairs and found a sturdy mule, two donkeys, and a cart. The donkeys led the way with the mule pulling along behind them. The mule cost over 400 yuan, but old Pigeon Turd was pleased with him. The donkeys also looked fine, even though they each cost 300 yuan. The cart, in excellent condition, cost us 500 yuan after a lot of hard bargaining (the team selling the cart first wanted 600 yuan but we finally got our price). By June the transactions had been completed, the loan was approved and we had our cart, just in time for the first harvest. It was with some satisfaction that members of the new team could pause during their work and see the cart roll by with members of both teams sitting on top of the freshly harvested grain, actually talking to each other.

We all wondered whether the merger would last beyond the first year, and it did. Part of the reason was that the brigade leaders had been right: productivity did rise, so much so that the annual work-point value in 1972 was 33 cents. The rubber-tire cart and the sesame-oil press were bringing in a substantial cash income, and the planting and harvesting of wheat and corn had been made easier by the larger combined fields and more mechanization. Household income had risen and, as you know, nothing pleases a peasant more than to get a few more yuan to spend. The increased prosperity had subdued the old rivalries between the two teams. There certainly were quarrels and arguments between us, but for the time being the higher income made us tolerate each other. Then, too, the new team committee was doing a good job. It tried hard to avoid favoritism to one team or the other. The new team leader proved to be a good choice. He was as fair as could be expected under the circumstances. He didn't always work well with his deputy, but that was to be expected. The brigade kept a close eye on what was happening and so did the Party, through its members on both teams.

Now it is 1975 and the two teams are still together, although there have been problems. The team committee had to be reorganized in the second year and now it has two deputy leaders, one from each of the old teams. There was a major dispute involving work points, and members of our team accused the recorder of giving extra work points to No. 4 team. There was a big argument over the sesame-oil press. The peasant in charge (from our team) was accused of spilling extra sesame oil and secretly giving it to his uncles and relatives from his old team. Last year no one worked in the fields for ten days because each team accused the other of getting an unfair advantage in labor assignments. So there's lots of bickering going on, but as long as they have a good work-point value, the new team will probably stick together.

The Accountant got the post on the brigade level that he was after, and he's no longer an active part of the team. However, Da Dui is still hanging around the brigade, waiting to become a full-fledged cadre. His personal life got in the way of his ambitions — he was caught in an affair with a married woman and the Party decided the time wasn't ripe to promote him. Pigeon Turd is doing well. He became animal tender on the new team and continued to sell pigeon shit. With the higher work points he was able to get enough cash to buy a small cart of his own. He admits that he may have been mistaken in opposing the merger so strongly at first, but he also says, "As long as we get our work points, we'll cooperate. But what happens when there are bad times? Then we'll remember why we never got along for generations in this village."

Maybe he's right, but in the meantime the merger has worked and it's as I told you at the beginning — the change isn't big, but it's for the better. In the old days nothing ever changed in the countryside, unless it was for the worse and by means of the landlord's lashes. Yet now there are ways to improve your livelihood and we have a voice in these matters. The brigade didn't use force to convince us to merge; we had to discuss everything and work it all out. And that's another thing, peasants sitting down and discussing decisions like that. Who would have imagined we would be able to do that? To be able to cast aside clan rivalries — that's a big sign of progress. So, as I said at the beginning, it isn't all mud and shit in the countryside. Peasants have come a long way forward. True, life in the cities is better, but we don't have to be ashamed of what we are. Sometimes when I talk with some of those sent-down cadres, who are soft and useless and can't do anything with their delicate, long hands, I wonder just who is better off. But that's another story to tell. One day I'll tell you about Big City Cadre, who came to our village for two years. He brought his own bed. We had to throw water on his courtyard every day because he couldn't stand the dust. We laughed at him for two years, although I admit most of us envied his fancy wrist-watch and high income.

I'm an old man and like to tell stories. I think I ramble a lot, and please forgive me. I did want to tell you a bit about the countryside and about what it's like to be a peasant who has seen the changes over fifty years. I feel funny sitting here in Hong Kong telling this to a foreigner. If it wasn't for the chance to see my brother after being separated for forty years, I never would have come here. I'm going back next month, that's for sure. I miss my village very much.

Chairman Mao's Letter to Li

SINCE 1968 over seventeen million Chinese young people have been sent from the city to the countryside to live and work with the peasants. It has been a controversial policy, disliked by most city youth. The large majority of refugees escaping from China have been "sent-down" youth who decided it was better to leave China than to stay in the countryside. Peasants also were critical of the policy, complaining that sent-down youth were an economic burden on the team, "empty rice bowls" that had to be filled by the peasants' labor, because sent-down youth often lacked the skills or the will to do their share of agricultural work.

Some young people were able to adjust and they stayed in the villages, settling down and raising families. A few became rural administrative cadres, specialists, or teachers. They are examples, albeit a minority, of the ideology behind the policy of bridging the gap between town and country. In this story, both Dongli and the narrator are touched positively by the possibility of being a "bridge," trying to work and live among the peasants.' They are resigned to their fate and respond to it in a constructive individual way, although ultimately the priorities of the larger system of which they are only a small part determine their future.

Chairman Mao's letter to Li Qinglin is an authentic document, cited at various times in the Chinese press. Three respondents were able to produce similar versions of Li's letter, and the text reproduced here was copied down by one respondent and brought out of China. There is nothing that is especially startling in the contents of Li's letter. His complaints on behalf of his son

*were voiced by countless other parents and youth over the past
ten years. What is interesting is that Chairman Mao chose to ease
the growing dissatisfaction by responding to Li's complaint in a
public fashion, and that he personally offered concrete assistance
to alleviate the worst hardships of sent-down youth. After 1973
there were cosmetic changes in the sent-down policy: young
people were not generally sent so far away from home; local authorities were given more money to help the youth adjust to rural
life; they were more likely to be put together with other youth in
teams rather than with the local peasants; their chances of returning to the city were somewhat enhanced by the reopening of
the universities, which began to admit a few candidates recommended by commune officials. Yet, in 1979, the authorities
continue to send urban youth to the villages and it is still difficult
for those now in the countryside to return to their homes. There
have been unpleasant demonstrations by young people demand-
ing urban residency and jobs. It is likely that this very sensitive
policy will be restructured in the near future, a development that
will be watched closely by the ten million sent-down youth who
remain in the Chinese countryside.*

I REMEMBER IT WAS AUGUST 1973 when I was summoned
to a special brigade meeting at which a county official read out
an important document. It was a Party document and I think it
was No. 21.[1] Its main subject was Chairman Mao's letter to a
schoolteacher, Li Qinglin. Li had become fed up with his seven-
teen-year-old son's critical economic situation down in the countryside and, after fruitless attempts to have local cadres do something, Li decided to write a letter directly to the Chairman. The
wonder of it all was not just that the Chairman actually received
Li's letter, but that he sent a reply. Mao's reply signaled an im-
pending change in the policy of sending youth down to the countryside, and so the Party summoned the twenty sent-down youth
in my brigade to hear the text of Chairman Mao's letter.

I had been working in the village for nearly three years,
having been sent down in 1970 from the Guangdong county town
where I was born and raised. I was twenty-one then, a headstrong
girl who had strongly resisted being "mobilized" for nearly a year.
First I managed to get a doctor's certificate that said I was in bad

health and needed to rest at home. Then through family connections my parents found me a job in a small local factory. But that job only lasted for three months. Finally the local authorities put pressure on my parents and on me to stop hanging around town. So I said I would go, but then managed to delay my departure again because my mother was sick and I had to help out at home. After a year of all this, however, I ran out of tricks. Actually some of my friends had already gone to work in agriculture and their reports weren't so bad. One friend had become a cadre in his brigade and was talking as if he might stay in the country forever. He didn't live that far from town, and I saw him several times. He even told me that if I liked life in the countryside maybe we could get married and live together in his brigade. He wasn't joking about liking the countryside, although I wasn't quite sure about the seriousness of his proposal. He said, "You should stop hanging around the towns and cities. There's no place for you there. There aren't any jobs and, besides, young people have to experience life, find out what life is really like. The best place for that is among the peasants. You can serve the masses and also have a good career, especially if you go to a commune that's close to the city." He sounded exactly like the Party propagandists who were always trying to drum us out of the cities into the villages, but I knew my friend really was serious. This made me think it wouldn't be so bad, and I guess, in the back of my mind, marrying him didn't seem so far-fetched. He was good-looking and came from a solid family. His father was a cadre of good class background, and a girl might well be satisfied with him for a husband.

As it turned out, however, we didn't get married. As a matter of fact, we saw each other only once more during the next three years, and by that time he had a wife and I had met someone else at the brigade where I was sent to live. Now Dongli and I were sitting side by side, listening intently to what the county cadre was telling us about Chairman Mao's letter. After three years of working together I knew what would be going on inside Dongli's mind and heart as he listened impassively to the cadre's words. Dongli had said more than once when I was complaining about my lot in the countryside: "It doesn't matter how you serve the people. Whether you're sent to work on the frontier or to dig potatoes you must find virtue in your duty. If the Party wants you to stay in the city, then you can thank Heaven for your luck."

Dongli had wanted to be an engineer all his life, but then came the Cultural Revolution and in 1969 he was sent down from Canton. He resolved not to resist or sulk, trying instead to wipe out his disappointment by becoming the best and most active of the intellectual youth. Soon he was appointed deputy team leader and had a good chance of being accepted into the Party. Outwardly he was a model sent-down youth, hard-working and committed to a life in the countryside. When our group arrived in the village in 1970 the leaders appointed him to take charge and to help us get settled. At first I thought him obnoxious, with his talk about "serving the poor and lower-middle peasants." Then one day I realized that in his heart he was like me, just as scared and confused and disappointed with his fate as I was. After that we became close friends and I felt that someday we would marry. He taught me to be like the willow tree, "to sway in any political wind without fear of being knocked down." At the same time he told me, "To be a willow all the time is also dangerous, because people will see you are an opportunist without principles. So sometimes you must be a pine tree as well, standing straight and tall, regardless of the wind. That's what Chairman Mao teaches us, and I intend to apply his lesson carefully."

Now we were both listening to the county cadre reading the text of the Chairman's letter to Li. The letter was short, and it read as follows:

Comrade Li Qinglin, I now send you 300 yuan. I hope this can solve the immediate difficulty of your son's poor economic situation. There are many similar cases in our nation. I will find a basic solution for all of them soon!

(*signed*) Mao Zedong

The county cadre then explained how it came about that the Chairman had written this letter. Li was a teacher in a primary school in the province of Fujian, earning only 45 yuan a month. He had three children, and all were in the countryside. The youngest was sixteen years old in 1973 when he was sent to the village. All three children were unable to support themselves economically and the father used to send them money, but it wasn't enough.

At this point we all pricked up our ears. What a familiar story that was! Had any of us, with the possible exception of Dongli, been able to survive solely on our own merits economically in our village? We all relied on money from home. None of us could have endured the countryside (especially the girls) without outside help. We couldn't earn enough work points and we couldn't get enough from our private plots. So we were intrigued by the Chairman's grant of 300 yuan to Li and by the hint that the Chairman was finally going to solve the problem.

The county cadre continued: "Teacher Li had problems convincing the local cadres to help him. They told him they could not make an exception in his case because it was a matter of national policy, and so Teacher Li sat down and wrote the following letter to Chairman Mao."*

Esteemed Chairman Mao:

I sincerely wish you longevity [ten thousand years' long life].

I know you have been very busy attending to the cause of the country and world affairs and I should not dare to bother you at all. I am, however, most desperate at the moment so I dare to write to you.

I am a teacher at the Putian Primary School, Putian County, Fujian Province. Ever since Liberation I have busied myself in the Party's educational work, and have always been keen in participating in all past campaigns.

Your policy of "young intellectuals going to receive education from the poor and lower-middle peasants" was correct, and I wholeheartedly support it. In response, my son went without hesitation to a distant hilly area to receive his re-education.[2]

Now, however, he faces several difficulties. For example, take

---

*Other sources suggest that it was not this simple. Li tried three times to send the letter to Mao but it was twice intercepted by provincial Party authorities. Li was threatened with serious punishment if he continued to write such letters (*China News Analysis*, February 20, 1976). Another respondent said that the letter had reached the Chairman only because of a "connection." The son of a high government official attended Li's school, knew Li, and arranged to hand the document to his father, who in turn gave it to a "distant relative" of Chairman Mao's.

After the death of Mao and the downfall of the Gang of Four, Li was attacked and later arrested for being "the trusted follower of the Gang of Four in Putian" (Radio Fuzhou, January 28, 1977, and November 15, 1977). (I am indebted to Victor C. Falkenheim for this information.)

food rationing. He gets X catties of staple food and X catties of supplementary foodstuffs a year.[3] Even at the very best, this annual amount only lasts him for eight months. It may sound ridiculous, but my son can't even afford to have his hair cut.

Some city cadres made various excuses to recall their children back to the cities. For example, they say they are "needed for the cause of revolution" and for "backing up industries." We who don't have much personal influence have to stand by helplessly and see our children confined permanently to remote, barren, and mountainous areas.

At the moment I am still alive and can render him a little assistance. But I cannot imagine what will happen to him when I die.

Under such desperate circumstances, I can only turn to you for assistance.

(*signed*)   Li Qinglin

The county cadre paused and said: "That was an authentic copy of the letter that Li sent to our esteemed Chairman. You have heard the Chairman's reply and it is clear that the Party will, in accordance with Chairman Mao's instructions, take fundamental action in the immediate future. Let me now read from the rest of Party Document No. 21." The county cadre adjusted his spectacles and continued: "Our great leader Chairman Mao has personally taken the initiative to encourage young intellectuals to go to the countryside to receive re-education from the poor and lower-middle peasants. This immensely helped to revolutionize all young people's ideology. Some local leading cadres, however, have failed to grasp the essence of this great policy."

Suddenly Dongli sat up straighter, his eyes intently focused on the county cadre. The rest of us, too, were waiting for something to happen. There was tension in the air. Were our local cadres about to be singled out for major criticism, or was this just a routine phrase in the Party document? We were listening carefully because we had to take our cues from how the Party would criticize local cadres. If the Party document was harsh in its criticism of local cadres, then we would be expected to criticize our own cadres accordingly. We could foresee unpleasant struggles lying ahead.

But the county cadre only produced a vague and mild rebuke of the local cadres. We all breathed a sigh of relief. He said:

"Chairman Mao's policy has been poorly practiced. Should these problems not be remedied in time, considerable damage will be caused to the Revolution. It is hoped that local collective leadership will seriously study editorials of *Wen Hui Bao* [the important Shanghai newspaper] and other relevant documents, and give their immediate attention to the implementation of the 'Send the Youth Down to the Countryside' campaign." After hearing these words we knew that, though local cadres had been singled out for criticism, it was only a mild reproach, without any political sting. We weren't going to be involved in any struggles just yet. Something big was in the works, but we didn't have to worry about committing ourselves or confronting our cadres. The Party was only setting the stage for future policy changes to conform to the spirit of Chairman Mao's letter to Li. Things could improve for sent-down youth—maybe not to the extent of actually rescuing us from our rural exile, but at least there would be some change for the better. We were a pretty happy lot after the county cadre had finished speaking. We had seen some hope at last. The local cadres were relieved because they had escaped major criticism. Local peasants and cadres both saw economic advantage to themselves if the center would actually subsidize the sent-down youth. This would relieve a major source of tension between peasants and sent-down youth.

Afterwards Dongli and I talked quietly about the significance of what we had heard. "You must not assume that much will change," he said. "Youth will continue to be sent down as before. The documents don't give any hint that those of us now in the villages are going to find it easier to go back to the cities. On the other hand, the fact that Chairman Mao actually wrote such a letter and that we've been told about it indicates that there will be substantial changes in the future." He wasn't too optimistic that these changes would get us back to the cities. But Weiling, my girlfriend, was very excited. She was sure that by Spring Festival we would all be back in the towns and cities: "The Chairman is going to send us all back home, I'm sure of that," she exclaimed. "Back to Canton, to civilization. I can hardly wait!" She could barely restrain her enthusiasm, but I felt more like Dongli. I told her that if the Party was going to send us all back home, then the Chairman would have mentioned something like that in his letter. In my opinion there would be some changes, but I suspected they wouldn't have much of an impact on those of us who had been in the villages these past three or four years.

In the next few weeks there was plenty of gossip. We heard rumors that every youth who had spent three years in the villages would be returning home permanently before New Year's, and that this policy already was being carried out in one province. Another story said that girls would return home after three years but that boys had to stay longer. One "inside" story said that all sent-down youth would be instructed to return to the cities to go to higher specialized institutions and universities; then they would be returned to the countryside. And so on. We discussed the rumors among ourselves and were a bit uneasy. Black-Face Meng (he had a large birthmark on the left side of his face) said that we should keep quiet until we saw which way the wind was blowing. "Remember the Hundred Flowers campaign? Those who foolishly dropped their guard were later cut down ruthlessly." So we kept our thoughts mainly to ourselves and waited.[4]

At the end of September the county cadre again appeared to address a meeting of all brigade cadres and sent-down youth. Peasants were not invited to this meeting. There were twenty-eight people in the room when he announced that a new Party document, No. 23, had just been released, and that this document directly dealt with the sent-down youth in the villages. He smiled and said (I can remember every word as if it were just yesterday, because it meant so much to us — we felt that our whole lives hung in the balance): "Following the lead set by our glorious leader, Chairman Mao, the Party has now approved important changes in the sent-down youth policy." I looked around and saw Black-Face Meng nervously trying to light his cigarette. Beside me Dongli and Weiling were both tensely straining forward to hear the cadre's words.

"The new Party document establishes the following," he said. "First, starting from now until 1980, all sent-down youth will be assigned either to existing state farms or to newly established youth units within communes. Sent-down youth will no longer be placed in existing teams and brigades. Instead, they will form their own teams and even their own brigades.[5] Sent-down youth will no longer live together with the peasants, but will have separate housing units. A section of land in each commune will be reserved for the exclusive use of sent-down youth, under the initial guidance and advice of the local inhabitants. These changes are to take place in the immediate future. Those youths who are already in the countryside, however, will remain in their current production units, which may or may not be restructured after the fall harvest has been completed." His last comment applied directly to us. It meant that for the moment there would be no change in status. By one simple stroke those of us already in the countryside appeared to have been cut off from the new generation of sent-down youth, just as the butcher cuts the tail off the dying ox.

Possibly sensing our feelings, the county cadre paused in his speech, cleared his throat, and added: "Remember that the Party is concerned for the happiness and welfare of *all* sent-down youth, in the past or future. For example, from now on any sent-down youth who has serious economic problems can get extra money from the state. If your yearly work-point value is less than 180 yuan, you can apply to the County Resettlement Office for a grant of 100 yuan.[6] You must, however, have worked a minimum of 120 days per year in the commune." We glanced at each other in surprise. This could mean that a clever youth might get away with working for only four months and then run off to hide in the city, returning just long enough to collect his 100 yuan. We all had plenty of friends who we knew would take advantage of this policy—they could spend well over half their time in the city each year and actually get paid for it.[7] "In future," continued the county cadre, "all new factory jobs will be open only to individuals who have spent a minimum of two years in the countryside as sent-down youth." This was no big deal since that was pretty much the current policy and the same exceptions apparently still applied: sons could "inherit" their fathers' jobs when their fathers chose to retire; communes that had special links with urban factories could continue to staff them with urban youth as the need arose; a son who supported aging parents was allowed to stay in the city and get first crack at a factory job; sometimes parents could keep one daughter in the city, to protect her against "uncertain" social relationships in the countryside.

The county cadre continued: "The Party is earnestly striving to take Chairman Mao's instructions to heart. You have all heard what the Chairman wrote to Li Qinglin, and now you are witness to the measures we are taking on your behalf. The future for

China's youth is bright, and we are grateful to the Party and to Chairman Mao. But we must also remain vigilant and oppose those who try to divide us, those who take cover under the flag of 'redness,' but who in fact wish to wave the black flag of reaction. The Party urges all of you assembled here, cadres and youth alike, to fight against the reactionary efforts of a few who wish to make socialism serve their own selfish ends. For example, there are those cadres who continue to abuse their positions by using the back door to pull their children out of the countryside. The Party is determined to stop these practices." I smiled to myself when I heard those words. This wasn't the first time that the Party was "determined to stop these practices." Not only did they always continue, regardless of the campaign, but those youth who were actually caught were rarely shipped back to the villages. It was like a game really. The cadre went on: "The Party ensures that local organs will look out for the welfare of sent-down youth, making certain they have enough food and proper living conditions. Where sent-down youth are economically suffering, the local authorities, together with other state organs, will step in and offer concrete assistance."

I didn't think much of that, and looking around the room at the local cadres' faces I don't think they thought much of it either. We were not a rich commune. The peasants could barely feed themselves. How could a local organ sacrifice anything extra for the sent-down youth? I suddenly recalled the words of my former team leader, Old Xu: "You are an unproductive lot, all of you. Despite all the propaganda, I know in my heart that we are worse off now, after you've come. We just can't afford to have so many of you eating out of our small rice bowl." Now the Party was asking people like Old Xu to provide even more from that rice bowl. So I didn't think much of this part of the speech, and I could tell that Dongli, Black-Face Meng, and Weiling didn't either.

The cadre went on: "Anyone who abuses or sabotages the Party's policies with respect to sent-down youth will be severely punished. By this we mean the severest punishment: full-scale surveillance, imprisonment, and even execution where necessary. Cadres and peasants who have forced sexual relationships with sent-down youth will be treated as counterrevolutionaries and executed. I can tell you that in Dongfang county an important

cadre has just been executed for raping two sent-down girls repeatedly over the past two years. He used his position to force
himself on women and has paid the price. The Party will not
tolerate such practices and will in the future deal harshly with
those who are found guilty."

[*At this point my respondent became somewhat flustered
and nervous, although she soon resumed her narrative as if
nothing had happened. Later, during more intensive question-
ing, it became apparent that she had a rape experience of her
own, but did not feel comfortable telling this story to a man, who
was also a foreigner. After a while she finally confided her story to
a female Chinese researcher and later, after the fourth interview,
she was willing to talk about it with me. Apparently not long after
she had been sent down to the commune, one of the commune
cadres took more than a fatherly interest in her work. She was an
attractive young woman. The commune cadre lived in the same
village and, under the guise of helping her learn about accounting procedures, began to make advances. At first she didn't realize what was going on but when she did, and resisted the man, he
grew more insistent, brought her presents, got her extra food
rations and other privileges, and tried to cajole her into sleeping
with him. She threatened to tell his family but he just laughed
and said, "I can do what I like with women here. Nobody dares
oppose me and you'll warm my bed just like the others before
you."
    One night he cornered her, saying that there was no point in
resisting any longer. She tried to get away; he grabbed her, tore
at her clothing, and pulled her down on the ground. She was
strong enough to fight back and then made a lot of noise. Luckily
someone heard and shouted, wanting to know what all the racket
was. The cadre ran off cursing. The next day he showed up with
scratches on his face, and the villagers winked at each other.
Everybody knew he had been after her. He didn't bother her
again, but after that she had a rough time. She didn't get any
privileges and the villagers treated her differently now, with far
less respect. "At least half of them were sure I had slept with him
all those times we were together. And the other half thought that,
if I hadn't, then I must have been really stupid to give up all the
advantages of having an affair with a top cadre. He got off scot-*

free after he had tried to rape me. No one ever criticized him; no one ever dared complain; but for me the next few months were very hard. Several times I had to fight off advances from other men, and one of them even said to my face: 'Why the false modesty? Your affair with the commune cadre is well known here. Take me as your lover now—I'm better looking and I'm younger too.' "

The experience caused her to withdraw from most relationships at the commune. It made her aware, she said, of how little the status of women had changed in that village, despite twenty years of Party propaganda. Top cadres could easily abuse their authority, and most people either did not care or were afraid to say anything for fear of "getting rid of the tiger in front in order to be devoured by the wolf in the rear." She felt the local peasants were especially backward with regard to such sexual encounters. Forced sexual relations were not uncommon, and even rape was seen as "part of the male-female relationship." "In passion there is violence," was a common local theme, and so was the saying, "A woman who first resists will then remain faithful forever." For a long time she was haunted by the memories and implications of the cadre's attempted rape. Only when she began to see Dongli did she slowly recover from this experience.]

After the county cadre finished his speech, Dongli and I talked about what it meant for us. We agreed that things had changed for the better for sent-down youth. The Party was obviously determined to make life in the countryside more palatable for us. The extra income would help those who had suffered economic hardship. Segregating peasants and youth in the future should make it easier for both groups: the peasants wouldn't be grumbling about having to put in extra work time to support us, and the youth wouldn't have to put up with all their petty criticisms. On the other hand, most of these policies applied to the incoming group of sent-down youth, not to us. We didn't need the income supplement, since over the years we had either become productive members of our village or had been receiving remittances from home. Separating us from the villagers after three years of living together was pointless—both sides had learned to get along and to tolerate each other's quirks and (more significantly) each other's major cultural differences. We were afraid that we had become too adjusted to rural life to constitute a problem to the Party. "Look," said Dongli, "they'll just leave us alone. They won't set up separate units for those already here in the commune, and the villagers in any case won't want to give up even a foot of their land just so we can form a separate group. Even if the Party twists their arms, we'll still suffer, because then we'll simply be given the worst land. You remember that piece of waste land, the seven hectares behind old Gao's house? That's what we will get and we'll be worse off than before Chairman Mao wrote that letter."

Two things seemed very clear to me. First, we weren't about to be sent back home, so all the gossip had been wrong. I told Weiling to forget about spending New Year's in Canton. "You had better instead think about composing revolutionary couplets attacking Confucius rather than dreaming about red packets (*hong bao*) from your family.[8] I think you'll be here for a long time." Black-Face Meng reminded us to keep quiet, saying that nothing was clear and that "the Emperor gives the most gold to the monkey who sits still the longest." Remember, he said, "Everybody listens to the noisy monkey, but he is also the first to be beaten." It was clear, second, that the Party was less concerned with the immediate futures of the millions of us already in the countryside than with the millions about to come. Black-Face Meng said that probably a whole new wave of youth was about to pour into the countryside and that the Party was simply smoothing out problems prior to their coming. "Just look," he said, "see how many youth have recently been sent down to the villages. The numbers are way up and they'll stay way up for a long time. The Party is too busy making sure they'll all be absorbed to worry about us as well." Dongli agreed with him, saying that it did seem as if the changes were destined for those to come rather than for us.

In the next twelve months, however, things did change. They didn't segregate us into a separate unit, but they also didn't send any more youth to our commune. Thus they were in effect phasing down the movement in our commune. More youth were now being sent to suburban communes closer to their homes, and more youth were being sent to separate units in nearby communes or to state farms staffed almost exclusively by youth. A friend of mine was sent to a state farm like that—he called it a "youth farm" — and said that it wasn't so bad. They all received enough food and the state made sure of their economic welfare by means of subsidies. The youth who went to new units inside existing communes weren't so happy because they usually received poor land (as Dongli had predicted) and found themselves rather isolated. The best off were those sent only a few kilometers from home, to suburban communes. When they became depressed they could just head home for a few days to recover. If they craved a taste of "city culture," they could get on a bus and be in the center of their hometown in an hour or so. We had none of these advantages, but the four of us continued to work out our personal accommodations to rural life — somewhat reluctantly to be sure, now that the promise of Chairman Mao's letter seemed unfulfilled for us.

I just kept on as I had without any illusions about the future. Dongli decided to throw himself completely into his work as deputy team leader, saying to me in private: "As far as going back to the city is concerned, I'm making my thoughts about that as 'blank' as Chairman Mao says a peasant's mind should be. Maybe in this way I'll be better off." Weiling was crushed when she suddenly realized nothing had changed for her. At first she moped around and did little. Then she became sick, so sick that they took her to the county hospital. She stayed there for several weeks and finally got permission to return home to her family to recuperate. That was the last we ever saw of her, and I wondered if she had recovered from her "convenient" sickness or whether, in fact, she had permanently slipped back to the city. Black-Face Meng stayed the way he was, for a long time saying little, following his own advice to keep quiet. Then one day he was gone, apparently to visit his sick father. He never came back either, and later we heard he had been caught trying to leave China, was in a detention camp in Southern Guangdong, and would soon rejoin his old friends in our village. But he never returned, and rumor has it that he did finally escape across the border to Hong Kong and now regularly sends money back to his family.

One day in mid-1974, Dongli was summoned to brigade headquarters and told he had a good chance of being sent to Canton to study engineering. He was informed that the brigade and commune leadership was recommending him strongly because of his excellent political and work record. The Party secretary said: "When you come back after four years, we expect you to make a major contribution to the technical level here, if not in this commune, then maybe as a technical expert at the tractor factory." Dongli was overjoyed at his luck. After four years his patience had paid off, and he was going to become an engineer. It was the chance of a lifetime and we both knew that, once he was a student in Canton, there was a good chance he would find a way to stay in that city forever. He had his ticket to a glorious future, but I wasn't destined to be so fortunate. There was no way that I could join him and so we were separated that summer. It was a bitter time for me. After four years we had grown very close, and now we had to be apart for a long time. Even if I managed to be sent back home, how could we be married and where would we live? Dongli would be in a bachelor dormitory in Canton and, even if I could get back home, I'd be in a town 150 kilometers away.

His letters came often and he was happy in his studies. For a long time I cried bitterly over my fate, but then one day something happened — I can't even explain it to you or to myself. I just decided to think more positively about rural life and less about leaving. For years I had strongly opposed being put in the countryside, but now I began to accept it. Maybe it was the business of harvesting that finally caught me up, or the rhythm of rural life. Whatever it was, I began to find value in what I had disliked. What used to bother me — the dirt, the gossip, the crudities of the peasants — no longer seemed relevant. My work as a team accountant was all-important and I was being useful for the first time in my life. Peasants argued with me about their work points; the other cadres consulted me about problems; I became involved in women's work. I was exhilarated and felt I had wasted four years of my life. Dongli's letters lay unanswered. I didn't care about what he was doing, I was that wrapped up in the life of my village.

For the next few months I completely shut out the outside world, resolving to live there forever. In retrospect that was the happiest time of my life. They told me I stood a good chance of becoming a Party member. I took an active part in the "Criticize Lin, Criticize Confucius" campaign, and in the campaign to "Study the Theory of the Dictatorship of the Proletariat."[9] Then one day the Party secretary shook me out of my euphoria by telling me that I was being sent home. I couldn't believe my ears. Why me? Hadn't I shown that I was willing to serve with the peasants forever? Wasn't I committed to living and working in the countryside? After five years, just when I had acquired the right consciousness, the Party was sending me back?

The Party secretary smiled at my questions and said: "Yes, that's all true and we're proud that you're such a fine example of Chairman Mao's teachings. But the matter is out of our hands. We've been ordered to return the eight sent-down youth still in our commune back to their homes. We cannot question such an order, and, besides, you're nearly twenty-five years old and still unmarried. Maybe it's best for you to go back home and find a husband. You haven't found one here among us, and now you're too old for any cautious man (there was that implicit reference to my 'rape' by the commune cadre). We will miss you, but perhaps it's for the best."

In this ironical way my life was again disrupted. I was being sent home to get married! In a rage I told the Party what I thought of the "great strides toward equality taken by China's heroic women." I stormed back home, not knowing what to do. Dongli and I had grown apart—how could I write to him after not answering his letters? My family was kind, but they couldn't adjust to "this woman, half peasant, half tiger," who raged about not knowing what to do. I found my life intolerable at that point, and so I went to visit a "sick grandmother" in Hong Kong. Only I'm still here now two years later, and the grandmother has died. I've found a husband and he can attest to my virginity when we married. So life has turned out better than I thought. Dongli, I hear, will soon become an engineer. Black-Face Meng must be somewhere in this city of four million, but I never see his birthmark in the crowds. Weiling I guess has disappeared—she may even be dead. Often I think about the four of us listening to the cadre reading out Chairman Mao's letter. Who would have thought that two short years later we'd be living lives so different, physically close to one another, true, yet in such different worlds?

Oil Man

CHINA'S ECONOMIC FUTURE is based on oil. If reserves, reported to be among the world's largest, can be developed quickly and effectively, then China will have the capital it needs to finance its massive modernization efforts. China's oil could pay for its large imports of foreign technology and could provide the energy to run its expanding industries. Much will depend on how China uses foreign technology and assistance in getting that oil into the refineries and out to the consumer. China's two major partners in these ventures probably will be Japan and the United States, both as suppliers of the necessary technology and, at least in the case of Japan, as ultimate consumers of the oil production.

The Oil Man's story turns out to be particularly fitting in the context of recent events. In the early fifties the Communists started exploring for oil, principally in the remote western parts of China. Later, when the Daqing fields began to develop, the focus shifted eastward and, by the mid-nineteen sixties, China declared itself self-sufficient in oil. The expansion of the fields at Dagang and Shengli, and the promise of more oil lying offshore, suggests that China will be among the future world leaders in oil production. The Oil Man was there during the transition from dependence on Soviet technology and expertise. He typifies China's stubborn insistence on developing its own expertise in this area and on moving ahead after the Soviet oil experts so hurriedly departed in 1960. The Chinese had to depend on Soviet technology and spare parts, but there were no advisers to give instructions. Still the Chinese managed to finish what the Soviets had

58

started, and the Oil Man could leave China satisfied that he had done a good job.

The story also shows that the rhetoric of the Cultural Revolution, in which "reds" were supposed to predominate over "experts," did not apply to an area so sensitive as oil production. The Oil Man tried to ignore politics. As a technician he felt that his job was to get oil for China. When politics intruded into Daqing briefly during the Cultural Revolution, the authorities in Peking quickly clamped down to see that production continued. Politics could not be allowed to jeopardize the all-important oil production. In recent times, the Gang of Four was criticized for reintroducing politics into oil production by attempting to sabotage the export of oil abroad, but by and large Chinese oil is an area that has remained above politics, a domain in which experts, both Chinese and foreign, hold sway to ensure China's development.

'VE HAD A GOOD LIFE, traveling all over the country, seeing the sights and living in dozens of places. If you take a map of China, there's almost no corner I haven't visited. Xinjiang, Qaidamu, Daqing, the south and the east, I've been to them all. Because I was an oil-drilling specialist, I was always on the go, spending a few months in one place then another. I went with a real sense of adventure, knowing that we were building up China. In the twenty years I was an oil man, we made spectacular progress. When I began there were only two or three fields, such as Yumen and Yanchang.[1] Then we found oil in Qaidamu and farther west in Xinjiang. We thought this was a real achievement, but then in the sixties and seventies we really developed our oil capacity, first in Daqing and then in Dagang and Shengli. You feel pride in China when you realize the magnitude of what we did. Remember, until 1965 we imported more oil than we exported, whereas now, in 1975, we ship oil abroad and can become one of the world's leading oil-exporting countries. I'm proud because we achieved so much and also because I participated in this historic rebuilding of China. I was right there in the early stages, especially in Qaidamu and at Daqing. I met Wang Jinxi, the famous "iron man of Daqing," and I even met Zhou Enlai once in Peking.

I went to western China the first time while still a student at the Peking Petroleum College. It was 1954 and a group from the college went to the Tsaidam Basin for six months to work in the oilfields there. We went to Daqaidam and Golmud. At the time, Daqaidam was a small town full of Tibetan and Kazakh minorities. The place was so isolated that we could watch the wolves running beside our truck. They had just started to build the city and it was in the middle of nowhere, where not much seemed to grow except parched grass and weeds. The climate was extraordinary; within one day the temperature sometimes changed by 24 degrees centigrade. I remember summer days when it was terribly cold at night and in the morning; yet at noon it could climb as high as 40 degrees centigrade. One summer evening it actually snowed. I never witnessed it myself, but I heard stories of truck drivers whose overheated vehicles stalled in the middle of the hot desert and who were found frozen to death the next day.

We had little rain, so water was a real problem. We needed water for everything, for drinking, for our crops, for oil drilling and recovery. It wasn't until 1958, when a pipeline was finally brought in, that we partially solved the water problem. We lived in tents at first and later on moved into dried-mud housing. Living conditions were primitive, but it didn't matter to us because we were young and enthusiastic. We were sure the oil was there, and over the next three or four years sank more than thirty wells. Most of them yielded oil of top quality.

Let me say some more about the weather. The basin covers an area of 300,000 square kilometers, but essentially it's an endless strip of near-desert, except along the eastern part where there's water. There were a few farm settlements, but most of the settlers were cattle-raising nomads of Mongol, Tibetan, and Kazakh extraction. The climate could not support a sedentary population, at least not on any significant scale. In the western section we had scarcely 50 millimeters of rainfall during a season. In the eastern part, away from the best oil deposits, there was 100 millimeters. The few rivers in the basin drain from the top of the rim into the center, and there you have a marsh that's so treacherous that careless travelers can get sucked down into the mire for good. What a place! Either you were pulled into the wet marshy land, or you died of thirst and heat on the nearby desert! But the most astonishing phenomena are the summer typhoons, which come from the north and west. Terrific winds lasting for two hours carry dust and dirt from the ground, and this gets spun into a gigantic cone. Sometimes there may be several of these cones in the sky at the same time, resembling the columns of a huge building. When we saw the cones approaching we dived for cover and waited for the storm to pass.

There's some agriculture, but it's marginal. There's too much salt in the soil, and this creates numerous problems. The best crop is grass, for cattle fodder. Sheep, goats, and horses are the main livestock, though there are camels and oxen too. But the high salt content adversely affects the quality of the grass and the drinking water. The larger animals suffer from foot diseases because of the salt. Still, despite the salt problem and the great hordes of mosquitoes that breed in the marshy areas, there has been progress in the area. I visited some of the state farms and they have been reclaiming land, leaching out the salt, and improving their irrigation networks. Nomads are now more settled and productive. They use water from melted snow and from underground systems to ease the chronic water shortage. In the years 1955-1959 I saw a great many positive changes and, when I returned in 1968-1970, the progress was continuing, and not just in agriculture. Golmud in 1956 had been a motley collection of mud huts, not much more than a watering place for Kazakh camel caravans. Sand dunes lay all around like burial mounds, covered with white thorn bushes and sand willows. If you made a loud noise, wild antelopes would burst out from the bushes. Well, in 1970 Golmud had grown to a city of 40,000 serving the oil and other mineral industries. You could still see camels and horses on the main streets in 1970, but the ex-herders who rode them now shopped for fancy clothes, hardware, and other supplies to take back to their nearby homes. When we arrived in the mid-fifties, you couldn't find a Chinese doctor and if you were really sick you might have to go to local traditional doctors for help. Then a handful of doctors and paramedics came, set up three tents, and carried out modest operations. When I came back in 1970, Golmud had a large new clinic and hospital with over a hundred doctors and nurses; this was one of four hospitals in the city. The medical tents were gone, although paramedics still made rounds on horseback to remote areas.

You know, the more I talk about those days, the more nostalgic I get. To see the way the place was transformed in less than fifteen years—that was impressive. Not just the oil wells and re- fineries either. Everything else changed too. The nomadic herd- ers settled down and were more prosperous. There was more water, and there were more goods in the shops at Golmud and Daqaidam and Lenghu. Where there had been camel tracks, there were now major roads; where sand dunes had stood, there were grain fields; where tents had flapped in the wind, sturdy homes existed. There were even brick homes in the area, al- though bricks had to be trucked in over 200 kilometers from Gansu province.

We started in the eastern part of the basin. Several wells had already been sunk by the time I arrived, and soon there were over 10,000 oil workers in the basin, mainly on the western side. We called Qaidamu a "sea of oil" because we knew there was plenty of it under the surface. By 1958 we had discovered 130 oil-bear- ing structures and had drilled 50 wells. Because the oil was close to the surface, we sometimes only had to drill a couple of hundred feet below the surface. The best wells are at Lenghu, and we went there in 1956 to do extensive drilling. We found oil at all levels, shallow and deep, from a range of less than 10 meters below the surface to over 3000 meters. The key discovery, however, was made in 1958, in an area called the No. 5 Formation. This is the source of most of the oil now being produced at Qaidamu.

I remember Lenghu in 1958. We pulled in the first gusher and telegraphed Peking the good news. A lake of oil appeared before our eyes, and hordes of technicians and workers came to Lenghu, pitched their tents, and got to work. There was no de- cent transportation. It was difficult to get our drilling equipment into the remote areas, and once we brought the wells in, we had to figure out how to move the oil out of Lenghu, eastward or south to Tibet. So the road builders descended on Qaidamu like locusts, and 2000 kilometers of roads were built in less than five years, linking Qaidamu to Tibet and to Xinjiang. The sections from Xining to Daqaidam and Golmud were developed and im- proved, and soon oil began moving eastward to the big refinery in Lanzhou. Still, we were limited by the transportation problem. It was impossible to build pipelines over such immense distances, and truck caravans often consumed up to 50 percent of the oil they carried. We only concentrated on the best wells, from which oil flowed the easiest, so as not to increase our already high costs. We also ran into tracking problems[2] because the oil-bearing layers were strangely positioned. What happens to these wells after they have been used for a while is that the pressure in the oil strata drops and this causes sand to collapse into the well. Often this means abandoning the well — at least that's what happened in the sixties. By the early seventies, however, we reopened some of these abandoned wells by a water-injection method we had been using at Daqing, the big new oilfield in the northeast. In 1970 we were building a 40-kilometer pipeline for the oilfields, and once it was completed we could pump water into formerly abandoned wells and radically increase production.

I learned from Soviet advisers at the Petroleum College, and I read Russian textbooks on oil drilling and exploration. In Qaidamu there were quite a few Russians. One of our joint stock companies was in oil development, and we imported most of our basic oil exploration and extraction equipment from our Soviet "elder brothers." Over half of our new capacity in crude-oil production in the fifties came from Soviet-aided oil projects. I remember one Russian who worked with us, first at Golmud and then at Lenghu. He was called Fuluoerfu [Frolov] and he sweated all the time. He was always drenched in sweat and smelled like a camel in heat. He wasn't a bad fellow and we learned a lot from him, though he didn't like to admit he was wrong. Several times we questioned his techniques and suggested better ways of doing things. He always shook his head and repeated the same words in broken Chinese: "Elder brother's tools, elder brother's trucks, elder brother's experience — let elder brother decide." Compared with some of the other Russians I had met, he was actually a good fellow. He liked to drink a lot and chase after women, but he knew how to find oil and that's what counted.

By 1959 there were nearly 200,000 oil workers in Qaidamu, and oil production had risen rapidly. We had made great strides in the west, at Qaidamu and also at two other fields farther west in Xinjiang [Karamay and Dushanzi]. Still China was not yet self-sufficient in oil and we relied heavily on the Soviet Union. Then two things happened that decisively changed the course of China's petroleum development. First, the dispute with the Soviets escalated and they packed up and went home in 1960. Second, we discovered a huge reservoir of oil in the northeast at Daqing that would enable China to become self-sufficient in production by the mid-sixties. The abrupt departure of the Soviets was a terrible short-run blow because they left unfinished projects and took their blueprints back home. We were thoroughly committed to Soviet equipment and couldn't switch over to Chinese-made boring machines or diesel engines just like that. In the long run, of course, getting rid of the Soviets was the best thing that ever happened to China. We learned to be our own masters and found that we knew just as much as the foreigners did, if not more. We developed Daqing on our own, and now we are a world leader in oil production.[3]

I was in the west about half the time between 1954 and 1959 while I was at the Petroleum College. Usually we went in teams for four to six months at a time. By 1958 I had finished at the college and was working on oil drilling at Lenghu, which was then a real boom town. This was where I had met Fuluoerfu, the Russian. In 1959 the ministry began reassigning oil workers from the west to the northeast, and I came back to Peking on my way to the northeast in the fall of 1959. In Peking we were told by top officials of the Petroleum Ministry that we had achieved much success and deserved to be congratulated, but that our greatest work lay in the future, in the northeast. The oil was there. Tests had shown an enormous quantity to be situated between Harbin and Qiqiha, in the Songliao plain. A discovery well had been completed in September, indicating that oil was there about 1000 meters below the surface in an area up to 1000 square kilometers. Preliminary studies showed that the oil was relatively easy to find and was recoverable at low cost. Now at last we had the promise of oil right at the doorstep of China's heaviest industrial concentration. We didn't have to think about transporting oil 2500 kilometers or more. The question was, how quickly could we get production rolling, especially without any help from the Soviet Union, our former elder brother?*

---

*Most evidence indicates that development at Daqing began in the late fifties, with initial Soviet assistance. The Oil Man insisted he had not been aware of any prior Soviet presence at Daqing, but then added, "Even if they had helped us at the beginning, they probably only slowed us down, maybe even deliberately sabotaged drilling and production." Soviet experts told me in Peking in 1975 that "without our help Daqing would still be a semi-barren wasteland."

It wasn't easy. I remember arriving in December and seeing nothing but a bleak snowy landscape. It was cold and depressing and the ground was frozen solid. Drilling was impossible under those conditions, and we spent the first weeks familiarizing ourselves with the area. In the midst of all this the Soviet advisers suddenly pulled out and we were left with half-finished projects, useless designs, and machines without instructions. By the spring of 1960, after a harsh winter, we were a subdued, disappointed lot. Food was scarce; our flimsy shelters barely kept out the cold; and the excitement generated by the Petroleum Ministry in Peking had left us. But then, as the snow melted and the ground thawed, we went around with the survey teams and talked with geologists and again became enthusiastic because we knew the oil was there. We lacked equipment and had to do things on a makeshift basis. But that was all right because we knew the results would be worth the effort — final independence from foreign domination in oil production.*

The symbol of this effort was Wang Jinxi, the so-called iron man of Daqing. I met him once in 1962 or 1963 (I can't recall for sure). He was burly, with a moustache, and he was an impressive fellow all right. Whether he really did everything that they said he did — well, that doesn't really matter. I doubt that he "slept on a pile of drill pipes and that the drill bit served as his pillow" — I doubt that very much. Seems to me he slept like the rest of us. He was the type, though, who could well have said that he would dig for oil with his hands, if it was necessary! I'm not sure about his riding a motorcycle around the oilfields spreading the Thought of Chairman Mao. No doubt there was a lot of exaggeration in the press, but he was a model worker and that's to be expected once the press makes a campaign. He definitely existed and he wasn't the only one who worked day and night to bring up the oil. He just happened to be there at the right time. I heard he died just after the Cultural Revolution of natural causes — too bad, because as a hero he was more believable than either Lei Feng or Wang Jie.[4]

*For a more lyrical description, see *Peking Review*, September 26, 1969: "When there were not enough vehicles and hoists, people carried the equipment. In the absence of water tanks and water pipes, they used basins and buckets to bring water from hundreds of meters away. As there was no housing, they pitched tents or dug caves in the ground for shelter. There were no vegetables when they arrived, so they ate wild herbs. It was with sure dogged revolutionary will that the heroic people of Taching [Daqing] built the world's first-class oil field in three years' time."

We used a water-injection method in order to keep a constant pressure in the well. It keeps the oil flowing for a much longer period. It's a tricky procedure. If you pump in too much water, then water goes into the wells in great quantities and destroys them. This actually happened in the early years. So we conducted many experiments and eventually worked out a water-injection procedure that took into account the differential degree of permeability of various types of oil-bearing strata. The new method now controls the speed, direction, and flow of the underground water over an entire formation and not just on a well-by-well basis. The method proved so successful that it has been applied in other oilfields, such as Yumen and Qaidamu, where irregular production can be enhanced and accelerated by judicious use of water injection.

The water-injection method was the big Daqing achievement in technological development, but there were others. For example, we began to find Chinese substitutes for the imported seamless steel required for our pipelines. Because Daqing crude oil has a high degree of paraffin wax and a viscosity with a high solidification point, it must be heated in winter. At Daqing, we developed and improved these heating systems. We also developed a smaller and much lighter oil-collecting tree to replace the "Christmas tree" equipment that you use in the West.[5] These were important achievements, though I think the main achievement lay in the fact that we were able to do all this without foreign assistance once the Soviets had packed up and left China. We discovered out of necessity that we could duplicate and improve upon foreign technology when it was vital — not in every case, but enough to give us confidence and to get the oil moving into our industrial areas.

The key word was "production," that was what Daqing was all about, how to get as much oil as possible out of the ground and to the consumers. Unlike Qaidamu, transportation was not a major problem. A railway was close at hand, and the first shipment of oil went out by train in 1961. Now, most of the oil goes out by pipelines, to the ports of Qinhuangdao and Luda and to the giant Peking Petrochemical Works. Oil production at the wellhead is organized into six or seven production divisions. The size of a division depends on the area or the number of wells under their control. Each division is subdivided into brigades and teams, like the teams and brigades in a people's commune. For a while I was attached to the No. 4 team of the No. 6 brigade of No. 1 division. We had fifty-five people in our team and were responsible for thirty wells. Team members were responsible for providing the manpower required to operate all wells and to inject water. The team had to perform a number of specific tasks: adding a demulsifying agent to the crude oil once every twenty-four hours; heating the crude oil during the cold weather in order to keep the oil flowing through the pipes; dewaxing the vertical oil pipes by lowering a scraper 500 meters every twenty-four hours. The speed of the oil flow had to be checked daily. There were many other tasks involved in ensuring that oil production would continue smoothly. Sometimes there were accidents. I recall a major fire in one well back in 1963. It took ten days to bring the fire under control and return production to normal. We carried out stringent safety precautions and started by fencing in each well. No smoking was allowed inside the fence. You couldn't even carry matches in the enclosed area. We had fire extinguishers, sand boxes, and other fire-fighting equipment. Most of the oilfield workers were former soldiers who had been demobilized in the late 1950s. They formed the nucleus of our team — thirty-five of the fifty-five in our team came from the military. The rest were local peasants, an occasional specialist like myself, and some sent-down youth.

Daqing was officially declared a "model" by Chairman Mao in 1964. I remember reading it in the *People's Daily* and feeling quite proud. We were made a model because we had found oil against all odds. Daqing was an example of self-reliance and of courageous work spirit, and it was this spirit that was emphasized nationally. Later they broadened the emphasis to include Daqing as a model community that combined town and country, workers and peasants, specialists and ordinary people. It certainly is different from other oilfields I've been in. At Qaidamu, for example, we lived in two or three large oil cities and went out to work in the fields, returning periodically to our homes in the cities. In Daqing, because of the large size of the Songliao oilfield, because transportation was accessible at most places in the area, and because there were large tracts of arable land throughout the area, we didn't have to concentrate people in two or three big cities and we could live right beside the wells. So the population

was spread out in some forty or fifty villages and over one hundred and fifty residential areas. The central villages have a population of about 5000 each. There is one big city, Anda, the gate-
way to Daqing, but the rest of the 400,000 people are well
dispersed.

After the Cultural Revolution began, we used to hear a lot
about how Daqing was the model for China's industry. Actually I
never really thought that much about it. To me it was just an oilfield that had proved successful. I didn't do any farming and I
didn't live in any family household. I always lived in bachelor
dormitories, so for me there wasn't that much difference between
Daqing and any other place. I did feel that Daqing was special
because it was an example of what China can do on her own when
foreign assistance is unreliable or unavailable. We took over from
the Soviets and made the thing work. I often wondered what
old Fuluoerfu thought when he heard how successful we had
been at Daqing. The hell with elder brother's tools, his trucks,
and all his experience — we did it ourselves. I used to mark the
rhythm of the oil pumps by singing "the hell with Soviet elder
brother" over and over again, just to pass the time away.

I left Daqing in 1967, just in the middle of everything, to go
back to Peking. (That's when I met Zhou Enlai at a big meeting.)
Production never stopped during those years, but it might have
been slowed down. In 1967 there was dissatisfaction, and I remember there were struggles among certain groups in the oilfields. I never really understood the issues, but I recall that dis-
gruntled local residents — the farmers in the communes — protested against the higher wages being paid to oil workers. Some
60 percent of the oil workers were ex-soldiers and the army was
taking command of things. The struggles at Daqing never were
very serious. I heard that 10,000 workers planned to march on
Peking, but by that time I was already on my way to Qaidamu for
a second stay. I never expected that there would be much of a
problem at Daqing because we needed that oil, and any major
stoppage in production would be seen as treasonous. We had a
local saying: "A drop of oil and a drop of blood are equally precious; neither must be spilled." There were some political casualties. Yu Qiuli, the head of the Petroleum Ministry and Kang
Shien, a vice-minister, were criticized and replaced.[6] Some Party

officials were removed and replaced by the army. The Party heads in my team and brigade were both criticized but remained in their posts. In their case it was more a matter of making them confess to being arrogant in their work style rather than accusing them of being outright followers of anti-Maoist policies.

I left for Qaidamu in the midst of the Cultural Revolution and stayed there till 1970. I got married a few months before to a fellow oil worker in Peking. She and I had been classmates at the Petroleum College, and then she married a fellow classmate who later died in an accident. So when I was back in Peking we decided to get married. I was in my mid-thirties and she was thirty-four. It worked out well for both of us; all those years living a bachelor's life in the oilfields had been hard and I was lonely. Those few months in Peking were a honeyed time of my life. But before I really had a chance to savor my new life, they sent me off to Qaidamu and we were separated for over two years, except for one short visit. I wasn't sent to Qaidamu as punishment—don't think I was one of those sent-down cadres. It was just my luck that they needed oil-drilling specialists and I had been there before. Probably it was just as well that I was thousands of kilometers west of Peking during the Cultural Revolution. Nothing much really happened in Qaidamu; it seemed that the farther away you got from Peking, the less excited people were about the political battles at the center. That suited me just fine.

I never had any political ambitions and I always kept my mouth shut and my eyes and ears wide open. My class background was fine (middle peasant) and I probably could have joined the Party, but those things never interested me. What I only wanted to do was to find oil, to work in developing China's oil production. There wasn't much that Chairman Mao's little Red Book could tell me about that. We used to wave it around and talk about how Chairman Mao inspired us in our work and how Liu Shaoqi had betrayed us, but I never took that seriously because the state needed oil and I could help them get it. There were many specialists like me who did their jobs and were left alone in the midst of all the political struggles. No bunch of half-baked Red Guards could ever replace an oil specialist. We were already in the vanguard because we were showing everybody that Chinese specialists could do a better job than foreign experts. So they left us alone and this suited me fine. You know, an oilfield isn't like life. It's a special place and politics aren't that important.[7]

After Qaidamu I came back to Peking, got reacquainted with my wife, and lived a good life for about a year. Then they sent me to Maoming, where they were working on oil-shale production. I stayed there a few months, enjoying the warmth and fresh fruit and vegetables of the south. After that, I was sent to Fujian where we had discovered oil. We knew there was lots of oil offshore, in the Taiwan Straits, but we couldn't begin any serious exploration there because of the security problem. How could China hope to defend any oilwell located in the middle of the Taiwan Straits? I worked there for nearly a year before being recalled suddenly to Peking. My wife had applied to leave China. She was an overseas Chinese who had come to China in the forties and now wanted to be reunited with her family. I had to decide whether to stay in China as an oil man or go with her to an uncertain future outside my homeland. I finally decided to go with her and, once the authorities learned of my intentions, my days as an oil man were over. I stayed in Peking doing nothing for another year before they finally gave me my exit visa. The day I left was the most difficult in my life because I loved my work, my life, and my country, and was suddenly giving it all up for an unknown future.

[*In 1975 the Oil Man was reunited in Hong Kong with his wife and was living with her relatives. He had not found a job. He was depressed because his background as an oil-drilling specialist was not of much use to him in Hong Kong. He hoped to emigrate to a nearby Southeast Asian country to work in the oil industry, but he was experiencing difficulties securing a visa.*]

Down with Stinking Intellectuals

INTELLECTUALS ARE A PROBLEM in any political system, but in China the relationship between the authorities and the intellectuals has been especially difficult. In the fifties, Chairman Mao asked intellectuals for their criticisms in the Hundred Flowers campaign. They responded with a vengeance, convincing Mao and other leaders that letting loose the reins on intellectuals had been a grievous error. During the Cultural Revolution, a major thrust of the Maoist group was against intellectuals and the policies associated with them. Jiang Qing, Chairman Mao's wife, personally presided over a massive purge of artists and writers. China's new "revolutionary culture" consisted of a few carefully edited operas and plays that expressed the prevalent political view of the Maoist group. The same principle was applied to China's communications media, which were purged of people who opposed the policies of this group.

In education, a "revolution" also occurred. The universities were shut down for three years while political battles raged over the type of educational system that China ought to have in the future. Students were encouraged to join the Red Guards and to help Chairman Mao in his struggle to reform the educational system. Professors and teachers were criticized and confronted by students; some were beaten to death. There was fierce fighting among the students themselves, and the central leaders were deeply involved. By 1970, universities were reopening, with new curricula and a changed student body and teachers. Education was now heavily politicized and more polytechnic. Higher spe-

*cialized education was deemphasized. Courses were shortened to
three years. The new student body initially was drawn from
workers, peasants, and soldiers. Examinations were abolished.
Some reeducated teachers returned, but others were not allowed
to resume teaching. By the mid-seventies the first classes of these
new Cultural Revolution students were being absorbed into
China's work force.*

*This story takes place at Amoy University in Fujian province.
The confrontation between students and teachers was so violent
that one professor committed suicide by jumping into boiling
water. Later, the violence subsided and the process of institution-
alization of the new policies began. We see how the new changes
in curriculum occurred, and what happened to theory in practice. By 1975 the narrator's own revolutionary commitment was
altered by events in a way that he would not have expected back
in 1966.*

*Today in China the elite component of education has been
restored. The emphasis again is on quality rather than on mass
education. Examinations have been reintroduced, and the
chances of workers, peasants, and soldiers reaching university
have been significantly reduced. China has thus moved away
from the radical educational experimentation of the Cultural
Revolution to a system resembling the one that existed before
1966.*

WHEN THE CULTURAL REVOLUTION BEGAN, I was twenty-three years old, a third-year chemistry student at Amoy University in the city of Amoy, my home-
town. I had a natural aptitude for my studies and was doing well.
My political record was clean and I was an active member of the
Youth League. I had fallen in love with a classmate, and we
planned to get married as soon as I graduated and the state assigned me a job. That was still a year off, however, so in the
meantime I was indulging myself in the pleasures and excitement
of youth, spending time with my girlfriend and being fully caught
up in university life. When the first big character poster[1] appeared in Peking, we didn't really know what to do. Peking
seemed a long way off, and so we waited cautiously for the provincial Party leadership to respond. Who could have predicted
that a few months later we would be toppling these leaders and

dragging the powerful Ye Fei and his wife out to face mass public criticism in the streets of Fuzhou?[2]

All classes were stopped, and the university was in confusion. What was going on in Peking? What were we supposed to do? Who were the targets? Who would take the lead and strike the first blow? The safest course was to attack the most visible targets — the teachers, especially those who had a known bad class background. Party and Youth League members put up big character posters like those in Peking, using the same words and themes. We attacked a few professors and lecturers who should have been criticized long ago, either for their poor attitudes or their zealous worship of foreign things. Some posters merely observed that "Professor Wang has more books published outside China on his bookshelves than Chinese books," and then asked the question "Why?" Others referred to "Jiang, who has never mentioned Chairman Mao's Thought in any of his lectures," and added that this poster was a "solemn warning to Jiang to change his ways at once or face the wrath of the masses." Another poster referred to "the dozens of teachers who have been hiding their reactionary backgrounds from the masses who want to criticize them."

Between June and November 1966, we locked up almost every university department head, deputy department head, professor, and lecturer. Every day we rounded them up and read them quotations from the works of Chairman Mao. We marched them off to the student dining halls to eat the same food that the students had to eat. No more fancy meals for them in the special professors' dining halls. No more getting fat on meat and fish while students were eating grain and leftovers. Every day they had to clean the lavatories and carry out the night soil. At night we made them write confessions "asking Chairman Mao for punishment." If we didn't like what they wrote, we made them do it again and again until they clearly showed how they had demeaned the Party and Chairman Mao in their lectures, how they had ignored socialism, and how they had deliberately spread the bourgeois life style at the university. Once every three days we had a small struggle meeting, maybe with a few hundred persons, and once a week we mobilized a large struggle meeting with over a thousand people in attendance. That's when we really gave it to them. By that time, covered with honest dirt and night soil, fancy clothes and leather shoes looking no better than a peasant's clothing, their once-proud voices stilled by the fierce criticism of the assembled masses, they were a sorry spectacle indeed.*

Most of them deserved their fate. Chairman Mao was right when he warned us always to be on guard against intellectuals. You can't trust intellectuals. They resist the Party line, become arrogant, develop a bourgeois way of thinking, and worship foreign things. Take old Wang, for example. When the Red Guards went to his place and took it apart, it was full of fancy scrolls and feudal Chinese art. Must have been worth a fortune. We dug out foreign coins and books, and you should have seen the furniture! He had closets full of leather shoes, fancy clothes, and junk like that. He even had a servant living in that apartment doing the cooking and cleaning. How can a socialist society tolerate people like that teaching the young? True, he was a leading specialist in physics and we needed his skills, but was it worth the cost, to keep this stinking bourgeois remnant alive to infect students with his rotten way of life? Students who took Wang's classes never liked him. He treated us with contempt and barely noticed us. All he ever did was show up to lecture and then leave abruptly. We could never talk with him, never ask questions. There were many others who were arrogant like that. Old Jiang taught mathematics as if feudalism had never left China. We had to repeat theorems and equations endlessly; examinations were thrust upon us without warning; we could never talk out in class. It was just the way education used to be in the time of the Manchus. We tolerated Jiang because he was a good mathematician, but was it worth perpetuating a feudal relationship in order to learn mathematics?

The most pernicious of the teachers actually were the younger ones who lived a proletarian life style on the surface, but underneath yearned to be even more bourgeois and feudal than the "old" intellectuals they allegedly scorned. I could forgive most of the old intellectuals for the way they lived and thought. After all, can you discard the habits of a lifetime? Is it possible to hide one's class background? Can a tiger hide his stripes? But that

*Struggle meetings were an important aspect of the Cultural Revolution at all levels, in all organizations and units. At these sessions individuals were singled out for mass criticism. It was a way to fix blame, to focus attention, and to maintain revolutionary spirit. For more details see "Kill the Chickens To Scare the Monkeys," "Return to the Motherland," and "My Neighborhood."

group was dying out and was being replaced by a new generation of scholars loyal to socialism and to Chairman Mao's Thought. At least that's what I thought. In fact, a lot of the newer, younger teachers began to act just like their older bourgeois colleagues. Deng, in the chemistry department, was one such example. Only thirty-three years old, from a working-class background and a Party member, you'd think he'd be a model for all to follow. So it seemed on the outside, but his students noticed otherwise. You could see the repressed arrogance in him, and it was clear he was a Liuist* through and through. For him, being a Party member and an intellectual was a double chance for personal gain. He was a perfect example of what Chairman Mao calls "a fish swimming with the current," actually worse than that because he already had become an out-and-out bourgeois in his work style and thought. Maybe it wasn't always that way with him. Maybe at the beginning he had truly wanted to "serve the people" and had only become corrupted along the way by the Liuist spirit of the times, which bred complacency, material acquisitiveness, and spiritual decay.

You see, I fully agree with Chairman Mao's analysis of intellectuals, that you have always to be on guard against them and that you must strive to remold their outlook and build up "an army of proletarian intellectuals which can serve the proletariat." At Amoy in 1966 none of this was happening. Not only were the old bourgeois intellectuals still in command, but they were gaining supporters from the so-called new army of proletarian intellectuals. The whole educational system needed changing because the way it was then reinforced the old feudal gap between teachers and pupils, theory and practice, elite and masses. In fact, education had become elitist all the way down the line. I had a friend who attended the elitist Fuzhou Number One Middle School, one of China's Red Banner schools. Although probably 20 percent of China's senior middle school graduates managed to get to college, I'm told that over 70 percent of the graduates from Fuzhou Number One School went to universities. That school stressed academic performance over anything else. Politics were a

*Follower of Liu Shaoqi, China's number-two leader in 1966, who was criticized and purged by Mao. In the "struggle between two lines" during the Cultural Revolution, those who opposed Mao were defined as Liuists—following the bourgeois and revisionist policies of Liu, who was branded "China's Khrushchev."

low priority. If you failed to keep up, you were expelled. Every day you had homework in five subjects and there were weekly and monthly tests. When the time came to prepare for the university entrance examinations, the school went to unbelievable lengths. At the beginning of each new school year, in the fall, the director of the Fujian Provincial Education Department (the wife of Ye Fei, first Party secretary of Fujian) would give a report at the school, to the senior grade-three students. She would say: "Fuzhou's Number One Middle School has been a Red Banner school for five successive years, and this year you must not let the Red Banner fall down. You must make your finest effort at all costs and I will offer my personal help."

The university entrance exams started on June 20, but already after the New Year (January-February) the senior grade-three students began to prepare for them. They moved right into the school and lived there until the exams were over. The school gave them a daily food subsidy. Homework was greatly increased and the students were issued a variety of study cribs and outlines to supplement their regular materials. Three months prior to the exams, the entire school launched a campaign of "performing good deeds." The lower-grade students were mobilized to do something each day for those students who were preparing for the entrance exams, such as washing their clothes and blankets or going to the dining hall to get them their food so they wouldn't have to take time from their studies. That was about the only "collective" part of the whole enterprise. With such special treatment, no wonder so many graduates wound up each year at such famous universities as Qinghua or Peking. Jiang Nanxiang, the Minister of Education at that time and a real Liuist, highly praised the school and the Fujian Provincial Education Department, especially for the way in which students prepared for the university entrance exam. I remember seeing Fuzhou Number One Middle School written up in provincial and national papers and journals. The school's deputy principal was even elected to the National People's Congress. Representatives from other schools came to visit Fuzhou, to "learn from its experience," and Ye Fei himself wrote a special inscription for the school: "Already at the top of a pole a hundred feet high, but still striving further ahead."

With schools like that serving as models for the rest of China, no wonder our universities were so badly in need of revolution. Schools like Fuzhou Number One Middle School perpetuated and enhanced elitism, the worship of expertise, and careerism. If you were an ordinary worker or peasant, you had little chance of getting admitted to such a school. The vast majority of students in Fuzhou were the sons and daughters of urban cadres. Here was one way in which the elite and its hangers-on could keep on top. Students in such schools cared little about politics. To them, the correct political line was something you had to know and be aware of, to make sure your career would not be harmed by any political miscalculation. No one took Marxism-Leninism very seriously at that school because, as my friend put it, "What mattered on the university entrance exams was how well you had prepared your subject and how you compared with other candidates. Of course you needed to know what was going on politically, but that was easy enough to learn, in comparison with trying to memorize a physics text."

At Amoy one could see the results of such a system in the increasing number of elitist and careerist youth who cared little for political work and did their utmost to avoid dirtying their hands. These were the students who let the professors dominate them, practically in a feudal relationship, and who didn't object to their arrogance or their blatant bourgeois practices. You see, these students had been trained to put good grades and careerism ahead of everything else. They would have sacrificed the very Revolution itself, I'm sure, for a good job in Amoy or Fuzhou. But the Cultural Revolution came just at the right time to put a stop to these practices. Chairman Mao's message to students like myself was clear enough: we needed a thoroughgoing revolution in higher education, and if the current Party leaders could not do the job, then let the students do it for them. The only way to get rid of careerism and elitism in higher education was to destroy the old system and rebuild it on revolutionary principles. So that's what we tried to do.

Of course it wasn't easy. There was plenty of opposition. First of all, the entrenched elite didn't want to give up any power. They were afraid that big changes would unhorse them, and they were right. At the outset they tried to deflect the criticism onto others. This was a brief period when their interests and those of the radicalized students coincided, because they made the bour-

geois professors the first targets. But that was as far as they intended to go. We saw it just as a beginning, mere lip-service to
Chairman Mao. We wanted to "struggle" the real class enemies,
the fish swimming with the current, those from the supposedly
"right" class backgrounds, such as Deng. But once we expanded
the struggle to attack members of the Party, we found ourselves
alone. The big political leaders wanted no part of that; they were
willing to attack old "safe" targets but were afraid to expand the
struggle for fear of being criticized themselves. So that's when we
suddenly found ourselves in direct opposition to people like Ye
Fei.

Then there was opposition from the students. There were
two sides in the struggle in Amoy, the careerist "have" students
from upper-class Fujian families versus the "have-nots," who were
the less privileged, more politically conscious Amoy student body.
It wasn't an easy struggle because, as I said, many of us were se-
duced by the privileges of careerism and elitism and were blind to
the costs of our actions. By 1966 we had a student body that had
no true peasants and only a handful of workers; a student body
that tried to avoid any type of manual labor by saying: "I serve
the people best by being a specialist — anyone can plant rice or
dig ditches, but how many can speak English or understand
quantum physics?" Only a handful of students cared about politics or worried about what had happened to the Revolution, and
those like myself were sneered at for "using politics as a way to
make up for lack of talent" or for being "toads who think they can
eat swan meat."[3]

The struggle among the student groups was hard and unpleasant. There was bloody fighting; friends fought against
friends and a few people lost their lives. I blame the big political
leaders for this. They were behind the reactionary students,
egging them on. They hoped that all radical students would be
driven out of the university and then their positions would be
secure. Of course it didn't happen that way.

Finally, there were the intellectuals. On the surface, this
seemed the easiest group to eliminate. We struggled them at the
university and made them write confessions, jet-planed them and
made them wear hats.* While we were in control at Amoy, no
professor was immune from criticism, and all bowed their heads
before the student masses. Old Wang and Jiang wound up doing

honest farm labor in the Fujian hills. It was probably the first time in their lives that their smooth bourgeois hands had experienced real hard work. Others couldn't stand the struggle and criticism sessions and became ill and died, practically in front of our faces. I took no pity on them, nor on the handful who committed suicide by jumping out of their apartment windows or the one who threw himself into one of our famous hot springs and boiled himself to death. There are casualties in any revolution. As Chairman Mao said, "We are not having a dinner party here, it's a revolution." So why feel sorry for a few who died? Without violence there can't be positive change. The problem with intellectuals is that they're the easiest targets in the beginning, but the hardest to get rid of in the end. It seems that intellectuals and Marxism-Leninism are in basic opposition, and you can't trust any intellectual even if he is a Party member. There's that tendency on the part of intellectuals to act independently, outside the Party line. There is that danger of elitism and careerism, and the steady slide into bourgeois class consciousness. So it wasn't an empty slogan when we ran around shouting "Down with Stinking Intellectuals!" We were trying once and for all to solve the problem that Mao so clearly saw.

Between 1966 and 1968 events at Amoy followed the same pattern as elsewhere in China, at least as far as I know.[4] The student groups took the initiative but were then split apart by factionalism. The old Liuist Party apparatus tried to stop the revolutionary movement, or at least coopt it for its own self-preservation. Bloody fighting broke out and people were killed. The army was called in and did not always choose sides wisely. Those of us who supported Chairman Mao found ourselves beset by enemies on all sides, and not infrequently we fell to quarreling among ourselves. Our hearts burned red in support of Chairman Mao, but we did not always know how to use our powers. It was only a matter of time before we lost the initiative, and then the question really was, would the new power holders carry out the

---

*In jet-planing a person, you pull both his hands behind his back and push him forward so that he looks like a plane taking off. People were made to wear hats physically and symbolically. The hats looked like dunce caps and were used in formal criticism sessions. Once you had been given a political hat, that is, had been made a bad element or a counterrevolutionary, then you had to wear that political hat until it was formally removed. For more on this point see "The One Whose Girlfriend Turned Him In."

educational changes that were necessary to make the system "serve the masses" and prevent elitism from entrenching itself again?

The army moved into Amoy to take over. I was one of the luckier Red Guards. Since I wasn't a member of the 516 group, they didn't get me for being an ultraleftist. I expected to be sent down to the Fujian countryside along with most of my peers, but to my surprise I was assigned to the city of Fuzhou not far away to work at Fuzhou University, to help them in their campaign of "cleaning up the class ranks." This campaign was different from the struggles that had taken place in the early stages of the Cultural Revolution. This was no blind struggle, but a well-organized, well-planned, and systematic classification of the university teachers, in all departments, according to their family background, personal history, and performance and attitude during the Cultural Revolution. Such classification was done by the Party branches of the various departments. So, because I was a chemistry graduate, I was assigned to the chemistry department and spent the next year sorting out class backgrounds and exposing and criticizing those who had landlord, rich-peasant, counterrevolutionary, bad-element, and rightist backgrounds. While we were busy with the clean-up, we also were discussing the future form and content of China's higher educational system. The curriculum was going to be radically revised; more emphasis would be placed on practical education; the examination system would be abolished, and university entrance would now be biased in favor of workers and peasants; the old professors might be allowed to teach again but under the strictest supervision, after they had first been reeducated through political study and hard physical labor.

The year passed and, because of my good political record and strong academic achievements, I had high hopes of staying on at Fuzhou to help in the transition to the new university system. Instead I was sent down to teach in a rural school in Shanxi, thousands of kilometers from home. It was a primary school which also had two classes of junior middle school. I taught mathematics there. This type of school was a product of the Cultural Revolution. Attaching junior middle school classes to local primary schools made it more convenient for peasant children to attend school. They didn't have to walk long distances to get to school anymore, and so they were encouraged to stay in school for a longer period of time. My students were commune children from several villages within a radius of three kilometers. We had no real textbooks since the old ones had been discarded and replaced by "draft" texts compiled by the Shanxi provincial educational reform group. I gave no exams and my students were required to do almost no homework. Aside from attending classes, students had no other responsibilities. School discipline here was quite different from what I had known in the city. The children frequently left in the middle of classes to do agricultural work. Some used to bring their little brothers and sisters along, babysitting them during lessons while the rest of their household worked.

I didn't have to prepare very much for such teaching, and actually all I had to do was to read from the draft textbook and then repeat what I had said several times until the students understood. The level of learning was really low, and it was my first big disappointment since I had been caught up in the Cultural Revolution. It wasn't that the conditions were that bad in the countryside; we all know how backward the rural areas are, especially when it comes to middle school education. And it wasn't the primitive living conditions either, because I was used to all that. Nor was I homesick for my family and my girlfriend. I missed them, but we had been separated several times over the past four years. What really bothered me was the huge gap between what we had been talking about in Amoy and Fuzhou and what in fact was going on in China's villages. There I was, with a new curriculum, in a "revolutionary" educational setting, and the students weren't learning anything. I could hardly get them to add and subtract, let alone do junior middle school mathematics. They'd never stand a chance of getting to senior middle school, not to speak of university. The draft texts were shallow and abridged. If this was the outcome of so much struggle and bloodshed—apathy and mediocrity at the local level—what would it be like at the top, in China's universities?

I soon had a chance to find out because in 1970 Fuzhou University had officially reopened, admitting its first large group of new students since the Cultural Revolution. There had been a number of trial student intakes as early as 1969, when two hundred were admitted to the departments of physics, chemistry, electrical engineering, mechanical engineering, and education. These were special two-year experimental classes, and all these students had graduated by 1971. By then it had been decided to set the length of university courses at three years. The student body numbered seven hundred, about 20 percent of the old enrollment, but it was to increase regularly in the following years and now there are several thousand. The university had a staff of six hundred, including four hundred teachers and over a hundred administrative cadres. They needed more teaching staff, and so I was reassigned from Shanxi to Fuzhou to work in the chemistry department as one of the new revolutionary teachers. Actually I was only a lab assistant who was supposed to be on lab duty six days a week, eight hours a day, and was paid 40 yuan a month (compared with the average professor's salary of 150-200 yuan a month). I never worried about the salary, since housing and food together only cost me 20 yuan a month. I couldn't spend it anyway. It made me wonder how those professors managed to spend all their money.

Leaving Shanxi wasn't easy. I had grown fond of the slower pace of rural life and had made some good friends. Actually I had fallen in love with another sent-down youth, a girl from Fujian province who was also teaching, and we were reluctant to part from one another. (As it turned out, we never did see each other again.) It had been good to be away from the political struggles in the cities, to get down to basic rural life and understand it better. I came away with a better appreciation of the difficulties of peasant life, but I headed back to Fuzhou with some misgivings about the kind of educational revolution we had accomplished. In Shanxi, at the bottom, the fruits of the Cultural Revolution had seemed meager. Would it be any different at the top, in a big urban university?

Returning to Fuzhou was an odd experience. Professors whom I had earlier struggled and criticized and called stinking intellectuals were now my colleagues and greeted me affably enough, almost as if nothing had ever happened. Others had simply vanished into thin air, to be replaced by young staff like myself, or not at all. There was a stiffness about the place, an air of uncertainty as to what was going to happen. The euphoria of three years past seemed to have been replaced by a kind of wariness. What would the new system be like? Could the "reeducated" teachers get along with those who had purged them and were now either their colleagues or in political command? What would the new curriculum be like, and what kinds of students would be admitted? The answers to most of these questions came quickly enough: the new system was a disappointment because it ultimately failed to provide a better educational system, and it didn't eliminate the abuses and problems of the old system. The reeducated and struggled old professors did not get on well with their revolutionary colleagues. In their hearts they burned for revenge, and our relationship with one another was only minimally formal. Who could trust them to follow the Party's revolutionary line in the future?

As for the new curriculum, I had mixed feelings about that. After my experience in Shanxi I wasn't surprised at what I found at Fuzhou. The old texts had been repudiated, but the new study materials had not yet been produced because the teachers in each department were supposed to compile the new texts themselves. Since most of these teachers had been struggled and criticized during the Cultural Revolution, they weren't about to make any more mistakes in print. They didn't intend to be accused of taking the old bourgeois road again. The political activists themselves couldn't compile textbooks; after all, they weren't chemists or physicists or mechanical engineers. Furthermore, they themselves weren't exactly sure what should be in the new texts, except (to be safe) a lot of politics. The teachers played it safe by compiling materials of a very general and shallow nature to avoid any controversy. In this they followed the lead of the middle schools, where the new teaching materials resembled political tracts. For example, the old history texts had been abolished and replaced by drafts that consisted almost entirely of the works of Chairman Mao and Lu Xun's articles. All foreign names had been removed from texts in physics, chemistry, and mathematics, resulting in such absurdities as the renaming of Mendeleev's periodic system of elements as simply "the periodic system of elements." Newton's universal gravitation became "universal gravitation." Such kinds of "revolutionary change" caused amusement and resentment, and people didn't know whether to laugh or cry. One of my colleagues, another lab assistant, broke his usual deliberate silence about such matters by asking me one day, "Is this what we spilled our blood for, to remove Mendeleev's name from a university text that has now been diluted to middle school level? What's so revolutionary about that?" In truth, I could not answer him.

But we were excited about the new students who were selected from among the workers, peasants, and soldiers, from the progressive class elements that had been loyal to Chairman Mao. The education section of the Fujian provincial revolutionary committee had assigned quotas to all organs in Fujian. These organs then recommended students to be sent to the designated university (Amoy, Fuzhou, Fuzhou Normal, and so on). In selecting successful candidates, the local Party committee emphasized personal class status, social relations, and political performance. Age and educational level initially were not important factors. As a result, the first groups of students were politically strong and the most mass-based group that had ever attended Fuzhou. They were willing to learn and many of us, especially the younger teachers, really tried to teach them. But unfortunately it soon became clear that enthusiasm and the right political line just weren't enough to produce competent mathematicians, physicists, or chemists. Chairman Mao's Thought can move mountains,[5] but you also need preparation and native intelligence to get specialists. The worker-peasant-soldier group, by and large, had good intentions but lacked everything else. We tried to build them up academically and to teach them as much as possible, but they were only at the university for three years, and over half of that time was spent in political study and practical work, in factories or the fields. The practical work was important and necessary— it's just that they needed about three more years after that in the classroom just to get up to a decent university level. We were reduced to giving university students remedial instruction, at a middle school level. Great for equality, but what were we accomplishing? The new worker-peasant-soldier groups were ill-equipped to go out and teach others; yet they were going to be sent to rural schools just like the one I had taught in, to become permanent teachers, thus only perpetuating the relative backwardness of the rural areas.

At the same time, the old urban-bourgeois-elitist students began to reappear at Fuzhou. How this happened is typical of the way in which the privileged groups manage to find a way to stay on top. First, an increasing number of the worker-peasant-soldier students actually turned out to be the sons and daughters of urban cadres who, after being sent down to the countryside, had managed to be selected by local communes to go to university in the city. This was, of course, carefully arranged by the cadres involved. So scratch a "peasant student" and you might find the son or daughter of a local city cadre underneath. Second, a few bright students became exempt from being sent to the countryside and were admitted directly to Fuzhou, usually students gifted in mathematics or the sciences. These exceptional students thus could gain admittance to the university by special means. Third, after it became clear that the worker-peasant-soldier student group was of too low an academic level, an unofficial quota system was established, allowing more children of other classes to be admitted to Fuzhou. This was a face-saving decision which helped to raise the academic level of the student body and at the same time once again gave official access to the elite for its sons and daughters to attend university. By 1975 at least half of the Fuzhou student body were the sons and daughters of urban cadres and intellectuals, even though statistically it was claimed that less than 20 percent were from that group.[6]

With elitism creeping back in, and with the apparent failure of mass-based higher education, my disappointment turned into disillusionment. Many of my former Red Guard colleagues had either been killed or exiled or had themselves become careerists. The old bourgeois intellectuals were by no means dead; actually they had only been waiting for the wind to change. It was also clear that those of us who had wanted a new system of education were still a minority, and the feeble results of what we tried to attain had limited our power and credibility. In truth, I had no power, despite my record of loyalty to the Party and to Chairman Mao. Others, far less revolutionary than I, had taken over the key command posts. I was suspected by some because I had been too much the revolutionary when there wasn't any revolution any more. "Be careful!" one of my friends used to say to me. "One day you'll wake up as a 516 element, an ultraleftist for sure. That's the way things are going in China now." I couldn't imagine that happening because I seemed to be moving away from radicalism the longer I taught at Fuzhou. Disillusioned with the effects of Cultural Revolution policies, I turned inward to my work and found a research project that occupied almost all my time and energies. Ironically, I gradually became the intellectual I had once scorned, buried in my work and avoiding any commitment to the political struggles of the mid-seventies. In early 1976, when a poster appeared criticizing me for having become a stinking intellectual, I knew it was time to go.

[*In 1973 the narrator married an overseas Chinese woman, the daughter of an engineer, despite strong objections from the Party organization. He simply said that he loved this woman and intended to marry her, regardless of the cost to his career. Maybe he had no ulterior motive and did not then realize that he was, in effect, buying a one-way ticket out of China with this marriage; in 1975 his wife applied for an exit visa and he decided to leave with her. Did he have any regrets about his decision? "No, for me it didn't matter any more. I had fought for an idea and seen it fall to pieces. I had been naive, thinking I could change the world so easily. Also, I found there was more to life than politics. I'm sorry for all those who were killed, but you have to fight for what you think is right at the time." He doesn't mind life in Hong Kong, works for a drug supply firm, and has two children.*]

Little Brother's Wedding

TRADITIONAL CUSTOMS AND PRACTICES play a major role in peasant lives. In the Chinese countryside the majority of peasants still follow the traditional lunar calendar with its large roster of festivals. One such holiday is New Year's, and then even the poorest peasant will try to put his affairs in order, eat a bit of meat, and think about his ancestors. Funerals are still conducted in the old style, with coffins and burials in the hills nearby: the Communists have persuaded few people in the countryside that cremation is a better system for honoring the dead.

Despite the Cultural Revolution and the "Criticize Confucius, Criticize Lin Biao" campaign, many peasants still think in terms of ancestors and household gods, ghosts and superstitions, and even clan loyalties.

Still it appears that, just as with Stalin's decision to let the Russian family alone, the Chinese leaders have made a number of compromises with tradition. Only the most blatantly feudal practices, or those in direct conflict with official policy, are being discouraged. A country wedding is an example of such compromise. The Party in principle opposes the concept of wasting resources on a large wedding but does little to stop it, knowing that the families involved are determined to have one. Large sums of money are spent (although if you have an equal number of sons and daughters, the costs of the weddings are eventually canceled out). Marriages are still arranged by matchmakers, but the bride and groom can decide, after they have met, whether they wish to proceed with the match. The woman is clearly inferior through-

87

out the ceremony, and everybody wishes that the lucky couple
will have many sons; yet the extra income she earns is a critical
element in the marriage negotiations. Furthermore, today the
prospective bride can reject a match if she so chooses.

This story describes what happens when a son marries in a
rural southern village. A ritual is carefully followed, with rules
spelled out over centuries of village life. Little Brother and his
bride have little to say once they agree to the match. They be-
come passive participants in a timeless traditional practice. The
wedding has almost nothing to do with romance and very little
with the concept of two people living together as an independent
unit. Rather, it is a household event (the addition of a daughter-
in-law to a household) and an economic transfer (one household
losing an able-bodied worker and another gaining that labor). In
China's cities, weddings are quite different. The household is sig-
nificantly diminished in the urban setting, and an urban wedding
is less of a social and economic institution. Romance plays a
greater role, the woman is more emancipated, and the couple
often winds up living as a separate unit. It will take a long time,
however, for the countryside to modernize its marriage practices
along urban lines.

LITTLE BROTHER was twenty-three years old when he got
married. I was unmarried at that time, aware that my turn
would come soon since I was the last of five children of the
Liang household, Fish Flower village in southern Guangdong. It
was 1974 and not the best time to have a country-style wedding—
not because the old-crone fortuneteller had picked an inauspi-
cious year, but because the authorities were cracking down on
feudal customs during the "Criticize Confucius, Criticize Lin
Biao" campaign. The commune leaders were making a big show
out of this campaign, and the brigade secretary had warned
everybody that large weddings are a sign of backward thought
and feudalism. I remember he came personally to our house and
told Father that the leadership would not sanction an old-style
wedding with a matchmaker (*meiren*), the expenditure of over
1000 yuan in bride price, a lavish feast, and all the other trap-
pings. "This is modern China," he told Father, "and we must stop
these backward practices. You can save yourself a big sum of
money if you have a small wedding. You've already married off

two children in the old style, so you won't be losing any face. You are a progressive peasant, with a good class background, and should set an example for the rest of the village."

The brigade secretary rambled on and on, but we could see that Father wasn't really paying much attention. He had heard all those arguments before and didn't take them too seriously. The Party hadn't objected when Big Brother and Big Sister were married off not long ago, and Father suspected that the brigade secretary was talking more for the record, on instructions from higher up, than from the heart. How could anyone expect a village marriage to take place without a bride price and without a wedding feast of at least ten tables? What the brigade secretary was suggesting might have been suitable in the city, where they don't care as much about the old customs and about family ties. But in our village a wedding was one of the biggest events in a lifetime. How could Father hold his head up among his village and clan if he did what the brigade secretary was suggesting? Anyway, didn't the secretary himself not long ago marry off his very own daughter in the old way? No one talked about it openly, but gossip said that the brigade secretary had received a bride price of 1000 yuan for marrying his daughter off to a family in a village 10 kilometers away. Not only that, but he had set out twelve tables of food for his guests and the gossip said that her dowry was as fine as anybody could recall. Didn't the brigade secretary attend the fancy weddings of others, eating their food, and joining in the festivities? It was clear, therefore, that one should not take the brigade secretary's words very seriously. "His heart and his mouth are not speaking to each other," that is, he was telling Father one thing but he meant something else.

What he was really saying was: "Old friend, I know you're going to have a big wedding and I'm happy for you, but you had better be careful with this wedding. There's a big campaign going on against feudal practices and you could get badly criticized. Then I'll be blamed as well. So make your arrangements quietly, try not to be too lavish, and if I don't attend your wedding, you'll understand why."

I suppose the brigade secretary's words did have some effect on the wedding arrangements. Our dealings with the matchmaker, who lived in another village, were done quietly, and only our family knew that we paid 50 yuan for her services. When we

were searching for the most auspicious wedding date, we found a
blind man in another brigade and paid him 5 yuan to choose a
lucky date for us. He said that the couple was destined for a
happy marriage—but we had already determined that by checking out the eight characters of their birthdates, also surreptitious-
ly because the Party considered that to be a feudal practice.
When we registered the marriage at commune headquarters, we
had to go to the brigade and get a letter of authorization. The
brigade leaders asked us if a bride price had been paid and we
had to lie and say that no money had changed hands between
the two families. Otherwise they would not sanction the marriage, since any money exchange violated the marriage law. Of
course, everybody always lied and said that no money had
changed hands. In the case of Little Brother's wedding, we paid
his future wife's family 500 yuan cash [about $320] as a bride
price, plus gifts and food totaling another 500 yuan. This had
been agreed upon after two meetings with the bride's parents,
together with the matchmaker. It looked like both sides were
pleased with the financial arrangements and, moreover, the
prospective bride and groom had met and seemed to like each
other. So that was a bonus.

The Father had been looking for a suitable bride for Little
Brother for several months. The matchmaker had first produced
a middle-peasant family with an attractive twenty-year-old
daughter. The prospective match didn't work out because the
families couldn't agree on the financial arrangements. The girl's
family wanted too much because the daughter was their youngest
child and they would be losing her income forever. They tried
twice to reach a settlement and it didn't work out. Also, Little
Brother knew the girl and didn't really care for her. So the first
attempt failed.

The second try was a disaster. The matchmaker found a
family of good class background with a strong, healthy, and
attractive daughter. Both parents agreed upon the bride price,
dowry, and wedding arrangements, and Little Brother seemed to
like her when they met. But the daughter was aloof and resisted
the marriage. It turned out that she fancied another young man
and wanted to marry him, but he had a bad class background
and her parents objected. When Little Brother found out she had
a boyfriend, he didn't want to marry her, and Father agreed

saying, "One shouldn't take a chance on used goods. She's like a broken shoe — once she's had a lover how can you marry her?" So the match fell through.

The matchmaker was on the spot because she had failed twice and each time our family had lost face. It was rare that two families could not agree upon a bride price, still rarer to find an eligible bride who openly resisted a match because she had someone else in mind. So the matchmaker had to find a suitable bride this time or else. Drawing on all the resources she had at her disposal, the matchmaker combed the surrounding area, visited teahouses, and finally came up with a candidate, the daughter of a peasant family in a neighboring commune. The bride's family wasn't rich, but their political status was excellent. Her eldest brother was a brigade cadre, her father a respected peasant. Because they were classified as "lower-middle peasants," the bride's family wouldn't demand too high a bride price. On the other hand, because our class status was inferior to theirs — we were "middle peasants" — they used that to their advantage in bargaining over the arrangements, saying, "Once our daughter enters your household, she will have suffered a loss in status. These days you know how valuable it is to be lower-middle peasant; middle isn't bad, but lower-middle is better."

The initial negotiations began. The matchmaker knew how much bride price we were willing to pay and what the bride's family wanted. The matchmaker arranged for both sets of parents to meet in a convenient teahouse. At this meeting the bride's mother took the initiative, inquiring about the size of our household, how many members earned a regular income, how many women were in the household. She wasn't at all pleased that Big Brother and his wife were living in the county town, or that Middle Brother had not yet married. (He was in the army, and who knew when he would return and settle down?) This meant her daughter would have to bear the brunt of the household work, even though I was still at home and my mother and Granny were in the household and were both able to perform household tasks. The bride's mother said that her daughter would have to do the work for everyone in our household. My parents said that the household work was not so difficult, especially since we were a middle-peasant family with savings and a small household. Only Granny, Father, Mother, and I were still at home, and that

wasn't so bad compared to other village households. Then the
bride's mother asked about the kind of housing the newlyweds
would get, and my father said that our house was large enough to
set aside two rooms for them. Father took a good look at the
prospective bride and wanted to know whether she was used to
household work and what kind of labor she did in the fields. Little
Brother and the girl sized each other up, too, at this meeting. It
was the first time they had met in their young lives, and they
didn't get an unfavorable impression of each other's looks. Little
Brother was handsome enough to pass inspection, and so was the
prospective bride. But they didn't talk to each other.

The next time the two sides met was to discuss the financial
arrangements. Both parents were willing to proceed further.
Little Brother had been pleased with his first glimpse of his prospective new wife, and apparently she didn't object either. Both
sides already knew through the matchmaker that they weren't far
apart in agreeing on a bride price. So the girl and her mother
came to our house, and we prepared a big formal meal to enter-
tain them, with nine courses. This was a critical time because
after dinner the man's side puts two packages of "lucky money" [10
yuan in big red wrappings] down on the table if they are interested in pursuing the match. The girl then takes both packages of
lucky money if she agrees, but only one package if she doesn't. I
watched the ceremony with excitement because I didn't know
what my parents had decided. When they put down the two
packages of lucky money I was secretly very happy because I liked
the girl. Would she pick up both packages? I expected she would,
even though her mother had been unhappy about her having to
work so hard in our household. I figured that was just a tactic to
be used for getting a higher bride price. Anyway, she picked up
both packages, stole a glance at Little Brother, and then everybody smiled and relaxed. For the first time she and Little Brother
spoke to each other and they seemed to get on well.

After that, the bride price was agreed upon fairly quickly.
They settled on 500 yuan cash plus seven sets of clothing, each
using four meters of cloth (that cost almost 200 yuan on the free
market), 30 catties of pork [about 33 pounds], 35 catties of wine,
40 catties of wedding cakes, 30 catties of rice, 8 chickens, 4 pairs
of shoes, a silver belt, and 2 ounces of gold jewelry. Altogether
the cash and gifts added up to over 1000 yuan. The 500 yuan

is called a "token of gratitude to the girl's father for raising the girl." It is a form of compensation to her parents for having spent money raising her only to lose her later to another household. Once she was married, they would lose her 7½ work points and suffer a loss in their household income. She would be gone forever to another household, so that's why we always give such a large amount of cash to the bride's family. Five hundred yuan is a year and a half's total household income, and when you add to that the other 500 yuan in gifts, plus the furniture in the two rooms that the newlyweds would get (a new bed alone costs over 300 yuan), plus the cost of entertaining twelve tables of guests at the wedding feast, then the wedding was costing us well over 1500 yuan. Where would all that money, which represented about four years' total household income, come from? Well, in part it comes back when you marry off one of your own daughters. Father figured that soon I'd be betrothed, and then he'd be getting most of that 1500 yuan back. Also we had some savings. One of our relatives in the next village quietly lent us 300 yuan. Father also knew that, once Little Brother's wife became a member of our household, those 7½ work points would become part of our household income, so we'd have a higher income once they were married.

Aside from the bride price the man's side also gave a sum of 50 yuan to the girl's mother. We call this milk money. It is a token of gratitude to the girl's mother for feeding her. When we gave it to her she burst out into tears, weeping and wailing, and so did her daughter. When everybody had quieted down, we drank a glass of wine and toasted each other in celebration of the engagement. The bride's mother was given the milk money once the engagement was formalized, but we paid only one half of the bride price to the bride's family. The rest we sent over to their house a few days before the wedding. I'm not sure why we did it that way; maybe it was because Father needed time to raise the cash or, more likely, one reserves half of the bride price until just before the wedding to make sure the bride won't back out.

It was agreed that the wedding should take place sooner rather than later. The wedding date was the 19th day of the lunar month because the number 9 is lucky. The young couple now had a couple of months to get acquainted, and they took advantage of this opportunity to go to the county town together to get photo-

graphs for the marriage license. They also went together to brigade and commune headquarters to register their marriage.
Legally they were now married, but they dared not sleep with
each other, not until they had bowed before the family ancestral
shrine and kowtowed to my parents on their wedding day. They
were legally married once they received the official commune
chop on the wedding license, but that means nothing in our part
of China where the village doesn't consider you married until
after the traditional ceremony. Even the most progressive cadre
never violates that rule, although there have been cases where
young couples sleep together as man and wife after they've registered their marriage. But these are usually couples whose parents
have refused to agree to a marriage, and they must live together
without having a formal wedding. What a blow to their parents!
But there aren't many cases like that.

Little Brother seemed happy with his prospective wife. He
didn't talk much about her. But he was pleased that he had made
his own decision to marry her. In the old days there was no
choice, and by the time you were twenty-three like Little Brother,
your marriage had long been arranged for you by your parents.
You never saw your bride until the wedding day, and sometimes
you were "married" while still an infant. Now even a girl can refuse to accept a marriage match. Some of the older peasants
grumble about this, saying that they have given the younger generation too much choice and the new modern way is bad because
it reduces parents' authority over their children. The other
criticism is letting young people decide whether they like each
other is unfair because it emphasizes shallow values such as good
looks. I remember an old peasant saying one day: "The new
system makes it hard to marry off an ugly girl. In the old days
you didn't even see her face until it was too late—and then it
turned out that she probably made a better wife than any of
those pretty ones. Now who will marry an ugly girl if he's seen
her once?"

In the days leading up to the wedding itself, both families
were making feverish preparations. The bride's household was
preparing her dowry, which included the following items: a
wooden chest, three sets of bedding, four sets of clothing, a sewing machine, seven sets of clothes (part of the bride price), a
beauty box (inside was a mirror, a comb, and a red ribbon), and

other personal items that a young wife would need in a strange new house. The dowry was brought over a couple of days before the wedding and was unceremoniously dumped in the young couple's bedroom. Then the day before the ceremony a female relative of the bride who had many children, especially sons, came and put the bride's things away carefully in the chests and drawers that the groom's family had put in the room. In the old days they say the delivery of the dowry was a most spectacular event, since big dowries were a sign of a good wedding match. In those days you placed fancy dishes and clothes and things like that in red carved chests and paraded them through the village so everyone could see how rich you were. Now we oppose big dowries, and the prospective bride arrives at her new household with only a few possessions.[1]

Both families held a wedding feast. The bride's family invited their relatives and friends to a big celebration the day before the wedding and set out nine tables of about eight people each. It cost over 100 yuan, and a lot of the food was provided in the bride price we had paid. Father had sent over the rest of the bride price the day the dowry arrived in our house. Our wedding feast was held the day after the bride's family had theirs. We set out twelve tables of eight people each, but there actually were more than 100 guests and we feasted in two shifts. The first-ranked guests were close family and then came other relatives, friends, and members of the team. We invited the brigade cadres and they came, even with the brigade secretary right in the center of things. He enjoyed himself and had too much wine by the end of the day. He complimented Father for keeping the wedding feast to a reasonable size, and he prudently refrained from mentioning the matter of bride price, although the whole village seemed to know to the exact penny what we had spent on every item, right down to the 15 yuan we spent in the county town on candied fruit.

Preparations for the wedding feast began several days in advance of the day, and several relatives came from other villages to help out with the cooking and serving. On the morning of the feast everybody got up early and we killed the chickens and ducks, hauled water, went to the market, and used all the nearby kitchens to prepare the meal. Some weddings have their own cook, but we wanted to prepare the meal ourselves. Big Sister and

Big Brother's wife took over the serving and cooking of the meal along with Granny and Mother, and I helped out too. Even the men were actively involved in the cooking. It was a tradition that on holidays the men would step in and do the cooking, so Father and Big Brother were busy along with the rest of us.

By 2:00 the guests had arrived and we began the feast, which went on for many hours. People came and went, and it was a noisy happy time. About 4:00 in the afternoon a group of ten young men set off on bicycles to fetch the bride. In the old days, of course, they used a red sedan chair and the bride was transported from her house directly to the groom's. Her feet were not allowed to touch the ground from the time she left her old home until she entered her new one. I guess it's bad luck for her future life if her feet touch the bare earth. Nowadays we use bicycles, although I can still remember seeing sedan chairs before the Cultural Revolution. Bicycles are much easier, and in some parts of Guangdong they use boats to bring the bride to her new home.

The young men traveled the 20 kilometers to the bride's village and stopped outside the gate to set firecrackers. Then they tried to "persuade" the bride to come to our house. It took about an hour, I was told, before she finally was persuaded to come out. She had been inside her parents' home, surrounded by ten girlfriends or "sisters" who supposedly were consoling her before she had to leave home, weeping and wailing. Actually they were all having a great time playing jokes on each other, getting the bride dressed in her wedding dress, and fixing her hair. She had had a permanent in town and so they didn't have to comb it up the way they did in the old days; she didn't wear a traditional "phoenix crown," just a red ribbon on her head and a red scarf used as a veil to hide her face. When she came out, the firecrackers popped (to scare away ghosts and monsters), and she wore a little mirror to ward off evil spirits. Someone held an umbrella over her head.

Then the whole party, young men, bride, and "sisters," set off, two on a bicycle, wobbling their way back to the groom's house. The longer the trip took the better, because no one expected to go to bed before early the next morning and they were supposed to drag the trip out to make the groom impatient. Finally, around 8:00, they arrived at the groom's house and Little Brother was waiting outside. Once again the firecrackers sounded, and the bride got off her bike and was carried to the door by two of my cousins. Now the guests and family were shouting all sorts of good wishes and traditional sayings. Some of the most common were: "May you have a hundred sons and a thousand grandsons" (*baizi qiansun*), "Have sons and prosper" (*tianding facai*). There were streamers with these sayings tacked up around the doorway. A woman relation of ours who had seven children, six of them males, came up to the bride and said, "You will have three boys and two girls if you're lucky," and then she helped her to the door, laughing and singing. At the doorway, my mother took a pile of grass and straw and set fire to it. The bride stepped over this pile of burning straw, which meant that she had entered our household without bringing in any evil spirits. Now she and Little Brother went to pay their respects to the household's ancestors. They knelt down in front of the family ancestral shrine — or, rather, where the shrine used to be, since the tablets had been destroyed during the Cultural Revolution. They burned incense and candles. Then they set out some wine, chicken, and five cups of tea in front of the shrine and bowed three times. After they paid their respects to the groom's ancestors, they got up and the bride paid her respects to her new inlaws. The bride paid her respects by washing her mother-in-law's hands and feet and by serving her tea. Mother replied by giving her lucky money wrapped in red paper, and the bride got lucky packets from the other important family members. Then she sat down and ate the head of a chicken. This signified that the bride now would be able to manage affairs in her new household.

At this point the bride was taken to the nuptial chambers where she rested for a while, together with some of the "sisters" who were helping her get settled. After about an hour she came out and joined in the celebration with our family and friends. The older people began to drift away, and soon it was time to tease the bride. That was a lot of fun and I had remembered it from Big Brother's wedding. Some of Little Brother's friends asked her to fill up a rice bucket using chopsticks; others asked her to light a cigarette for Little Brother. Then some even dared the couple to kiss — but they wouldn't do that. There was lots of noise and singing; the bride had to sing whatever songs we asked her. Finally after about two hours of this teasing, it was after midnight and the bride's "sisters" got ready to leave. The bride and groom went to their bedroom, but the young men at first

wouldn't let them close the bedroom door. Then they stood outside the house and yelled and shouted till early dawn.

So ended the first day of Little Brother's marriage. We were
exhausted and happy that it had all worked out and that the gods
had been appeased. The right traditions had been observed and
the bride was now part of our household. On the second day the
bride got up early and helped around her new household, getting
acquainted with the way things worked in our house and especially with her new mother-in-law. I don't remember that day, but
on the next day Little Brother and his wife went back to her village to pay respects to her parents. She stayed there for two days
and then returned to our house. A week later her mother and
some aunts showed up at our house with gifts, a courtesy visit. By
that time the debris from the wedding banquet had long been
cleared away, and Little Brother's wife seemed to be getting used
to the household routine. She stayed away from work in the fields
for a week altogether, but then started again as a new member of
our team, earning the same work points as before. In the old
days, brides were not allowed to be seen outside their new homes
for thirty days, but nobody bothers with that practice anymore.
It's a stupid superstition, that women have to stay indoors for a
month after they're married.

The wedding had gone off without any trouble, and even the
brigade secretary didn't complain. He had done his duty and had
warned us about not having a lavish wedding, and by local standards the wedding was about average—maybe a bit above
average. The matchmaker had done her work and only charged a
few yuan for doing an important job. Not only had she found the
bride and brought the two families together, but she also helped
organize the wedding preparations and the feast. The bride price
had been paid out and the bride's family was satisfied. The wedding was a true mixture of old and new. Bicycles had replaced
sedan chairs, but the couple still kowtowed to their elders and
worshiped ancestors behind the gates of their house. The matchmaker had brought the bride and groom together but, unlike the
old arranged marriages, the young couple themselves had decided whether they liked each other enough to get married. They
even spent time with each other before their wedding night. Peasant girls now have a choice in their marriage partner, and this is
a big change from the recent past. (On the other hand, you can

see from the ceremony that women are still second-class citizens in China—look at how everybody always wishes for sons and never for daughters!)

I left China in 1975, and it's been a year and a half now since Little Brother's marriage. My leaving wasn't a hardship for my family because they knew I would be sending back money from Hong Kong. So Father soon will get back all that he spent on Little Brother's wedding, even though he won't be getting any bride price for me in exchange. Things haven't turned out so well for Little Brother and his new bride. She gave birth to a baby girl and that was a big disappointment, since you want to have a son first. Then Granny became ill and suddenly Little Brother's wife was very busy around the house, taking care of Granny and the baby. She couldn't work steadily in the fields, and this reduced the household income. Everybody was grumbling and the happy time of Little Brother's marriage was over. Now he and his bride had become part of the routine problems of daily life in Fish Flower village, southern Guangdong. The excitement of the wedding was over; we had new relatives, new faces in the household, and family life continued as it had for as long as anyone could remember.

Return to the Motherland

ABOUT 40 MILLION CHINESE live outside the current boundaries of China, 95 percent of them in Southeast Asia, where they generally are either a minority within another Asian country or the dominant population in an entity that has an awkward political relationship with China (Taiwan, Hong Kong, Macao). Since 1949, the relationship between the motherland and these overseas Chinese has been complex and subject to a variety of pressures; for example, Chinese-Vietnamese conflict has been exacerbated by the presence of a large number of Chinese living in Vietnam. China at various times has urged Chinese living abroad, particularly the young and technically skilled, to return "to serve the motherland." Many Chinese who felt discriminated against in their host countries took up this offer, especially since the Communists provided free education, a chance to pursue a specialized career, and better food and housing than are normally supplied to ordinary citizens of China.

About 600,000 Chinese returned to the motherland in the twenty years after 1949. Ten million relatives and dependents of overseas Chinese also lived in China, basically concentrated in the two southern coastal provinces of Fujian and Guangdong. Many continue to receive remittances of money from their relatives abroad, a tradition begun generations ago when adventurous Chinese began leaving their families to seek their fortunes among the barbarians. For China, the overseas Chinese have been a mixed blessing. They are an important outside listening post and a source for exerting political pressure in Southeast

Asia. Yet they also constitute a major problem in China's foreign policy, especially in the conduct of relations between China and those Asian countries where overseas Chinese are a significant political factor. Moreover, China has had problems integrating returned overseas Chinese into its socialist system, partly because the returnees never fully shed their bourgeois habits and because the Chinese have been unwilling to grant returnees the equal status they desire. In the years following the Cultural Revolution, over 200,000 overseas Chinese have received permission to leave China, and most of them are now in Hong Kong. Ironically, having just washed its hands of so many overseas Chinese, China is again actively recruiting a new group of overseas Chinese youth and technical experts from Southeast Asia to return to help in the nation's current modernization drive.

This story chronicles Younger Brother's search for identity in China, through his various roles as student, revolutionary, tourist, steelworker, and farmer. Each of these experiences helped him to learn more about China and about himself. He listens carefully to the advice of Elder Brother, a Party member, on how to become a good Chinese citizen. After eight years he and Elder Brother arrive at different solutions to the problems of adapting to life in the motherland, and the two say goodbye in Canton, knowing they will probably never see each other again.

IT TOOK A LONG TIME at the border. I had many crates and packages, and the guards went through everything. Elder Brother had asked me to bring a sewing machine, a watch for his wife, powdered milk, peanut oil, canned food, western medicine, a transistor radio, sweaters, shirts, blouses. I had spent a hectic few days in Hong Kong with Elder Brother's trusted friend Li, who worked in one of the Chinese-owned companies. He helped me buy all the things Elder Brother had mentioned. Li kept saying: "How lucky you are to be going back to the Motherland! China needs young men like you to build her national economy. How I envy you! I wish I could return with you, but it is my duty to serve China here in Hong Kong." We bought everything that I needed and he saw me off on the train. I was so excited I could hardly sit still. To go to China at last, after thinking about it for so long! Elder Brother had already been there seven years, and I couldn't wait to see him and to meet his wife. I was going to a whole new life, to a place where everybody was Chinese. No more discrimination because I was Chinese. No more insults at the hands of foreigners (*waiguoren*).[1] In China I would be free and equal with all other citizens. China was welcoming me—old Li had said in Hong Kong: "China will send you to the best schools and provide you with a career in which you will truly feel proud to be Chinese." So, as you can imagine, with all these thoughts and images buzzing around in my head, I was euphoric when the train reached the border.

I hadn't been prepared for the long search through my luggage, especially since I had followed Elder Brother's advice not to bring in any sensitive foreign publications, and I took pains to declare all my valuables. I was very careful in exchanging currency and I made sure everything was written down and recorded, just as I had been instructed. So they didn't confiscate anything that I brought in, although most of it was unpacked and spread out on straw mats in a big shed. There were hundreds of us there, all "displaying our wares" to the officials. My Mandarin Chinese was poor and I didn't know Cantonese, so they brought over an officer who spoke Indonesian. "Why are you bringing in so many things?" he asked. I replied, "They are for my personal use and also gifts for Elder Brother and his family. My brother is a Communist, a cadre in the Returned Overseas Chinese Federation in Canton. He asked me to bring those things that are legally permissible, and I checked carefully in Canton with the Overseas Chinese Travel Service people there." The officials unpacked the sewing machine, thumbed through my books (all of them published by the Indonesian Communist Party), looked at the medicine I had brought for Elder Brother's bad heart, and then let me pass. The officer who spoke Indonesian said, "I hope you'll get rid of all this bourgeois junk by the time you get to Peking. If you want to be a good citizen of China, then you'd better learn to live like a regular Chinese." I thanked him and then got on the train to Canton.

What a difference between the two sides of the border! The piles of garbage that had been strewn all around the shacks in the New Territories were gone, and once inside China all you could see were neat fields dotted by villages, some new construction, and many people working in the fields. After the chaos and dirt of Hong Kong, my first view of the Motherland made me excited all over again. I had been a city boy all my life in Djakarta, and I had never lived in the countryside. I had heard that in China everyone had to work with peasants and live in the rural areas for a while, and I was eagerly looking forward to living on a commune. "Are these really people's communes?" I remember asking bemused passengers on the train. "How neat and clean it all looks. And the people hardly look like peasants, at least not through the window."

The train's arrival in Canton shook me out of my reverie. There was Elder Brother, wreathed in smiles, a bit fatter and shorter than I remembered him seven years ago. He looked just like any other Chinese in Canton, a blue and white figure in a blue and white crowd. I suddenly felt awkward in my colorful Indonesian clothes and resolved then and there to switch to Chinese clothes as soon as I had a chance. Elder Brother lived in a flat in central Canton with his wife and two children. He seemed happy and we talked together for hours about the family, especially about Father, with whom Elder Brother had argued many times before he left. "Is Father still so autocratic and reactionary?" asked Elder Brother. "All he thinks about is making money. How did you manage to get his permission to leave?" I told Elder Brother that Father had opposed my coming, too, but I knew I had to come. "You're my model, Elder Brother," I said. "Remember how we used to talk together in the old days at home? Your defiance of Father made a lasting impression on me. I had to come to China once you came here." Elder Brother said, "I'm happy you came, because China is where we belong, although I wish that our Father would have at least approved your return. But, remember, it will take some time for you to get used to life here. You've made a difficult decision, but it's a correct one. In Indonesia you will always be a second-class citizen. Here in the Motherland you will become a member of a vanguard, building a new China, the socialist society of the future. Life may seem hard at first, but once you shake the bourgeois dirt from your shoes, you'll adjust and be happy. Look at me, I've got no regrets at all. I never think of going back to Indonesia, even for a visit. I've got a responsible job and peace of mind. You'll even do better than I because you're still a baby, only eighteen, and have a college education in front of you. The future is all yours here."

I stayed in Canton with Elder Brother and his family over

New Year's. Then we parted because I was due in Peking to start studying at the Overseas Chinese Preparatory School there. I had taken Elder Brother's advice to go to Peking: "You can't speak Cantonese," he said, "and you have to learn Mandarin to have a good career in China. The best place for you is Peking. I have connections and can get you sent there. Also you're interested in mining and geology, and the best institutes are located in Peking. If you pass your university entrance examinations then there's a good chance you'll be admitted to the Mining Institute." Taking the train northward gave me a chance to see more of China, and to pass through places that had only been names on maps to me before: Changsha, where Chairman Mao went to school, the big industrial city of Wuhan, the Yellow River, Zhengzhou. People on the train were friendly—they knew, of course, that I was not a native Chinese even though I was wearing Chinese modern clothing. How? Well, every time I opened my mouth to say a few words of broken Mandarin, they knew. Also my haircut didn't look right, and I was smoking foreign cigarettes, which everybody borrowed from me with relish.

I was met at the Peking train station and taken to the school. The Peking train station was impressive—the largest I had ever seen, and the cadre from the school commented, "This station is a monument to the ten great months of effort by the people of Peking in 1958, when we built ten projects like this. Soon it will be your turn to build monuments for socialism!" I felt like jumping out of the truck and doing just that at once, especially when we drove through Tiananmen, by the Forbidden City and up Changan, past some of the buildings that had been put up in 1958—right past the spot where Chairman Mao and the Party leaders stood during October 1st celebrations, and by the Great Hall of the People where all of Peking's overseas Chinese had been invited at New Year's to meet with China's top leaders. Peking was very different from Canton. This was the capital, the center of everything (*zhongyang*), and the key decisions affecting China's destiny were being made here. The people seemed more sure of themselves, moved more deliberately, were taller, straighter, and less communicative than the southerners. It was the first time I had seen snow, and this made the city look even more empty than it already appeared, in contrast with Canton, where people lived practically on top of each other. The people, the cold, the special magic of Peking, all made me realize that it was here, and not in Canton, that my introduction to China really would begin.

The Overseas Chinese Preparatory School was located in the northwest part of the city. Our school was a city in itself. You could eat, sleep, shop, and carry out your small business activities within its walls. We had an indoor swimming pool, a large sports field, a bank, post office, and a state purchasing station, where overseas Chinese were allowed to sell their foreign-made personal items to the state for much-needed cash.[2] There were four dormitory buildings for the students. The school only admitted overseas Chinese students so there were no local students. At one time the school had 2500 students, and there were about 1800 when I came. The teachers were a mixture of overseas Chinese and locals, about half and half. I was lucky—most of my teachers were locals so I had some real Chinese to talk to. The school was divided into three basic groups: classes at the junior high level, at the senior high level, and refresher classes. The latter were for people like me who had a high school diploma outside China but now needed to learn Chinese and also to prepare for the nation-wide university entrance exams. Soon after I arrived, Teacher Bi, a local Chinese, came to meet me and introduced himself as the cadre at the school who looked after Chinese from Indonesia. He would help me get settled in, and if I had any problems I was to consult him. There were Chinese from fourteen countries at the school, and each group had its own version of Teacher Bi, a local cadre whose main job was to advise his charges, making sure they attended classes and stayed out of trouble. In my case there were no problems—I began Mandarin classes immediately, trying to remember the few phrases I had learned back home, and trying to shed my Fujian accent. I also attended brush-up classes, in which I learned about Chinese politics and history. Since I planned to make my career in mining or geology, I took special courses in science and mathematics.

The courses kept me busy, and I could see that I'd have to stay at the school another year before getting a decent score on the exams. My language was shaky, and I didn't have the background in mathematics. Elder Brother had cautioned me not to be impatient and told me that I would likely need a year and a half, so this wasn't a disappointment. It gave me more time to look around Peking, and just traveling about the city was an education. What a strange mixture of old and new — modern skyscrapers and old hutongs!* Lots of politics to digest; the slogans were all around me. And it was a *Chinese* city, for Chinese, with the few foreigners there under *Chinese* control. If the leaders didn't like them, they could throw them out. I could look some of those foreign dogs square in the eye and wait for them to blink and turn their faces away. It had been the other way around in Indonesia. Of course, I was a foreigner in Peking too. That's a fact I soon discovered. I looked Chinese and dressed Chinese, but my accent and my identity documents stamped me as "overseas Chinese." Even with a Peking-style haircut, my gold ring tucked in my pocket, and wearing all the right clothes, it was never long before some alert citizen would ask, "What country are you from, comrade?" There always seemed to be this gap, this awareness that I wasn't part of "them," and no matter how I tried, I could never close this gap, never make "them" feel that I was also Chinese. Elder Brother said later that he never felt that way, that he always felt at ease with anyone and they with him. But in Peking I sensed early on that the closeness with the Chinese people I wanted, that I was searching for back home, might also elude me here in China.

I tried to explain this to Teacher Bi, but he insisted that I misunderstood people's reactions. "They're not placing you in an inferior category," he argued, "only in a special category. You're treated in a special way because when overseas Chinese first come here they're different and need special attention. Some need a great deal of help to overcome the habits of a bourgeois lifetime; others are too eager to serve the Motherland and want to rush out before they know what to do; still others find life too harsh when they get here and lapse into dangerous ways, lying around and doing nothing. Those overseas Chinese who become 'steeled and tempered' in the ways of the Motherland are accepted as equal citizens, but this can take time." I understood what Teacher Bi was telling me and it did make sense. Not everyone, it seemed, was enchanted at what they found after returning to the

---

*One of Peking's characteristic features are the hutongs, small crooked alleys with their walled one-storey houses and inner courtyards. Though the houses lack inside plumbing and the streets are unpaved, hutong residents generally prefer living there to moving into larger new apartments with inside plumbing and other amenities.

Motherland. One student told me, "I'll stay in China as long as
Daddy keeps sending the money from overseas. Once the money
stops, I'm getting out of here." Another student asked me if I
wanted to join a small group that liked to go dancing and hang
around with foreigners. (They had heard that I had brought
along some foreign records and wanted to hear my music because
they said, "We're tired of the lousy music we hear day after day in
China.")

There was a group of over a hundred disaffected students at
the school who never attended classes, spent most of their time
down at Wangfujing (Peking's main shopping area), drank
coffee, and sold their things on the black market for extra cash. If
you sold a piece of clothing on the black market you got back two
to three times what the state purchasing station was willing to
pay. This group, composed of overseas Chinese from several
countries, deliberately wore their hair as long as they could and
strutted around in their western-style clothing with stove-pipe
pants and blazing colors, "just to make the Chinese mad." These
students were disaffected for a number of reasons. Some were fed
up with Peking and wanted to leave China, but had been denied
exit visas. Others had failed the national exams and didn't expect
to pass, or had been assigned to work or school in some place
where they did not wish to live. A few had wandered into Peking
from other schools in China and now were at loose ends until the
school, the Returned Overseas Chinese Federation, and the
Overseas Chinese Affairs Commission could figure out what to do
with them. This apparently was a chronic problem. Back in the
late 1950s our school had been singled out for the bad elements it
was harboring. A purge had taken place and most of these dissi-
dents were dispersed. Now they were back again.*

The overseas Chinese community in Peking was split basically into three broad ideological groups, as well as along na-

*For more on the situation of the late 1950s at the school, see "A New Atmosphere Ap-
pears in Overseas Chinese Preparatory School in Peking," *Qiao Wubao* (Overseas Chinese Affairs Bulletin), January 1958: "For a long time in the past, the School had more
than 100 students who were not assigned to classes or who had been assigned to classes but
were absent. Quite a large number of them were wicked elements who, while abroad, were
saturated with lethargic attitudes which despised labor and with selfish exploitative thinking. Day in and day out, they did almost nothing but steal, fight, assail women and
cheat—; when they returned to China, they refused not only to study but to accept
reform. As a consequence, they were for a long time not qualified to gain admittance to

tional lines. There were two extremist ideological positions and a
large group in the middle. The two extremist groups occupied
minority positions on the left or the right. On the right were
people like the disaffected students in Peking, who were openly
dissatisfied and went out of their way to criticize the Party and
government, hoping to provoke a response. Some were called
"do-nothing bums," who went around wearing western suits and
ties. They lived off remittances from abroad or from black mar-
keteering. Later many were arrested and sent to labor camps.
A few were given exit permits just to get rid of them. Then there
was an opposite group, the "progressives" or "activists." They
were called *jijifenzi* and were alternatively scorned or feared by
those who came in contact with them. Some accused the progressives of being "redder than the red flag" in order to gain political favors. Many of the other overseas Chinese called them radish
communists, *hong luobo*; like radishes they were red (progressive) on the outside but white (reactionary) in their hearts.
Generally the poorer overseas Chinese, those who had no rich
daddy sending remittances from home, were more likely to be
activists. The third group, which probably comprised 80 to 85
percent of the entire community, was in the ideological middle,
trying to get by without suffering any political disasters. Many of
the people in this group were older professionals and specialists
who had settled down to relatively secure jobs in the state system.
They were under no pressure to be red radishes, and they kept
their opinions to themselves.

The overseas Chinese group was also divided along national
lines. When you arrived in China you were classified by what
country you came from, and once settled in Peking you naturally
tended, out of familiarity, to associate with others who spoke your
own language and knew friends back home. Generally, except for
a serious quarrel in the early fifties between overseas Chinese
from Thailand and from Indonesia, there was no serious dis-

formal schools; or when they did, they soon left without authorization; or they violated
law and discipline and showed no signs of repentance after undergoing labor reform on a
number of occasions. They not only refused to accept education and reform, but frequently created disturbances. Some of these criminal activities of the wicked elements
have already been exposed in this *Bulletin* in its November 1, 1957 issue (see "We Cannot
Tolerate Persistent Wicked Elements Among the Returned Overseas Chinese Students,"
by Xu Lianchuan)."

agreement among the national groups. Certain groups preferred each other's company—for example, Asian overseas Chinese preferred the company of other Asians. The westernized, European overseas Chinese didn't want to spend time with us. They tried to ingratiate themselves with the other European foreigners in Peking. The Japanese overseas Chinese rarely mixed with the rest of us and were one of the best-behaved groups. The Indonesians were so-so. In Indonesia there had been two groups of Chinese—one was traditionally Chinese-oriented, and the other was western and modern. They had rarely mixed with each other in Indonesia but in China, because of the various pressures, they got along so well that they even intermarried, something that rarely happened back in Indonesia. In general, the overseas Chinese community tended to marry by country, or at least by language group. It was rare for an overseas Chinese to marry a Chinese local, but it happened, usually because the Chinese local was intrigued by the "exotic" prospect of marrying one of us and, possibly, by the promise of an exit visa if the spouse ever chose to leave China. If anybody could leave China, it would be an overseas Chinese. Even if he (usually a male overseas Chinese married a female local) had no intention of leaving, he might still be a good catch for someone from a mediocre class background. You'd never have a good political record if you married one of us, but if your own class background was petit-bourgeois or worse, then you'd never have a clean political record anyway. So why not marry a rich overseas Chinese who gets regular remittances from abroad and has a good job?

In those days, however, I wasn't so cynical and actually belonged to the group of young activists. I was far from being a red radish. I took politics to heart and joined the Young Communist League. My goal was to emulate Elder Brother, who had become a Party member only four years after his arrival. Teacher Bi one day said, "You have made great progress, and the Party is proud of you." So despite all the problems around me, the disenchanted students, and my feelings of not being accepted as a Chinese, things were going along pretty well. When the reactionaries in Indonesia turned on the Chinese in 1965, massacring countless thousands upon thousands, I knew I had made the right decision. Now there was no alternative—the gates had been locked for good behind me. My parents were safe, but after 1965 I really

never expected to see them again. In Peking, the 1965-66 school
year was progressing nicely for me. I had made progress in all
areas, and my Mandarin was getting quite good. I still had an
accent, but it was fading rapidly. I expected to do well on the
exams, and the Mining Institute looked like a real possibility. At
least that's what the school's Party secretary mentioned to me one
day.

   Then, of course, came the Cultural Revolution and everything stopped in its tracks, including my career plans. Students at
the school formed a Red Guard organization called "The East Is
Red." Our group later took an active part in the Cultural Revolution in the foreign affairs system, especially against the Overseas
Chinese Affairs Commission headed by Liao Chengzhi and Fang
Fang.[3] We criticized these officials for being revisionists and for
following Liu Shaoqi's mistaken policies. I participated in this
struggle and in addition was present when we criticized Chen Yi
and when the Iron Army of radicals stormed the Foreign Ministry
(more about that later). It was an exciting time for me. I joined
the radical Red Guard faction because I believed in Chairman
Mao and what he was trying to do. Admittedly it also gave a frustrated young man a chance to let off some steam, and it made me
feel I was finally a full-scale participant in China's revolutionary
socialist construction.

   Those were heady days for me—I roamed all over Peking
and became involved in the oddest things. During the "Smash the
Four Olds" campaign,[4] I had to make sure not to be a target myself, so I quickly got rid of my foreign clothes. I stuffed Grandfather's gold ring in a crack in the wall behind Chairman Mao's
picture. Then I joined in raiding Fang Fang's house (he was
deputy director of the Overseas Chinese Affairs Commission),
and we carted off all kinds of foreign goods, such as the expected
transistor radios, watches, and tape recorders, but also cans of
Ovaltine, glucose, piles of foreign literature, and western clothing he had been hoarding. Our faction became involved in a
gang war between overseas Chinese and Chinese youth. A group
of Chinese middle school students came to the Overseas Chinese
Village—the fancy area with special housing owned by overseas
Chinese—and started to make trouble.[5] Suddenly it was Chinese
versus overseas Chinese, and our radical faction had to rescue the
other group of overseas Chinese with clubs and homemade weap-

ons. It was short-lived but ugly. Then, when we had got rid of the Chinese, the two groups of overseas Chinese suddenly turned on each other. The other faction was a bunch of reactionaries and had been running around Peking fighting and stealing. So after we had rescued our compatriots we beat them up. That's the way it was in Peking in those days.

Everybody was coming to Peking on *chuan lian,** so I decided to do the reverse, to exchange experience with the rest of China. I left in the fall of 1966 for the south and west, hoping to see as much of China as possible and taking time to visit Elder Brother in Canton. Dressed in a green uniform, wearing a green cap modeled after the army's uniforms, a Mao badge pinned on my chest, I managed to find a seat on the train to Xian. I had my water canteen and a green canvas bag with the yellow characters "Serve the People" neatly printed on its side. My red armband with "East Is Red" was conspicuously displayed on my left sleeve. It turned out to be a sightseeing trip rather than one of exchanging revolutionary experience, because after the big events in Peking I wasn't much interested in provincial politics—anyway, I didn't really understand them. But just to see Xian, Yanan, Luoyang, and Hunan was worth it. I stopped at Changsha and managed to get to Shaoshan (Mao's birthplace). On the way I met all kinds of young people and almost no one noticed that I wasn't a "real" Chinese. It was a good feeling at last to be accepted like that. That was the first thing I told Elder Brother when we met again in Canton: "I'm a real Chinese now," I said. "I've made revolution, destroyed the Four Olds, traveled with the revolutionary masses all over the Motherland, and can speak Chinese almost without an accent. It's a wonderful feeling."

Elder Brother was happy for me, but I could see he was forcing himself to smile. "What's the matter, Elder Brother?" I asked. "You've changed—are you in some kind of trouble?" He admitted he was and explained that, as a Party member firmly devoted to the system, he had supported the first work teams. Then, when these teams were denounced for being Liuist, he was caught on the wrong side. He had desperately made a self-criticism, but it was too late. No one actually denounced him for supporting the

*This policy enabled youth for a few months to travel free of charge all over China to "exchange revolutionary experience" with youth in other cities. It was an unprecedented opportunity for young people to travel throughout China.

work teams, because Elder Brother wasn't a top cadre in his organization. But now for the first time since he came to China, he was afraid. "You see, I know how the system works, Little Brother. My record always was clean, but now there's a big black mark on it. I made a mistake and eventually I'll be called to account. It's inevitable. So that's why I'm glum and why I keep my mouth shut these days. I can't afford to make a second mistake. Little Brother, my whole life in China is being threatened, so forgive me if I don't share in your enthusiasm. Go and make revolution, and topple those who stand in your way. You can do it, but I can't because I've a whole career and family to think about."

The meeting with Elder Brother shook me up. How could he be guilty of anything? He had been a model Party member, unswerving in his loyalty to the Party and to Chairman Mao, yet there he was, trembling in his shoes, afraid that tomorrow's big character poster would focus on him and shatter his career. Gloomy days in Canton, and that visit was the low spot of my travels. I felt sorry for Elder Brother, but I couldn't believe that he would be struggled. He had been too loyal a Party member and most important, he wasn't a big fish, only small fry, and not worth struggling. At least that's what I thought as I headed back to Peking in a train jammed with crazy Guangdong kids on their way to Peking. Most of them had never been outside Guangdong province, let alone to Peking. Their high spirits made me feel much better after seeing Elder Brother. I told them about the Four Olds and about sacking Fang Fang's house in Peking. One of them said, "We're like blood brothers. You know, my older brother helped pull down Fang Fang ten years ago when he was doing his reactionary tricks in Guangdong. We got rid of him then, so they kicked him upstairs to Peking. Now he's been found out once more. Hooray for Chairman Mao!"[6] We "blood brothers" swapped Mao badges and enjoyed the trip north until Peking when we parted, the Guangdong youths to head for Tiananmen and I to see how the Overseas Chinese Preparatory School had fared in the two months I had been away.

It was 1967 and a big political showdown was about to take place, the attempt by ultraleftists to take over the Foreign Ministry in Peking. Two events in particular occurred: the public criticism meeting of Chen Yi, the foreign minister, and the storming of the ministry. I was there at both because the Iron Army took an active part and my friend was in that group. It was August 11th when the Chen Yi Liaison Station held a "Thoroughly Criticize Chen Yi Meeting" at the Great Hall of the People. Zhou Enlai, Chen Boda, Kang Sheng, Xie Fuzhi, and others attended the meeting.[7] It was called a meeting to "criticize" (*pi ping*) and not for the much stronger "down with" (*da dao*). Zhou had said he would only come if it were for criticism and if we were forbidden to shout "Down with Chen Yi." Of course we all came into the hall shouting, "Down with Chen Yi," "Long Live Chairman Mao," and "Long Live the Cultural Revolution." That was inevitable. There was singing and yelling of slogans back and forth. Then the top leaders appeared and we yelled, "Respect to Premier Zhou," "Learn from Premier Zhou." Chen Yi and Qiao Guanhua[8] followed and had to stand on the right corner and left corner of the stage. Soldiers were standing in the background.

Chen Yi made his self-criticism, which wasn't very strong, and we shouted, "Down with Chen Yi" and "Liberate the Foreign Affairs System." Suddenly members of one faction jumped on stage to grab Chen and force him to bow his head to the masses, but the soldiers immediately stepped in, a scuffle broke out, and Chen and Qiao were hustled out the back. Zhou and the other leaders also left the stage. Fifteen minutes later, when order had been restored, Zhou and the other leaders reappeared and Zhou then expressed cautious support for the radicals, saying that "it would be better now for you to criticize Chen in small and medium-size meetings instead of such large ones." The confrontation with Chen Yi was thus defused and the leadership had saved face for the moment. Then, however, the matter of Chen Yi became embroiled in factional Red Guard struggles, and the Iron Army decided to go to the Foreign Ministry to kidnap Chen. I remember going in trucks to Tiananmen and assembling in front of the Ministry. The kidnap plan was foiled because of confusion and various misunderstandings on the part of the groups that were allied. We stormed the gate and spilled into the compound. Windows were smashed and someone slashed the tires of a "Red Flag" limousine parked in the compound. Chen Yi couldn't be found. We were ordered to leave and there were soldiers all over. The top rebel leaders talked with Chen Boda inside the building, but none of our demands were met and we finally left in the evening, without Chen Yi. It had been an exhilarating experience. We didn't get Chen, but we had demonstrated our rebellious spirit. Everybody was afraid of us, right up to the very top leaders in the government and Party.[9]

A year later, however, the tide turned. Peking's youth were no longer in a favored position, no longer being used by the leaders to spearhead their attacks on one another. Now we were about to be shipped to the countryside. For some this was tantamount to exile, and they tried to resist. For others, like myself, it was one more adventure in a young life. The school had been closed since 1966, and after two years of hanging around I welcomed the chance of doing something else besides playing politics. The army showed up to help mobilize the school's students, and it turned out that I had three alternatives to choose from: the great northern wilderness (*Beidahuang*) in Heilongjiang province; an overseas Chinese state farm in the northeast; or a commune in Inner Mongolia. I chose the latter for two reasons. First, I was intrigued at the prospect of living among Mongols and, second, the commune included regular Chinese as well as overseas Chinese. At least I would be together with Chinese and not segregated on an overseas Chinese state farm or stuck in a wilderness area. I left with fifteen others in early 1969. It was cold and we wore padded jackets and sheepskin coats, carrying our padded blankets. The state had provided these free of charge and had also given 400 yuan to help us get settled, to defray the cost of housing and furniture. We could keep anything that was left over. The commune was in the richest part of Inner Mongolia, and it was half-agricultural and half-pastoral. The main crop was wheat. The inhabitants were 70 percent Han Chinese, the rest Mongols. The latter lived in their own villages and had their own production brigades. I didn't work with them, but I did talk with them often and visited some of the herdsmen out in the plains.

I enjoyed the four years in Mongolia, finally getting the opportunity to experience living and working among peasants in the commune and with workers in a Hohhot factory. It wasn't as bad as most city folk said, but it wasn't as exciting as I had imagined back in 1964 when my train had cut through the well-tended Guangdong rice paddies. The highlight of my time in Mongolia was my experience with the Mongols, learning about their fascinating ways and customs. I was invited to visit a Mongol family in their yurt, a tent made out of layers of felt blankets stretched over a circular wooden frame. The yurt is about ten feet high and has a small ring in the center which lets out the smoke from the stove. Once you get used to it, you hardly realize that you're inside a tent, because it has furniture and rugs, pictures on the walls, and all the comforts of home. I was given kumiss to drink[10] and was invited to sit in the place of honor, facing the male head of the household. Guests sat around the head of the household in descending order of importance, with the least important guest actually squatting by the door. I attended a banquet in this yurt, and we ate out of a large tub set on a table, filled with sweetbreads, intestines, and assorted parts of the cow. You cut off a chunk of food with your knife and then eat it with your fingers, washing it all down with gulps of a powerful spirit made of wheat (sometimes of mare's milk) that really knocks you out. The hospitality of the Mongols is known all over China, and I was fortunate to experience it myself.

The Mongols are a proud people who have barely been "tamed" by modern civilization. I think they're happiest on the land, away from other people. They especially love animals, and I guess that's why Mongolia has been called "land of five animals" (horse, cow, camel, sheep, and goat). Animals appear in all their sayings and proverbs. When a Mongol doubts that something will occur he says, "It will happen when the camel's tail touches the ground" (never). Another saying goes, "To speak words to a man who doesn't understand them is like throwing grain on a cow's horns." My Mongol friend at the commune once described his idea of happiness to me: "A man riding his camel is near heaven —that's happiness." I respected their love of nature, but opposed their treatment of women. A Mongol once told me, "Women have long hair but short brains," and there is truth to the view that on the plains a Mongol pays better attention to his horse than to his woman. Admittedly, the Mongol women look less than attractive in their long bulky gowns, whereas a galloping horse is a thing to behold, but that didn't justify the clear position of female inferiority. Even on the commune where they lived in regular houses and were "civilized," the Mongol men still treated their women in a feudal way.*

In Hohhot, which contained over 400,000 people, about 30

percent of the population were Mongols, 20 percent were Hui (Moslem), and the rest were Han. In contrast to the custom in the countryside, there were many marriages between Hans and Mongols in the city. Because of the intermarriages it wasn't always easy to spot a Mongol and, since it was a modern city, the Mongols generally wore regular Chinese clothing, reserving their traditional clothing only for trips to the villages and yurts or for special festive occasions. I worked in the Hohhot iron and steel mill, in the plant's steel-pressing section. The factory needed workers in 1971 and I decided to apply, since I had already spent two years in farm work. There were over a thousand workers in the plant and we worked pretty hard, although the plant wasn't producing as much now as it had before the Cultural Revolution, when it had an elaborate bonus system that gave extra money to the workers. I was happy with my pay, but several of the older workers were always grumbling that they hadn't had an increase in eight years. We lived in the factory dormitories and the housing was free, the food cheap. I ate in the factory dining hall and spent a lot of time getting to know the other workers. As it turned out, I was one of the few overseas Chinese working in that factory; there were three others but they had been there for some time and were technicians and engineers. One of these overseas Chinese, Old Yao, had come from Indonesia fifteen years earlier and we became friends. He had married a Chinese woman and was satisfied with his life. Old Yao told me, "I make over 100 yuan a month and can't spend it all. My living conditions are more than adequate and as an overseas Chinese I get an extra grain ration and extra cloth coupons. I can't complain, although right now I worry that my children may have problems getting admitted to higher educational institutions because of the policy of admitting only the 'best class elements.' That does bother me; also the fact that I'd like to travel abroad and see my family once more."

*For a good description of the woman-horse contrast, see J. Bisch, *Mongolia, Unknown Land,* (New York: Dutton, 1963), p. 44: "The Mongol reserved the deepest feeling any man can have for his horse; he loved it . . . The ungallant might even allege—there is more beauty in a Mongolian horse than there is in a Mongolian woman. 'She is hardly a stimulating sight when you see her shuffling along in an ankle-length gown, with her plump body and weather-beaten face,' one acquaintance said to me. 'But it is a magnificent and fascinating sight to see a Mongolian horse tearing along on its swift legs, with its mane and tail flowing behind it. If, in addition, you happen to be a rider yourself, able to enjoy the feeling of one-ness with the animal as it streaks across the steppe, then the pleasure is multiplied.' "

I wandered around Hohhot as much as possible, especially
the old city, which is like an ancient Chinese town with its muddy
crooked streets and one-storey houses. It had no modern multistorey buildings and reminded me a lot of the hutongs of Peking. The old city, in contrast to the new part of Hohhot, was
always teeming with people milling in the streets, at the market
stalls and shops, or haggling with peasants selling their wares on
streetcorners. Most of the Han Chinese lived in the new city,
where the housing is multistorey, the streets are wide, and there is
plenty of green space. This part of the city has the large state department stores, new theaters, a hospital with a thousand beds,
and other large public buildings. In this part, too, are the universities. Before Liberation* Hohhot did not have one university or
institute of higher learning, and now it has seven or eight, including the Inner Mongolia University, the Academy of Engineering,
the Academy of Forestry, the Medical College, and the Academy
of Agriculture and Animal Husbandry. The new section, therefore, has the face of a modern city, and it could have even been
more impressive if Ulanfu, the effective ruler of Inner Mongolia,
could have had his way. He wanted to expand the size of the city,
build whole new districts, a museum, a gigantic sports complex,
and a large railway station. It was said that he wanted to make
Hohhot "the Peking of the North," and he was criticized and removed during the Cultural Revolution.[11] Hohhot then stopped
expanding and, when I left in 1974, there hadn't been any significant new construction for several years. Still it was a pleasant
place, with its mixed population, the contrast between old and
new, and the fairly relaxed political atmosphere. I could have
stayed there for a long time, if a number of events hadn't occurred that altered my destiny.

I received a letter from Elder Brother that brought unpleasant news. He had been accused of being a royalist † and had
undergone rigorous struggle. Then he was sent, along with his
entire unit, to a May 7 Cadres School in 1969. His heart had
never been good, and now he was in ill health as the result of two

---

*"Liberation" is the term used by the Chinese Communists to refer to the transfer of
power into their hands. The official date of Liberation is October 1, 1949, but some areas
were liberated earlier and others after that.

†A supporter of Liu Shaoqi and others opposed to Chairman Mao.

hard years in the countryside. His old job was gone, and he was working at a lower-status job in the Overseas Chinese Travel Association. While in the countryside he had apparently become involved with a woman, and now this was complicating his marriage. He wrote me, "It is as I feared, Little Brother. All that I worked for has been destroyed. I'm in poor health, my personal life has been disrupted, I've been given a low-level job, and I'll be under a black cloud forever." I felt deeply for him—he had given up everything to serve China and there he was, in his thirties, despondent and a broken man. It wasn't fair and I brooded about the injustice of it all.

Then I received some bad news that affected me directly. I had asked to resume my interrupted career, now that the dust from the Cultural Revolution had settled. I wanted to go back to Peking to enter the Mining Institute. After all, I'd worked in the countryside for two years, put in two more years in a steel mill, had a good political record, and spoke almost flawless Mandarin. But they refused to let me pursue my career, saying, "The Party feels you can better serve China by staying with your present unit." Old Yao, the overseas Chinese engineer who was my friend, said, "Did you really think they'd let you go back to Peking? You're an overseas Chinese and you'll be near the bottom of the list of those who are going to be admitted to a place like the Mining Institute. Forget about Peking and resign yourself to living your life here in Inner Mongolia."

After ten years in China, after all my efforts to work hard, learn, and develop the correct political consciousness, I realized I wasn't prepared to spin out my life in a Mongolian steel mill. I had closed the doors on my birthplace and my family, but China was still reluctant to welcome me fully as one of its own. I was still a second-class citizen even in the Motherland (during the Cultural Revolution I remember once being called a "half-breed" by some brash young Peking Red Guards, and it now looked as if I would never escape that classification). No matter how pure my accent, how red my heart, how hard I worked, what clothes I wore, my documents still cried out: "Overseas Chinese." So I began to think more closely about my life and what I was doing with it. Did I want to stay a steelworker forever? Would I wind up the way Elder Brother did? What alternatives did I have?

About this time a new alternative had opened up for over-seas Chinese—leaving China permanently. So many overseas Chinese had become disillusioned with their lot in China that Peking finally decided to let them leave. They didn't know what to do with us so they took the easy way out, giving us exit visas if we wanted to leave. I first heard about this new policy from a friend in Peking, because at the beginning the policy was all hush-hush. People didn't know whether it was a rumor or actual policy, and individuals were afraid to apply for an exit visa if there was no such policy because they might be accused of all kinds of reactionary thoughts. But by 1973 it was clear enough. Overseas Chinese were leaving in large numbers, and a definite procedure had evolved. There was a long waiting list, but from gossip and a few concrete examples it appeared that almost every-one who applied eventually received an exit visa, although in some cases it took over a year. Now for the first time I thought seriously about leaving. If I left China, where could I go? Indo-nesia was out—I knew that the Indonesians wouldn't let people like me back in. I didn't want to go to Hong Kong, but it was the only alternative. What could I do there, in that wretched monu-ment to colonialism? Maybe I could find a toehold there, or may-be I could find another country to go to afterwards. Was it worth it? Would I find peace of mind there? Would I ever find a place where I wouldn't feel like a second-class citizen? For weeks I mulled over these questions. Was I being disloyal? Was I a traitor to the Motherland for even thinking of going? Did the Mother-land really care about what I did?

I guess it was the answer to the last question that finally made me decide to ask for an exit visa. I submitted my written application for an exit permit to the revolutionary committee of the steel mill. Then it was checked over by the political depart-ment before going to a higher-level department (I never did figure out what that department was) for endorsement. When the application was approved, I received verbal notification that I had to go to the Public Security Bureau to fill in an application form, taking along three passport-size photos. The procedure was time-consuming—it took more than a year before all the formal approvals had been granted. When I became impatient over the long delay, Old Yao advised me to try the backdoor, that is, bribe the officials.* "Don't you know," he said, "they all wait for something extra from applicants? A few well-placed bribes can save you six months." I refused to do this, although I had heard stories that corroborated Old Yao. A friend of mine told me how he had used the backdoor. It seemed that every time he went to the Public Security Bureau to ask about the progress of his application, the person in charge always smiled, looked him directly in the face, and said, "I'll have to study (*yanjiu*) the problem." One day my friend finally figured it out and got the message: *yanjiu* (study) sounds like *yan* (cigarettes) and *jiu* (wine). In other words, that official was waiting for something special from him, such as cigarettes and wine, as a bribe. Two weeks later my friend appeared at that official's office with several catties of the best spirits, some high-quality cigarettes, and several feet of the most expensive cloth. Within a month he received final approval of his application.

Once I finally received my exit permit I didn't dally but headed south, first to Peking and then on to Canton. It had been a decade, almost to the day, that I had spent in the Motherland, and now I was returning along the very same route that I had so blithely taken ten years earlier. I lived a whole lifetime in those ten years, was a student, steelworker, farmer, revolutionary, and tourist. I almost became a "real" Chinese, but found a permanent barrier that prevented me from achieving that goal for which I so desperately yearned. Elder Brother was of a different opinion. "China hasn't failed you," he said. "You've failed the Motherland. You came here like a romantic fool, thinking you could conquer the world, but instead it was too hard for you. Your stinking bourgeois roots remained inside you, and you couldn't accept what the Motherland was prepared to give you. So now you're going to run off to Hong Kong with your little bourgeois tail tucked between your legs." Harsh words from Elder Brother, and surprising words for someone who had been poorly treated by the very Motherland he still upheld. "I guess you and I are two different kinds of people," I said. "China can be proud of you. You have suffered so much and yet you are a true Chinese. I'm truly sorry that I've failed to measure up to your loyalty and

---

*See "Eating Pears in Fuzhou" for a longer discussion of bribery and the illegal use of the backdoor (*houmen*) to gain favors and privileges.

strength. I hope you forgive me, but I can't stay." We embraced with tears in our eyes because we knew that we would probably not see each other again. "If you ever have a chance to see Father, tell him that I wish him good health and his forgiveness." Those were the last words Elder Brother spoke to me before I boarded the train for the border.

At the border it took a long time, and I remembered ten years ago when I arrived, loaded down with crates and packages and crazy dreams. Now I had a suitcase and a canvas bag, that's all. I had about 100 yuan that I could exchange at the border. I still had Grandfather's gold ring, which I put on my finger for the first time since 1966, when I boarded the train on the Hong Kong side. It was a whole new world once more, and I wondered if I could come to terms with it now. After all, I had no place left to go.

[*He had some distant relatives in Hong Kong and they helped him get a job. He went to night school and learned Cantonese. In 1976 he managed to emigrate to West Germany, where he is studying at a university.*]

Eating Pears in Fuzhou

*IN TODAY'S PERSPECTIVE, with the Chinese authorities
themselves criticizing many past policies, the comments made by
this narrator, an intellectual from a well-connected Fuzhou family, may not appear as critical as they were in 1975. He preferred
to write his comments, saying that he felt more comfortable with
a written format. What appears here is a condensed and edited
version of his hundred-page essay on the Communist system in
Fuzhou, a city that remains essentially closed to foreigners.*

*The narrator is especially critical of the increasing privileges
and powers of the military in China. During the Cultural Revolution, after he had seriously weakened the Party structure, Mao
turned to Lin Biao and the Chinese Army to help restore order
in China. The military quickly moved into key civilian decision-
making posts, in many areas running the newly formed revolutionary committees that were governing China. By 1970 every
important committee, administrative or production-oriented,
had its military component. A year later, however, with the
downfall of Lin Biao and with the reintroduction of restructured
Party committees, Mao began the process of disengaging the
army from effective political power. He only partially succeeded
in this task, and even today in the post-Mao era it is evident that
the army's role in the power struggles at the top has been a decisive one, and that the military now exerts a much more powerful
influence on politics than it did before the Cultural Revolution.*

The practice of "using the backdoor" is not something that has suddenly developed in China. It was practiced long before the Cultural Revolution, but the irregular supply of commodities in recent times, plus the increased use of the backdoor by the military, inspired the narrator's wrath. He makes the point that it is impossible to prevent the use of the backdoor in a socialist planned economy where goods are in scarce supply, but that at least it should be possible to prevent the most privileged from using the backdoor to increase their already substantial stock of benefits. He argues that the masses should be allowed to use the backdoor, but not the elite.

He attacks the increasing privileges of a small minority and its control over the rest of society. He questions whether the Cultural Revolution helped to eliminate the gap between the elite and the masses, or whether it simply entrenched a new elite in power. These are harsh criticisms, but they have been recently expressed publicly on the walls of Peking and other cities. Those same walls even contain occasional criticisms of Chairman Mao, which the narrator rejects because in his opinion Mao "had the right ideas but couldn't always persuade the other leaders to follow him."

CHAIRMAN MAO TELLS US, "To know the taste of a pear, you must eat the pear." What he means is that you cannot understand life from the outside, by only reading books or by just sitting around thinking. You have to experience life in order to understand it. As the Chairman says, you must "learn to swim by swimming." Many foreigners come to China mistaking theory for practice and their dreams for reality. They never get to eat a pear. Maybe what I have to tell you will make China more understandable because I lived in China and can write of the bad as well as the good, of failures as well as successes. Not all our pears are sweet to eat; some are rotten and others have never ripened, so the China I present to you will not be one-sided, but it is a fair picture, at least to one who has lived there. That means it is also a view of China that some people may not wish to hear. I write about common things known to ordinary people, not about abstract ideas or about what goes on at the top of the system, among the elite. There is not always glory in the everyday routine of ordinary men.

I was born and grew up in Fuzhou. Like every other person
in this world I have a deep affection for my hometown. I think of
her always, praise her achievements, and pity her failures. Fuzhou is special, but it also mirrors China in that it combines the
old and the modern, the backward and the advanced, the poor
and the prosperous. It is a city that perfectly carries out the government's maxim: "From not having to having, from small to
large, from primitive to modern." All are present there. From the
Gushan hills in the suburbs you can get a full view of the city.
In the southeast lies the industrial district, with its forty-year-old
power supply station which, gorging itself on coal, supplies a
third of the city's electricity. The buildings of the Fuzhou No. 2
Chemical Factory, the result of frenzied construction during the
Great Leap Forward in 1958, are located there, modern factory
buildings whose products are sold throughout our country. Nearby is the new railway station, an eye-catching building. Not far
away from this station where diesel engines come and go is a
parking lot for the three-wheeled carts of the Fuzhou manpower transport station. The old and the new: diesel locomotives
on the one side; on the other, men still pulling three-wheeled
carts, competing to transport the city's wares. Twenty-five years
after Liberation we still rely on coolies in modern Fuzhou.

Fuzhou was the provincial seat of Fujian province even before Liberation. Now its population is 650,000, twice that of
1949. About 200,000 have a regular job, and probably another
200,000 are middle and primary school students. Many residents
have overseas family connections and receive regular remittances
from abroad, making their lives much easier. Because Fuzhou is
so close to Taiwan it is a high-risk defense area. Many soldiers are
posted there and few foreigners are allowed in for that reason.
We also keep out foreigners because Fuzhou is a shabby city in a
poor part of China. Traffic is chaotic and the public transportation system is woefully inadequate, a clutter of pedestrians, bikes,
carts, trucks, and squawking fowl. You can either get run over by
a dilapidated bus or by a moldering honey wagon.[1]

The city is made up of four types of buildings. One type was
built by foreigners before Liberation, mainly in the area where
the old foreign consulates and villas once were located. The best
of these buildings—they are "homes" in the western, capitalist
sense of the word—are now occupied by the Fuzhou Military Dis-

trict and used as guest houses for the families of high-ranking officers. The less attractive ones have been turned into schools and into government and Party offices. Those in the worst shape, some of them propped up by wooden supports, were given to the municipal Housing Administration Bureau, which rents them out to ordinary people. These houses are the very dregs and ought to have been torn down a long time ago. The Housing Administration rents them out cheaply; a square meter costs about fifty cents a month,[2] and they are never maintained because the Housing Administration refuses to spend money on them. One building collapsed while I was there and killed about two dozen people. It was so old and rotten it just fell apart. We all knew that it was the city's fault. No one had ever fixed a single crack. City residents jokingly say that the Housing Administration's motto is: "If the house is still standing, it doesn't need to be repaired, and if the house has fallen down, then it doesn't need to be repaired." I had a friend named Wang who lived in Changshan district. He lived in a building that used to house the American consulate. It must have been an impressive place once, but now it's in one hell of a mess. The stairs are cracked; the plaster on the walls has come down; doors and windows no longer fit; the wooden floor is gone, probably used for firewood. There used to be inside water toilets, a real luxury, but they don't work anymore and the bathrooms are used for storing coal. But it's cheap and my friend paid only sixty cents a square meter. The Housing Administration comes regularly to collect the rent but never makes any repairs. Sometimes my friend had to prop up a wall or fix a window, so he had to scrounge up the materials and workmen through the backdoor and do it all himself.

The majority of Fuzhou housing is of a second type, one-storeyed houses, forty to fifty years old. The former owners had worked with sweat and blood to build these houses, but when their grandchildren inherited them, they also inherited bad luck. In 1956, the Party launched a socialist transformation campaign to change private enterprises into socialist ones. Owners of private housing in Fuzhou were only given enough space for themselves and their families. The rest of their buildings were often turned into public property without any state compensation. Then these homeowners were branded as "landlords," "industrialists," or "merchants." For their grandchildren it was a double disaster: not only had they lost most of their property, but they had suffered a major political setback. "So what?" you might say. "They probably deserved it. Why pity them?" Well, I do pity them because many were blameless and didn't deserve such a fate. As the saying goes, "The color-blind shepherd kills many white sheep before he finds the one that's black!"

This type of housing is also cheap because it's so old and poorly maintained, with no toilets or kitchens. Residents squat on "night stools," whose contents are then placed outside each night for the honey-wagon collectors from the local communes. Our city is famous throughout China for these night stools.

But the old gives way to the new, and gradually that old housing is being torn down so that new factories can be built and crooked streets can be widened. Sections of new housing have begun to appear here and there, "new villages"[3] comprised of two- or three-storey buildings. These houses have a kitchen, but usually no toilet. Four or five buildings form a "village," and the rent is less than a yuan per square meter. The trouble is that families don't want to live in them, regardless of the cheap rent and their new condition. People are used to their own houses and regard the family as an independent unit. We would rather live under one roof in a crumbling old building than share one floor with five, six, and even ten families. No one wants to give up his little plot of land and his little courtyard. Old people are almost impossible to pry out of their homes. They put up the fiercest battles, although the government always wins out in the end because, once they knock down your old house, you've no choice but to go to one of the new "villages." Occasionally you might manage to slip in with friends, sharing a room or part of a room in an old house, but since it's illegal to sublet space to individuals, this does not happen very often. Anyway, who has the extra space to let one's auntie move in? As it was, we were always gasping for more space.

A fourth type of housing is reserved for the elite, and for them space is hardly a problem. A section of Fuzhou, in the northern part, contains many fancy villas for top-ranking cadres and military officers. An area called the Generals' Buildings housed, for example, the commander of the Military Region, Han Xianqu, and many of his deputies. High-ranking provincial Party officials and revolutionary committee cadres live in a special district on West Lake, one of the loveliest areas in Fuzhou. It costs over 300 yuan per square meter to build some of this housing. No wonder the common people took advantage of the Cultural Revolution to unseat some of these new emperors by ransacking their houses! Some of them had indoor swimming pools, hot springs right inside, and indoor toilets. Can a high cadre be expected to carry his night stool out to be emptied every morning?*

The highest buildings in Fuzhou are the eight-storey Telegraph Building and the seven-storey Overseas Chinese Hotel. After these two were completed in 1958, no more buildings higher than five storeys were built. I'm not sure why this decision was made, whether it had anything to do with earthquake dangers, security, or cost, but the central authorities issued an order banning "high, big, and foreign" in construction. Maybe it was an attack on the Soviet Union, since we had used Soviet architects, blueprints, and construction methods all those years. Some local skeptics thought they knew the real reason for reducing the height of buildings in Fuzhou. You see, after the Telegraph Building was completed, a horrible thing happened. It tilted to one side. There was a big scandal, and now Fuzhou has a Chinese Leaning Tower of Pisa, though it is not exactly what we want as a tourist attraction.

These have been a few lines about my hometown. As you can see, it is an ordinary city, no different from many others in China. If we are poor now, it is because we were far poorer before Liberation. If the city looks shabby and there are only a handful of new buildings, it is because our dreams can never keep up with the reality of life. Life was never easy for the masses, and it is still

---

*This description of the opulent life of Fujian high-ranking cadres is corroborated by another account, that of Ken Ling. My respondent thought that Ling's account was "too critical at times, and not always accurate." But he observed that Ling's description of Ye Fei's life style was quite accurate, based on his personal experience in Fuzhou: "the space occupied by Yeh and Wang [his wife] was twenty times that occupied by an average worker . . . in the living room was the floor, inlaid with an elaborate flower design of expensive woods that must have required a lot of people's labor . . . more than 100 bottles of expensive liquor and cigarettes and tea, almost all imported" (p. 136). Ling had once visited the home of a high-ranking cadre during his student days and recalled that "they had rugs on the floor, huge empty rooms, food of all kinds, and, like an Emperor's throne, a magnificent indoor toilet finished in grand style." Ken Ling, *Revenge of Heaven* (New York: Putnam, 1972).

not easy today. But there has been progress and we have survived difficult times, though not as gloriously as our Party propagandists have said. (What can be farther from reality than a Party propagandist's words?) We all exist in a world of dualisms and we Chinese in particular are used to it. Fuzhou is a good example of all the contradictions that abound in China. Perhaps the sharpest of all these contradictions, and the one that is hardest to resolve, is that between elite and masses. What I wrote about the leaders' luxurious housing is only a part of this contradiction. How is it that, despite Chairman Mao and despite the Cultural Revolution, the privileged few still manage to scoop away the extra rice from our bowls and take it for themselves? How is it, after nearly thirty years of Revolution, the laws of Heaven seem unchanged in Fuzhou? Those at the bottom seem destined to stay there, while those at the top gorge themselves on the fruits of Revolution. I am not bitter, only puzzled at how this came about.

Everybody in China knows about the backdoor. It means using your personal connections to bribe people with money or material goods so you can get something you can't obtain through normal ways, through the "front door." Using the backdoor has been a common practice in China, but it really flourished during the chaos of the Cultural Revolution. Now it is a major part of our life. When you have scarcities and a privileged group, then you have a society full of backdoors. The backdoor can be found at the top, in government organs, in the Party, the army, through the entire system right down to the very bottom. The general gets his marble bathtub through the backdoor, and the ordinary worker his "Flying Pigeon" bicycle the same way. People take the backdoor for granted and do not regard using it as something disgraceful or "antisocialist." On the contrary, those who know how to use the backdoor are regarded as clever people, whereas those who don't are considered stupid.

We in Fuzhou are well known throughout China for using the backdoor. All our commodities are in scarce supply and many necessities are rationed. For example, each month, aside from the grain, cloth, and cooking-oil ration, a resident is entitled to receive only one catty of pork (other types of meat are just not available), one half catty of sugar, three eggs, 45 catties of coal, one piece of soap, and five packages of cigarettes. This is hardly enough and, if you have a surplus of any commodity, then you head for the backdoor to get extra meat, more coal, or whatever you want to bargain for. That is how the backdoor operates at the lowest levels. It is really an informal system for bartering and redistributing food and a few necessities of life. How does it work exactly? Well, let's say a friend or relative works in a meat shop, a department store, or a coal shop. This friend sets aside a special cut of meat, puts you at the top of the waiting list for a Shanghai-made radio, or hoards some lighter-flints[4] for you. People cooperate because there is never enough to go around. If you stood in a regular line without using personal connections, you'd never get anything, even if you had coupons and money, unless you dealt directly on the black market and that is too risky a business. You might be able to buy rationed foodstuffs on the free market,[5] but the prices here are too exorbitant, sometimes four and five times the state price.

When my sister worked in a Fuzhou hospital she met patients who worked in meat and coal stores. Through this backdoor she got extra catties of meat every month and several extra catties of coal. Then, when the coal sellers and meat clerks or their friends came to the hospital for treatment, my sister made sure they didn't have to pay the registration fee. They could get free injections and free medicine. My nephew was a bus conductor, and whenever any of my family or his friends rode his bus they never bought a ticket. He just looked the other way. One of my friends was a doctor and he furnished one-week sick-leave certificates in exchange for favors. A middle school teacher nearby would give your child good marks in exchange for a substantial gift, such as a dacron shirt or some chickens, ducks, or fish. A friend of mine who worked in the big Fuzhou department store told me that shipments of scarce commodities such as wristwatches, bicycles, radios, and clothing never made it to the shelves but were secretly sold by employees to their relatives or friends, or bought by the store clerks themselves to give as gifts to their superiors. The store managers usually were the biggest offenders, taking the best of everything for themselves. Ordinary employees didn't have to worry about being caught since the bosses were doing it too. Anyway, as long as the store received the full price for the goods, it was fulfilling its plan and that's what counted.

All this is common practice in China and no one gets excited, since everybody, somehow, sometime, uses the backdoor for personal needs. It reduces dissatisfaction and it gives ordinary people a chance of getting something. What makes the common people angry is the abuse of the Big Backdoor by higher-level government, Party, and army officials. This is a backdoor that really makes a difference, a backdoor based on one's political background; it determines one's social and economic position. Top cadres use the Big Backdoor to keep their children from staying in the countryside. The central authorities prohibited sent-down youth from returning to the cities to look for a job, but cadres used their influence to have their own children or their relatives' children assigned to live and work in Fuzhou, even after their residence permits had been permanently transferred to a rural area. The niece of the secretary of the Fuzhou Party Committee (who was concurrently deputy chief of staff of the Fuzhou Military Region) was sent down to the countryside, but in less than three months' time, under the pretext that she was not fit for physical labor because of illness, she received medical authorization to return to Fuzhou for treatment. I wonder who her father's doctor was! Afterwards her "permanent residence" (*hukou*) quietly crept back after her to Fuzhou. Then she studied for one year at Fuzhou University and finally was sent to study at the Shanghai Foreign Languages Institute. How amazing that her "illness" vanished so speedily, the farther away she got from the Fujian countryside! Here's another case: a high official in the Fuzhou shipyard managed to have his daughter, who was still a first-year junior middle school student, assigned to work in a local rayon mill. He just telephoned a colleague of his in the Civil Affairs Section of the provincial revolutionary committee and this friend got her a job. Not only didn't she have to go down with her class, but a year later she was quietly admitted to university, after having established her credentials as a worker.

There are over 200,000 educated youth in the Fujian countryside, and some have been there already four or five years. But I bet you'll hardly find any children of Party officials among them. They were all pulled back to Fuzhou through the backdoor a long time ago. In a well-publicized letter to Chairman Mao in 1973, protesting the poor conditions that his son was enduring in the countryside, Li Qinglin wrote that children of cadres, even of low-ranking Party cadres or junior army officers, had all sneaked back to the city a few short months after they went down supposedly for three years to a lifetime. They used their parents' position to creep back home. Some had never even left the city. Those who remain in the countryside are children of families who have no political pull or economic force. Their fate will be to remain in the countryside forever.[6] When the people see this sort of Big Backdoorism they are bitter and angry, but we dare not express our anger openly for fear of being accused of "Opposing the Dictatorship of the Proletariat," of "Undermining the Sent-Down Youth Program," or even of being "Active Counterrevolutionaries."

Not too much is written about how the army uses the Big Backdoor. In shops reserved exclusively for army personnel you see rows and rows of goods that have long vanished from the regular stores, if indeed they ever were for sale in those stores. In the shop located at the Fuzhou Military Region's headquarters you could buy top-quality cigarettes, powdered milk, a wide range of the best liquors, wristwatches, bicycles, and clothing. I once asked the wife of an army officer to buy me some granulated sugar and milk powder for my daughter, who was sick. If you had a proper connection you could get these army dependents to buy such things for you. The army dependents, seeing a good thing, were busy buying up everything. They bought huge stocks of cigarettes, sugar, and spirits and sent them back to their home villages, building up a nest of favors and obligations at home to make life after demobilization more pleasant. For a time there was a big outflow of commodities from the army shops, and finally Commander Han Xianqu prohibited army dependents from buying anything not for their own personal use. This hardly slowed down the buying, but it did make people a bit more cautious.

The central authorities provided army dependents with many special benefits. For example, wives of officers who had served for fifteen years were entitled to employment, with a salary from 32.5 yuan upward. Maybe that was reasonable in theory, to give the wives a chance to earn an income, but in practice the majority of these wives were village women over age forty. Some only had a primary school education and others were illiterate. Yet because of their husband's position, they were given desirable jobs in modern factories with an income as high as 37.5 yuan a month.[7] Some of these illiterate officers' wives even managed to get classified as technicians in large organizations. The silicon laboratory of the chemistry department and the jet research center of the mathematics department of Fuzhou University had fourteen army dependents on their staff. Ten of them were over thirty-five years old. Only one had a middle school education. Eight had a primary school education, and one couldn't even write her name clearly. Can you imagine that, she couldn't write her name and yet she was employed in Fujian's most prestigious university! They had no education, but didn't care to advance themselves. They didn't want to dirty their hands and were afraid of hard work. They spent the day doing nothing. Every week they went on sick leave for a few days, and they used their husband's position to make life miserable for others. The local leadership was unhappy with their presence, and a top Party cadre at the University privately told me that army dependents were incompetent, difficult to control, and a drawback to serious research.

The example of these dependents shows the fine line that exists between reasonable privileges that accrue to an elite and the abuse of the backdoor by that elite. Originally, only officers' wives secured employment through the backdoor. Then the central authorities legitimized what was already a common practice for officers' wives. That's the danger of the backdoor when it is used for big things, such as permanent economic gain, because soon the dependents of junior army officers will also demand and get these "rights"—just wait and see. Already junior officers use the backdoor to move their dependents into the city from the countryside. First they illegally get their dependents' residence permits transferred to Fuzhou, and then they use the backdoor to get jobs for them. Meanwhile rural masses and sent-down youth are forbidden to live in Fuzhou for any reason, and for them finding a job in the city is like discovering a grain of uneaten rice during a famine.

The central authorities did make an effort to limit these abuses. Mao himself argued that using the backdoor could lead to the downfall of the Party and to national disaster, and in 1973 and 1974 we had major campaigns against the backdoor. In Fuzhou, in mid-1973, I remember attending a mass meeting of 50,000 inhabitants presided over by Commander Han. The theme was "warmly hail Chairman Mao's letter to Li Qinglin, and resolutely put an end to the malpractice of using the backdoor." We were told that Chairman Mao was angry at cadres who used their personal influence to pull their children back from the countryside. The deputy head of the Civil Affairs Section of one city district confessed he was guilty of accepting bribes in return for illegally finding jobs in the city for a dozen educated youth. He was sentenced to ten years. A cadre in the municipal public security bureau had accepted bribes from overseas Chinese who were trying to get exit visas. Some of them had paid as much as 7000 yuan in order to get exit visas. He was sentenced to death and executed.

Yet harsh measures alone cannot solve the problem because almost everyone, from the top Party and army cadres down to the local levels, uses the backdoor. Everybody is guilty, and if the backdoor is eliminated the top cadres will have to turn themselves in and admit their own guilt. Even though the central authorities issued orders attacking the backdoor, that was only a hollow campaign in which a few scapegoats were selected. Most of the big fish got away. The problem is not to eliminate the backdoor—I don't think that can ever happen anyway. Used in moderation the backdoor actually helps spread scarce commodities around. At the lowest levels the people really don't mind it. Indeed, for many it's like a sport. But when the elite use the Big Backdoor to entrench and enrich themselves at the expense of the common people, then efforts must be made to stop them. Chairman Mao was right in attacking the backdoor, but even his will wasn't strong enough. Maybe the masses have to be more vigilant, but I weep for China, because I know that the masses are incapable of stopping the leaders from doing what they want.

One reason that the masses are so powerless is because we are so carefully controlled. The leaders may have made political mistakes, such as having us build backyard blast furnaces in 1958, but they sure know how to control us. It is a system that is especially impressive in a big city. The police and the public security office know everyone's business, and therefore people rarely speak their minds to each other. We do what we are told. The lowest level in the control system is the residents' committee. It is a most effective organization for supervising the daily life of citizens. Fuzhou has about 150 of these committees, which means that on the average one committee supervises 4000 people. Forty police station branches in turn supervise the residents' committees, and they are under four district public security bureaus. The district public security bureaus are under the jurisdiction of the city and the provincial public security bureaus. The public security network is well-disciplined and centralized, commanding our respect and fear. They control our dossiers and thus can determine our fate.

Each residents' committee has a chairman who is a Party member, four or five vice-chairmen who are not necessarily Party members though they must have a correct class background, and several activists who usually are middle-aged women without regular jobs. The committee's activities are distributing food, cooking-oil, and other coupons to residents;[8] inspecting the environment and trying to keep the area tidy; helping to mobilize high school students to go down to the countryside when it is their turn. Those are the stated functions of these committees, but in fact their main activity is to supervise the activities of every household and to guard against social and political deviance. The residents' committee, in cooperation with the local public security office, knows everything about you, especially the bad things, such as who has a bad class background, who has relatives in Taiwan, who has committed political mistakes in the past, and who has been convicted of a crime. During the Cultural Revolution the residents' committees were purged of many of their members. People with suspicious class backgrounds had wormed their way into key positions on these committees, hoping to gain personal political insurance. They were removed in the "Purify the Class Ranks" campaign, and were replaced by people drawn from the ranks of the "five red elements,"[9] that is, those with pure class backgrounds who supported Chairman Mao's line. In those days we held special training classes for new members of these committees so that they could better understand their role in the community. Party activists explained how the committees worked and what individual members' duties were.

The committee approves applications for employment, requests for housing space, and permission for residents to have guests stay on their premises. Whether you apply for a permit to leave China or to get married, you need official approval. The committee can make your life hell if it has a bad impression of you, or if it decides to take revenge against you. You never know just who is working for the committee. Where we lived, the committee used a number of secret activists who regularly reported to the public security office. When a guest arrived from out of town these "secret agents" kept tabs on him and asked questions to find out what he was doing. I recall that in 1973 the residents' committees and public security offices carried out several large-scale residence registration investigations, to find out who was illegally living in the city. They came in flying squads, in the middle of the night, searching for these "black people." The campaign was a success because they ferreted out many illegal residents. It is hard to hide in a system that so effectively controls your everyday life, from food rationing to marriage, from your visitors to where you go at night. I think it is harder to move from one part of Fuzhou to another part than it is to fly to the moon. It is easier for Americans to go to the moon than for Chinese to get around the strict residential control system.*

Another form of local level control is the urban militia, which emerged in 1958 when Chairman Mao officially reorganized the Peking militia. This marked the formal establishment of the urban militia throughout China, and Fuzhou immediately set up its own militia, organized into two parts, ordinary militia and basic-unit militia. Joining the ordinary militia was easy. Men between the ages of fifteen and forty and women from eighteen to forty-five with a good class background can join the ordinary militia, but recruitment for basic-unit militia is stricter. If you have relatives with a bad political record or relatives living abroad, you can't join the basic-unit militia. The basic militia uses old weapons that the army no longer needs and it periodically trains with live bullets. It is on the alert during air-raid drills and patrols sensitive areas in and around the city. It is formed into a division led and trained by the municipal military garrison. Big factories and organizations have their own militia battalions and companies, and an armed department or people's defense section in large factories and organizations supervises these militia units. All militia units in Fuzhou are under the direct leadership of the military garrison. The militia is

*For more on the work of residents' committees, see "My Neighborhood."

tightly organized and, when the order is given, it can assemble within minutes. That is because we need the militia for coastal defense and for the organization of civil defense in case of attack by Taiwan. In nearby Amoy, the militia is fully armed with modern rifles. Members are accurate shots, in good physical health, and absolutely loyal to Chairman Mao. Each has his own skills, such as swimming, mountain climbing, and boat rowing. It is a very mobile organization, closely tied in with the local army units, and forms a reliable reserve force for the army. The Amoy militia accurately expresses Chairman Mao's saying: "Joint defense by the army and the people's militia."[10]

You had to take part in training and patrols, and you had to attend political and technical classes. Many people didn't want to join because that left them with no free time whatsoever. If you had the right qualifications you had to join, otherwise you'd be criticized. You might use political influence, or the backdoor, to "prove" that your work was too important, or that you had other spare-time duties, if you wanted to avoid serving in the militia, but this wasn't easy to arrange. When the threat of foreign invasion was greatest in 1958, people were willing to serve, but when the militia spends most of its energies as it now does in looking for domestic class enemies, then fewer want to join. Those who are most eager to join usually are trying to gain a political advantage to protect their own questionable status, or they are outright political opportunists.

When the militia carries out its fight against domestic class enemies, that's when the people come under its control. The militia supervises "black elements" in neighborhoods, factories, and enterprises, guarding them and often isolating them as punishment. It stands guard outside sensitive areas to keep strangers away and patrols the streets at night to protect against bad elements and class enemies. The militia arrests and investigates criminals, in conjunction with the public security organs. It can even execute criminals, under the guidance of public security organs. I witnessed the execution in 1970 of a rapist-murderer, who had forced himself on a thirteen-year-old girl. When she threatened to tell her family, he strangled her to death and threw her into a stream. He was immediately caught and within days was sentenced and executed in the neighborhood. That murderer deserved what he got in this case, and the masses dispensed justice

on the spot. Most of the time, however, it seems that the militia
just checks up on other people and is there to remind us that the
Party, the army, and the public security apparatus control everything. The militia is effective because one part of the people is
used to check up on the other part. People thus wind up distrust-
ing one another, and those at the top preserve their power. I hesitate to say this, but using the militia seemed to be Chairman
Mao's clever way of giving people an illusion of democracy while
perpetuating the rule of a small group of leaders.

I've mentioned political control, and you can see that at the
local levels the masses are subject to a great deal of it. The same
applies to control over economic life. You just can't go out and
look for a job in the city because these jobs are carefully parceled
out, even the lowest such as street cleaners, transport workers, or
toilet cleaners. Almost every unit has to hire its workers through
the Fujian provincial revolutionary committee. The committee
decides how many workers can be hired in Fuzhou, acting in
accordance with nationally determined quotas. If the central
level says "no more jobs," then we can't hire a single person in the
city. The central level also imposes harsh restrictions for any
urban jobs that are available: rural residents cannot be employed; sent-down youth are not eligible for urban employment;
those with a bad class background do not qualify. As the system now exists, you apply for a job through the neighborhood
revolutionary committee, which submits the application to the
district level. That level passes it on to the municipal revolutionary committee and then it goes to the appropriate department in the provincial revolutionary committee. If any one
of these bodies rejects the application, your chance for legal
employment vanishes into thin air. Each year the number of new
workers is strictly controlled, and in 1972 Fuzhou hired only 5000
new workers. Even this number was above the limit allowed, and
the province was heavily criticized by the central level, which issued a document criticizing "those local organs that disregard
national employment norms."

Educated youth suffer the most from these restrictions because they cannot find work in the city, even a low-level job
in neighborhood street workshops. The province allowed a few to
return to the cities in 1971 and 1972, but by the fall of 1972 the
central authorities abruptly announced that as of December 8,

1972, no more educated youth could be recalled to the cities and that youths supposed to start work after that date were to be told there were no jobs for them. This order shocked those who had official assignments ordering them to report to their new jobs after December 8. They refused to return to the countryside and stayed at the factory to which they had been officially assigned. Finally, after several months there was a compromise: they could "temporarily" work at the place to which they had been assigned and were given an allowance of 13½ yuan a month for living expenses, barely enough to keep from starving. There were 20,000 of these temporary workers in the city, and three years later in 1975 they were still getting 13½ yuan. They willingly worked at such starvation wages just so they could remain in Fuzhou. That's one lesson to be learned from this example: no one wants to work in the countryside. The bigger lesson, however, is that the authorities have a tight system of economic controls. They tell you where and when to work and you have no choice. If you can use the backdoor, or if you are genuinely lucky, like the 20,000 youths who finally got permission to stay in the city, then maybe you can occasionally bend the system a bit. However, the vast majority get no such lucky breaks. The few "legal" jobs that exist are reserved for those who have a proper urban residence permit. The state decides who can stay in the city and who can't. It tightly limits your mobility, and if you can't move around, then it's much easier to keep control over what you are doing.

I've talked about our system while hardly mentioning the Communist Party. From the time the Party under the leadership of Chairman Mao obtained political power until just before the Cultural Revolution, the Party's leadership has always been sound. That is because China has a one-party system. There are several so-called democratic parties, but they have no power at all and exist only because the Party wants a democratic face. The Party enjoys high prestige among the people, and this is due to the serious attention it pays to propaganda. As early as primary school, one learns how great the Party is and how brilliant Chairman Mao is. The school curriculum is devoted to telling us that Chairman Mao is the greatest leader of all and that the Party is our savior. A Chinese youth practically from birth knows that the Party is good.

Before the Cultural Revolution the Party's position seemed impregnable. From the center down to each organ, school, factory, and enterprise, the Party committee was the dominant leadership group. The Party's policies were swiftly relayed to everybody through this network. The Party also controlled the Youth League and the Young Pioneers, further reinforcing its supremacy. When you joined the Youth League it was the most glorious thing in your young life. You felt proud wearing that red scarf around your neck, and you knew that the path to success lay in doing a good job in the Youth League and later in attaining Party membership. To be a Party member meant that you entered the ranks of an elite — less than 3 percent of the population — an elite that ruled China as effectively as any of the best emperors, such as Kang Xi. Of course, many played the game of joining the Youth League and the Party only to gain privilege and status. And why not? Youth League members received priority in entering university and were given the best jobs. So the idea was to be as "progressive" as possible and take an active part in all social activities and in physical labor, to ensure admittance to the Youth League. Only 45 percent of eligible students were admitted to the Youth League.

To join the Party is more difficult, and you must undergo a long testing period. You have to have a good class background, and it is almost impossible for persons of landlord, rich-peasant, counterrevolutionary, bad-element, or rightist background to become members. You must work well, be active in all political campaigns, and respond fully to the policies of the leadership. In short you have to show yourself as being obedient to the Party and to Chairman Mao. The effort is worth it, however, because the gains are great. The key positions in any organ are staffed by Party members. Children of Party members have a far better chance of getting into university and then obtaining a good job. High-ranking Party members get all kinds of special privileges, ranging from better medical care to special shopping rights.[11] On the other hand, Party members have greater responsibilities; a Party member is, after all, not an ordinary person. He is a leader and a symbol of the dictatorship of the proletariat. With such people you never speak your mind or even hint at any disagreement.

Before the Cultural Revolution many people were politically

active, living exemplary lives, even though they had no hope of joining the Party. These were people who had either a bad class background or a bad foreign connection. There are lots of them in Fuzhou because they have so many relatives overseas. They worked hard, actively spoke out during meetings, and periodically "reported the state of their mind" to the Party. They knew they could never be admitted into the Party but figured that, by being active in this way, they could curry favor with the leadership and secure their livelihood. They hoped this would ensure them against being attacked for their class background. The Party knew this and manipulated these people for its own ends. In this way potential dissident elements could be coopted by the leaders. No wonder there were so few criminal activities in China. We had a secure and calm country then, probably more secure than any place in the world today.

The Cultural Revolution changed this balance, maybe permanently. First, it disrupted and almost destroyed the system of control and direction that had been carefully built up all these years. It put the Party's role into question, raised doubts about its policies and the quality of the members. Second, the army's sudden rise to prominence showed that there were ways other than the Party to get into power. The army was a new route that opened right up to the top. Third, the delicate balance that had kept China calm was destroyed. Now criminal activity was much easier because, when there is chaos, bad elements emerge and multiply. Finally, those who had been coopted by the Party —those non-Party activists who had bad class backgrounds but nevertheless had worked hard for the Party—were the first targets for struggle. The lesson to the rest of us was clear. You can't hide your class background, no matter how well you serve the people. When the next campaign comes you'll be a primary target, no matter how pious a citizen you've been. I think all of us had forgotten too quickly the lessons of the Hundred Flowers campaign.[12]

Before the Cultural Revolution the army had the twin tasks of defending the frontiers and suppressing domestic class enemies. It did not meddle much in politics; indeed, it seemed separated from the administration of the nation. In those days before the Cultural Revolution the army stayed out of politics, and it was a good thing. Then came the Cultural Revolution and everything changed. Mao got rid of his political enemies and tried to make China a more revolutionary society. But the entrenched leaders resisted these changes, and Mao had to turn to the army to maintain himself in power. He proclaimed Lin Biao, who controlled the military, as his close comrade-in-arms, and he met millions of Red Guards in Peking while wearing a military uniform, thus confirming the army's new power. Soon military control commissions run by the army were set up, replacing the paralyzed Party committees. The military moved into the top posts and began to appoint its loyal followers to key positions in provincial government. Beginning in 1969, every key official wore a military uniform, from the chairman of the provincial revolutionary committee down to the number-one person in a local school. The commander of the Fujian Military Region was also chairman of the provincial revolutionary committee. The head of the city government was also deputy head of the Fuzhou Military Region. The military men were in power until 1971 when Party committees were finally reestablished. Even after that, the military men stayed on, becoming provincial, municipal, or other key Party secretaries. They took advantage of their new power to entrench their own interests, getting extra food and benefits, jobs for dependents, and exemption from policies that applied to ordinary citizens. The sons and daughters of the military did not have to go to the countryside, and when there were no fish to be found in the city markets, the Fujian military was happily picking its teeth clean with bones from the finest local fish supplied from its own sources. The people were angry but, because the military has the power of life and death, nobody dared to speak out.

Mao sensed the dangerous nature of the military, and as early as 1969 he tried to stop its growing power by ordering members of military control committees back to their units. But he was too late, and many military leaders did not want to listen to him. Lin Biao knew that Mao was trying to curb the military's power. That's why Lin wrote in his conspiratorial statement ("Minutes on the 571 Project") that, after 9.2 [the second Central Committee plenary meeting of the Ninth Congress], the military was being suppressed by Mao.[13] Mao relied on his own prestige to win that struggle against Lin, but it also served as a warning. The military had to be curbed, and in 1972 Mao ordered the abolition of the military propaganda teams, whose purpose had been to supervise the activities of personnel in all organs. Then in 1973 he ordered all military men in regular state organs, except for the number-one military person in each organ, to leave and return to his former military unit. Mao launched a campaign against using the backdoor, mainly directed at the abuses the military had carried out in order to enhance itself. In 1974, Mao suddenly transferred and reassigned the commanders of China's eight military regions, and they had to report for duty at their new posts within ten days. They could only bring along their wives and children and had to leave their subordinates behind.[14] This was deliberately done to prevent them from staying too long in one place and from creating their own "independent kingdoms."

Today the power of the army has been cut back, but it still is not like it was before. Many top officials now have a military background and strong loyalties to the military. Many of them think the army should be running the country and not the Party. One military man who now holds a civil post in Fuzhou told me bluntly in 1975: "Chairman Mao says that 'the Party must command the gun and the gun must never be allowed to command the Party,' but I say, 'One hand shall hold the gun and the other hand shall hold political power. With two hands we shall win.' " This military view is dramatically opposed to what Mao said, and it shows how reluctant the army is to give up the power it gained during the Cultural Revolution.

As you can see, I wish there were some way to get rid of the military's influence. The old system of undivided Party rule was the best. If the Party made mistakes, they were correctable. Party members understand the masses far better and can work more effectively with them. The masses do not fear the Party as much as the army. The military takes advantage of the system by using the Big Backdoor. There was much good in the Cultural Revolution because it attacked entrenched interests, but the Cultural Revolution did one bad thing—it got the army into our civilian affairs, like a fox in a chicken coop, and now we cannot get it out. I think it was an unfortunate setback for China that the Cultural Revolution happened the way it did. True, we got rid of some secret counterrevolutionaries and we fought an important struggle against bourgeois ideas, but the long-term costs may turn out to be greater than what we gained.

You may think me somewhat harsh because I do not hesitate to criticize what has happened in China. But, as I wrote at the outset, one must have a realistic view of China. Nowadays people like to paint life in beautiful colors, and as a Chinese I must admit I'm proud to see this. Yet one must be fair; you can't expect every one of the Chairman's pears to taste sweet and juicy, and daily life in China is anything but sweetness for the vast majority of those who live there. There is a good and a bad side to everything. Maybe I've emphasized the latter, but I could have also told you far worse. If you can get a picture of a China that is changing, a mixture of all things, a nation recovering from a shock, then I've achieved my purpose. If you come away saying, "Well, the backdoor is probably all right if it were kept small and out of the hands of the top leaders," then I will be happy. We'll need control for a long time, but it should not be abused by those at the top. If the leaders could really follow Chairman Mao's advice, "to trust the masses" and not try to separate themselves from them, then China's achievements, already significant after only twenty-five short years, could be even more impressive in the future.

[*He left China in 1975 and now lives in a Southeast Asian country where he works in a publishing house as a part-time editor. In the perspective of post-Mao China, his written comments seem less critical today than when he wrote them in Hong Kong in 1975. For example, today even Chairman Mao is not immune from criticism, but for this man Mao was sacrosanct, a leader who "stood above the rest of us by his deeds and his thoughts."*]

Frontier Town

NEARLY A BILLION PEOPLE live in China, and most are crammed into a small area in the eastern part of the country. The western part of China, comprising the Tibetan highlands and the desert basins and mountains of Xinjiang and Inner Mongolia, has over half of China's total area but less than 5 percent of its population. Ethnic minority groups such as Tibetans, Uygurs, Kazakhs, and Mongols comprise a large percentage of the area's population. In all of China minority groups make up about 6 percent of the population, but in Xinjiang and Tibet the minority groups outnumber the Han Chinese. Because of the area's size and strategic significance, the sparse population, and the low number of Han Chinese, efforts have been made to "colonize" the area more extensively and to secure the loyalties of the native population. Border confrontations, first with India and now with the Soviet Union, have necessitated the deployment of large numbers of troops and have also hastened the development of a better communications-transportation network linking the western frontier and the populous areas of the east. Today highways and railroads are beginning to cut across the area, and jetliners routinely land in Urumchi. The frontier is being joined more closely to the rest of China, but it is a slow and expensive task, only partly hastened by the current Sino-Soviet confrontation which has led China to build up its vulnerable frontier regions.

In this story a former resident of Shanghai is relocated to the province of Qinghai, in the northern part of the Tibetan high-

144

*lands. After a two-week train trip he arrives and soon finds
himself in a factory that is making rifles in the middle of nowhere. Gonghe is a typical frontier town, in which expansion is
taking place in all directions and with an openness not
unlike similar towns in the American west in the nineteenth
century. The narrator himself draws the comparison between
cowboys and Indians in the United States and Han Chinese and
Tibetans in Qinghai.*

*He is fascinated by the Tibetans and describes many of their
customs—some that he likes, such as the penchant Tibetan
women had for Han men—and others that repel him, such as
burial customs or the way Tibetans clean their tea bowls. He
points out that the Han Chinese give the Tibetans special treatment and are careful to maintain good relations with them.
Although he appears to have a good relationship with the
Tibetans, he also patronizes them, and in that respect he is very
much a Han Chinese.*

I WAS DISPATCHED TO GONGHE in 1968 at the height of
the Cultural Revolution. It was clear that my job as a translator
in Shanghai had been "indefinitely suspended," and the authorities assigned me westward to work in Gonghe. Having never
traveled anywhere else in China, I found the 3000 kilometer trip a
real experience. At first it was exciting just to be on a train going
somewhere but gradually, as we worked our way westward past
Zhengzhou and toward Xian, it became tiresome. At one point I
was stuck in Luoyang for two days and had to sleep on the railroad
platform. It began to dawn on me, as the lush Shanghai area
faded farther and farther behind, just how remote and isolated I
would be. Gonghe was in the province of Qinghai, one of the
poorest and least populated parts of China, an area of long and
cold winters with short hot summers, not far from the source of
China's sorrow, the Yellow River itself.[1]

The train took me as far as Xining, an old Chinese city that
used to be a trading center and military outpost dating back to
the sixteenth century. To me it seemed like an overgrown village
that had spilled its boundaries into the neighboring countryside.
I was amazed that over 300,000 people lived there and that the
majority were Han Chinese. I stayed there overnight and the next
day got on the back of a truck heading out for Gonghe, a trip of

150 kilometers over rough asphalt. The road passed through hills and valleys that were at times bleak and empty, reminding me of what I had imagined the American wild west would look like, based on a movie I had once seen in Shanghai. "Where were the cowboys and the Indians?" I asked myself, and later of course it turned out that I would be one of the cowboys and the Tibetans would be the Indians.

We arrived at last. The trip had taken a whole day because the truck broke down several times. My first impression of the place was disappointing. It was a real frontier town huddled together in the middle of nowhere, a mixture of square clay and sun-dried brick Tibetan houses, a few fired-brick buildings, ramshackle wood huts, and even tents. The dust was everywhere, blowing in from the nearby desert, getting into your eyes and mouth. To the south lay the vast empty reaches of the Tibetan highlands and the road to Lhasa; to the west were mountains and beyond that the marshy wastes of Qaidamu Basin, where oil had been found in the mid-fifties. To the north of us, less than 100 kilometers away, was the largest body of water in the area, Koko Nor, also called "Blue Sea" by its Chinese name Qinghai, after which this frontier province, in this strange remote area, was named. Farther still to the north were huge mountains and behind them the barren wastes of Gansu, the Gobi desert, and the Chinese-Mongolian border. I was a long, long way from home and I felt very lonely.

Yet, despite the isolation, the place had a good spirit about it. People were more informal than back in Shanghai. The farther away you get from the center, the more at ease you are politically. We were much more relaxed out here; maybe this was due to the relaxed ways of the Tibetans, who made up a third of the city's population. The Tibetans considered Gonghe to be their city and preferred to call it by its Tibetan name, Chagbug-chag. The city was the administrative center of the Hainan Tibetan autonomous region, which had a population of about 275,000 people. The entire province of Qinghai had a population of 2.5 million (about a fourth the size of Shanghai) with 600,000 of those Tibetans. Of the 30,000 residents of Gonghe, about 10,000 were Tibetan. Han Chinese had been settling in Qinghai for generations, and some of the old families claim that their ancestors came to the area back in the Song dynasty. They came then as exiled convicts and criminals. Now they are by and large engaged in agriculture. They are called "Qinghai people" in deference to their ancestry.

The major influx of Chinese into the area, however, began more recently in the 1950s. This group, sent from the east, is made up of soldiers, administrative personnel, university graduates, industrial workers, and sent-down youth. The Chinese run the city, but they defer to the Tibetans all the time. It is Chinese policy to favor minority groups and to give them better treatment than the Chinese get.[2] This makes it easier for the rest of us because the authorities cannot give benefits to a minority group without giving them to the Chinese as well. One example of this had to do with birth control. The authorities let the Tibetans have as many children as they wanted. That is central government policy. If a Tibetan had so many children that he was in financial difficulties, the state would lend him money to tide him over. The policy toward Chinese was quite different. If you had a fourth child, you could not get a legal ration coupon and that child could not be legally registered. So you were discouraged from having more than three children. At least that was the policy. But out in Qinghai it wasn't enforced because it set a double standard, and both the local Chinese and the authorities didn't want to enforce it. I think that another benefit was the absence of major political conflict that was going on elsewhere. The struggles of the Cultural Revolution seemed almost irrelevant out there on the frontier — how could you "purify the class ranks" of the Tibetans, many of whose leaders still worshiped their own religious idols openly, without fear of criticism? Nor could you lose face by setting Chinese to struggle against Chinese, letting Tibetans stand by and watch. So the political struggles of the center were muted in Qinghai.[3]

After I arrived, the authorities gave me a dormitory room and two days off to recover from two weeks of steady traveling. Then they put me to work in a factory that manufactured both agricultural machinery and rifles. In one part of the factory we made shock absorbers, attachments for small hand tractors, electric dynamos, and wooden horse carts. In another section we produced rifles. It was strange to be making these guns in the middle of nowhere. The Mongolian border must have been 700 kilometers away, with deserts and mountains protecting us from attack. It wasn't very likely that any enemy would be attacking us and, if they did, those puny guns wouldn't be much help. My friend who was in the army agreed with me. We often talked about it together, though of course we never said a word to anyone else.

I was put to work in a special unit of ten persons (cadres, technicians, and workers) in charge of rifle production. This particular gun had been tested by the army in the area, and was distinguished for its durability. I was told that, even after over 3000 rounds of firing, the gun was so durable that the barrel only wore down by less than a millimeter. Frankly, that didn't mean much to me because I was no weapons expert. They had assigned me to that factory principally to translate English-language materials and books on automatic and semiautomatic rifles. The materials were mostly American. How they wound up in Gonghe, in the depths of China, was a mystery to me. Why hadn't the books been translated back in Peking or Shanghai or even Xian and Lanzhou? Why were they sent to this way-out place to be translated? No one ever knew. The director of the factory did say, however, that they had studied carefully all the available foreign materials on rifles and had selected the American ones. "Of the foreign guns," he said, "American, Czech, or Soviet, the American-style rifles are the most suitable. That is why we are making them here." Strangely enough, the factory produced thousands of shiny new rifles, but had no bullets for them. If the enemy had appeared suddenly, like a Qinghai summer storm, we would have been blown right out of town without firing a single shot. Anyway, the rifles really weren't for us but for the Lanzhou Military Region, which was stockpiling them for the future.

Most of the factory equipment was made in China, but we did have some Polish and West German machines. We were trying to make these machines ourselves or at least hoping to learn exactly how they functioned and how we could modify them to suit our needs. Aside from my regular translations of materials on guns, I often was asked to translate English materials found inside the packing crates. Mostly this was a sheer waste of time because I ended up translating crumpled-up old newspapers and inspection slips or pieces of paper that had mistakenly fallen into the crates. Once there was a lot of excitement because someone had fished out a diagram that looked like some sort of electronic weapon, but after starting the translation I quickly realized it was a diagram for the inside of an ordinary TV set. Still I took my time and finished the whole translation, since I didn't have that much to do. There were only so many books, pamphlets, and reference materials that needed to be translated, and when I was not translating I was supposed to be doing manual labor — filing down gun barrels or gathering up scrap. To avoid such jobs I took my time and became adept at spinning out translations for days on end. A twenty-page manual could thus use up six weeks of loving care and keep me off the factory floor. I worked this system well for over a year and a half and only spent a few weeks on the floor doing manual labor, but then Monkey Tongue Wu showed up in 1971; he was a good translator who also was politically active. He didn't mind working on the shop floor, getting his hands dirty, and there was no way I could keep slowing down the translations once he arrived. So from that time on, I spent a lot of time in manual labor and had my hands full just keeping up with Monkey Tongue. I was a better translator than he was, but he had a better political sense and the confidence of the factory's political leaders, so I was careful never to cross him.

Even though we were in a Tibetan area, almost every one of the eighty workers was Chinese and we spoke to each other in Mandarin. We were a motley group, a mixture of active soldiers, demobilized soldiers, workers, and technicians from the coastal areas, young people, and a few local residents. The factory was a Han Chinese outpost. There were only two Tibetans and four Moslems in the entire factory. We weren't even under local control; the factory was too important for that and was administered jointly by the Administrative Region and by the Military Region. Actually, military trucks from the Military Region and the Hainan Military Subregion constantly moved to and from our factory bringing in raw materials (wood for the rifle butts came up through Sichuan all the way from Guangxi province; the trigger mechanisms, which were English-made, and the metal sheets for the cartridge holder, which came from Japan, were brought down from Xining); the finished guns were carted away to secret storehouses in Gonghe, Xining, and Lanzhou. The factory apparently was self-financing in the nonmilitary end. Income from the sale of agricultural machinery covered the cost of production (salaries of workers, administrative costs, and cost of raw materials). But the rifle making had to be heavily subsidized and, given the large investment in rifle production, it was evident that the combined operation of the factory, civil and military, operated at a net loss that was covered from the Military Region budget.

The factory was run by a Party committee that dominated and controlled the factory management (the revolutionary committee). The head of the Party committee was also the factory director. His two key subordinates were army men, from the Military Subregion. In general, despite the heavy investment in military production, the military kept a low profile inside the factory. They let the Party and the technical experts run things, and they rarely interfered. There was a good relationship among the top cadres, perhaps because they were all Chinese. I don't know too many details, but the cadres did have a certain air about them. They dressed well, associated only with one another, and tried to maintain the best possible relations with the local minorities. The director of our factory used to say to the rest of us: "Remember, we Chinese do the deciding around here; but we must do it softly so we don't irritate the Tibetans."

The working conditions weren't bad. We worked a standard six-day week, forty-eight hours altogether. The building was new and actually in better shape than most Shanghai factories I have known. Because we were on the frontier, we received extra benefits, such as longer holidays, better food, and income supplements to compensate for the higher prices. Most important, the factory arranged to get jobs for wives and children. This was a good way for a household to supplement its income. A wife might be able to earn as much as 60 yuan a month making sun-dried bricks or collecting stones for road building. This was not much below a worker's average income of 72 yuan per month (wages were 20-25 percent higher on the frontier than in Shanghai). Sometimes the factory offered short-term employment for casual laborers. Then they would hire dependents. There was always a scramble for these jobs because they paid over 50 yuan and provided extra household income. Everyone tried to get such a job for his wife. You needed good connections, however, so you would ply the responsible cadre with gifts of fresh fruit and vegetables or with a Shanghai trinket that you had carefully hoarded for just such a purpose.

Our food ration was generous. Workers got 34 catties a month, and cadres got 30 because they didn't work as much with their hands. Dependents also got 30 catties a month. The food ration was distributed at the factory and was made up of 70 percent flour and 30 percent lesser grains. We got very little rice, which bothered me because I was a "rice-eating" Chinese back in Shanghai. It was hard for me to adjust to wheat and barley in my bowl. Most of us ate in the factory cafeteria, where they gave us a choice of three dishes each day. Households that cooked their own meals had to buy vegetables and other foodstuffs in town. The supply was pretty meager, but occasionally the factory cafeteria bought a large load of vegetables trucked in from Xining and then sold an extra portion beyond its needs to factory employees. The factory grew its own potatoes and rape seed for cooking oil. We all had to work on the factory farm during planting and harvesting, sometimes three days a week. Once in a while we got extra potatoes, but there was always a shortage of cooking oil. If you had connections or used the backdoor, then you could always manage to get cooking oil. We received a half catty of sugar per month, and since I didn't use sugar I traded my sugar coupons for pork coupons. It was supposedly illegal to trade coupons like that, but I didn't care since everybody did it, including the cadres. And I loved to eat pork; it was one of the few pleasures I looked forward to. I hated mutton and couldn't stand the stinking smell of it, couldn't stand the greasy taste. You could buy mutton freely, without coupons, in the town market, but most Chinese like me just didn't like to eat sheep meat. We only got a half catty of pork per month, the same amount as the sugar and cooking-oil rations. Prices of basic foodstuffs were only a few cents higher than in Shanghai, but vegetables and fruit were three times more expensive. Many consumer goods were just not available, and those of us who had come from rich Shanghai wished we had brought more stuff along with which to barter for scarce items. Monkey Face Wu may have toed the political line closely, but he also brought a suitcase full of sweaters, extra padded clothing, and a package of scarce flints. He was the best fed of all the workers after he finished bartering off all that stuff. If someone could have brought along a new bicycle from Shanghai, he could have sold it for two or three times its regular Shanghai price.

I lived in the factory dormitory, in a room with three other workers. In my spare time I read the Xining and Lanzhou papers, which were available a day after publication, and the *People's Daily,* which arrived five days after its publication in Peking. By that time you knew all the important news from listening to the radio, so there wasn't much that was new. Of course, you had to read the editorials and the leading articles to be sure what the current political line was. On Sundays I had the day off and did laundry or sewing, wrote letters, walked around the town, visited friends. There wasn't that much to do because there weren't many new films or artistic productions. Every once in a while there'd be a visiting artistic troupe, but they had a limited reper-toire and played the same stuff, such as "Red Detachment of Women," over and over. The army showed films regularly, but there too they were the same three or four movies all the time.

After a while I began to get to know some Tibetans, and that made all the difference. The Tibetans are a warm and friendly people, and my experience with them was a happy one. I had a Tibetan girlfriend whom I visited in a nearby commune. I even ate that stinking mutton with them, using my bare hands, drink-ing tea mixed with salt and sheep fat and poured into a bowl that had been specially "cleaned" for me.* Later I found out that the bowl had been cleaned with dried sheep dung and then dried with my host's dirty shirt, "as a mark of respect." I used to watch their archery contests and their horse races; they are superb horsemen. Tibetans living in towns are more "Hanized," that is, more like us with respect to clothing, food, and hygiene. Town Tibetans regularly wash their hands and face with soap, but those who live in the rural areas wash only three times in a lifetime: when born, when they marry, and when they die. They like to eat their mutton almost raw, dipped briefly in boiling water, with their hands and not with chopsticks. They don't normally eat pork and they don't like to speak Mandarin Chinese. On the other hand, you'll find quite a few Chinese who have learned to speak

*Tibetan "tea" is brewed in water for a long time and soda is added. It is put in a long wooden tube together with butter, salt, and more boiled water. Then it is whisked by a special tool that mixes all the ingredients thoroughly. After it is poured in your cup, you add another chunk of rancid butter, taken from a skin pouch hanging nearby. For many Tibetans, tea is both a drink and a soup, to which they add some barley (*tsam pa*), the Tibetan staple grain, and then drink in large gulps.

Tibetan. Even I could speak it passably enough after five years of living there.

Given that there were so many modern Chinese around, I found it surprising how much of the Tibetan life style and customs still reflected their feudal past. I expected that they would be imitating our customs, wearing our clothes and speaking Chinese, but only a few towndwellers did that. They preferred to follow their old customs, and the authorities didn't seem to object so long as they were peaceful and didn't try to reestablish the old feudal class system. Some of their customs were quite surprising to me—for example, the way in which they bury their dead. Actually they don't bury them at all. The body is carried up by relatives to the mountains, usually to some barren rocky area. The corpse is hacked into small pieces and then scattered in all directions as food for the vultures, who gather quickly in large circles. Before they cut up the bodies, they blow large horns. When you hear those horns blowing, you know that a Tibetan has died and his flesh is now being offered to the birds. As a matter of fact, the ceremony is called "feeding the birds" (*ja tor*), and often they strip off the flesh with knives and hack the bones into smaller pieces to make it easier for the birds to feast. Sometimes they burn sandalwood to attract more birds. When the bones have been picked clean, they gather up the rest and crush them to pieces, into a powder. They do all this because they believe that, after the body has been eaten by vultures and has disappeared, its spirit is finally free to go to heaven; they call this ritual "heavenly burial." In the old days they sometimes dumped the corpse into the river and let it decompose there, but we don't allow that anymore because it can cause disease.

I couldn't understand such a barbaric custom and never actually saw it happen, but I knew it did go on regularly. An even worse custom had to do with their treatment of old people. When old people are no longer able to work, their children just put them outside the hut or tent and leave them in the open air, lying there. They are fed by the family until they die. I thought that was a terrible thing to do, although at least it wasn't done in the cities anymore, just in the remote rural areas.

Tibetan women have a great deal of sexual freedom. They think little of sleeping with a man before they are married nor even of sleeping with several men after marriage. In the olden days some women had several husbands, usually brothers from the same family, and whichever brother was spending the night with the shared wife would leave his shoes outside the door to let the others know. Tibetan women enjoy sex and consider it as natural as eating or sleeping. They have to show they are fertile and can produce a child, and the child doesn't have to belong to the legal father. So there is lots of sex before marriage, even with Han Chinese. Actually Tibetan girls liked to boast of their Han Chinese conquests to others. Sometimes it was embarrassing to hear the Tibetan women talk so openly about such a personal thing, but to them it was natural. One big problem, however, was that as a result of all this promiscuity (which was not exclusively confined to Tibetan women after a while) there was a high rate of venereal disease in the area. We were always being told by the Chinese doctors how to detect, cure, and prevent VD, but I think it almost reached epidemic proportions at one point, mainly because the Tibetans didn't pay any attention.

Disease is a serious problem in Qinghai, even though many medical graduates have been sent from the east. The two main problems are VD and typhus. In the summer of 1970, there was a terrible typhus outbreak in our area. It started in two communes and spread like a desert storm. In one of the communes 280 people died in one week; in the other, 500 died in two days. The whole area was quarantined for three months—nobody could get in or out. You couldn't even mail a letter. All traffic was stopped except for medical teams that arrived from Peking, Tianjin, Lanzhou, and Urumchi. They couldn't save those who were already infected and dying, but they gathered all of us together in several large meeting grounds and sprayed us with some kind of disinfectant. We all put on white masks and had to drink special water brought in containers from outside the area. Over a three-month period the typhus was stopped, but over 2000 had died in the region, all in the rural areas.

The Chinese doctors are upset that the Tibetans are still so backward with regard to hygiene and medical knowledge, especially in the rural areas. The doctors realize that little can be done about it, so long as the Tibetans are protected by government policy, but they are concerned that more epidemics can occur because the Tibetans don't like to change their habits. For example, Chinese doctors are appalled at the custom of putting newborn babies into a leather sack with dried sheep dung on the bottom "to keep the sack clean." The Tibetans are slow to change this custom, and consequently many infants die in the first few days of their lives. Tibetans have a very high infant-mortality rate. Ironically, even though rural Tibetans are slow to change, they nevertheless respect Chinese doctors highly—sometimes more highly than their own leaders. I remember once being present when a Chinese doctor and a Tibetan county official went to visit a Tibetan household. In Tibetan custom, the host automatically gives the leading guest the seat of honor, but in this case it was the Chinese doctor who got the seat of honor and the best food, not the Tibetan official. I never would have thought that a Chinese doctor would get preference over a Tibetan official, who was an important local personage.

Basically I found the Tibetans to be friendly and intelligent, willing to learn from the Chinese, yet secure in knowing they could retain a large part of their own culture. In the cities Tibetans are more like us, in their dress and habits, but in the rural areas where most of them live they are still backward culturally. Even in the cities, however, you could find strange remnants of feudalism. I once visited a ruined monastery not far from town, and poking around the rocks I found a small praying Buddha statue, which I secretly took to my room and put in a corner. I thought little of it; just a souvenir of the local area and a reminder of the past. Well, one day a Tibetan came to see me. He was a brigade leader from the suburban commune where my girlfriend lived. He saw the statue and fell on his knees in front of it and began to pray. He begged me to sell it to him for any amount of money, but I didn't want to sell it and said no. He tried many times afterward to buy it from me, even offering 200 yuan. Not only was he a cadre but he was also a Party member, and he wasn't the only Tibetan who believed in such superstitions.

I spent five years there and can't say I regretted it. You got caught up in the frontier spirit, and living together with the Tibetans made life interesting. I took a certain pride in watching Gonghe grow from a dusty small town into a dusty city. A railroad was being built from Xining and, in anticipation of a large influx of future settlers, a new railway station, large hotel, and sports stadium were under construction.[4] A new post office building, theater, and public bath house had already been built, along with a truck terminal and an expanded bus depot. There were piles of bricks, tiles, and construction materials lying all around, and Gonghe was a boom town. For years the town was heavily subsidized by the central government, but now it has become more self-sufficient in its economy. For example, in the past, local wool was shipped to Xining for processing, but now the city has its own woollen mill. Technicians, workers, and knitting machinery have been brought in from Shanghai. Gonghe produces its own knitting wool, sweaters, and cloth, thus saving a great deal on transportation costs. The same goes for cattle and sheep raising. In the past we sent the animals to Xining for processing and storage. Now the city has its own cold-storage plant and a cannery that produces tinned meat for export to Pakistan. Cement plants, expanded mineral exploration (for asbestos), small coalmines, more retail shops — all this occurred while I was there. It was a period of real growth, and the city has more to offer those who came to settle there in the mid-seventies. You might still feel a little isolated and lonely, and life can get boring at times, but it's a simple place without the political passions that embroiled so much of China in the past years.

I left with mixed feelings. It had been a good time in my life and I had many friends. Near the end I met a Chinese woman and we began to make serious plans. But her father became seriously ill and she returned home. Then it seemed awfully dusty and dreary once more, and that stinking mutton smell wouldn't go away. I was glad finally to make my way back to the east, to the land of pigs and rice, and away from the land of stinking mutton and tea cups cleaned with sheep's dung. Later I got to Hong Kong and am about to emigrate to America, where I'll finally get to see the real wild west and real cowboys and Indians.

Kill the Chickens To Scare the Monkeys

WHEN THE CULTURAL REVOLUTION spread across China, observers' attention was focused on several spectacular confrontations in major Chinese universities, on conflict between Red Guard factions, and on the struggle between civil and military authorities. Chairman Mao reviewed a million Red Guards in Tiananmen Square, and posters blanketed the walls of China's major cities. Important leaders such as Liu Shaoqi were struggled and denounced in mass meetings. Hundreds of millions of Chinese daily waved their little Red Books while paying homage to Mao. Foreigners followed the big events fairly well and have a reasonably clear understanding of what happened. But we lack detailed descriptions of how the Cultural Revolution affected the daily operation of smaller, less visible units in the system.

This is a story that describes what went on in one Peking office during the Cultural Revolution. The narrator, a young cadre, describes some of his co-workers and what they did during this period. He shows how they were affected by events and what happened to them. Bao, the ambitious, hard-working ex-soldier, was transformed into a ruthless zealot who became known as the Imitation General. Zhong, the theorist, wound up on the wrong side and was sent down to the countryside. The director and his deputies, especially Emperor Fang, were removed from their posts. For a while the office was a miniature battleground of opposing factions, each "waving the red flag of Chairman Mao's Thought" through poster campaigns and struggle sessions.

Eventually, however, the struggle turned violent and several

157

*people were murdered or committed suicide. The army finally
stepped in to restore order. The Imitation General was accused of
being a leader in the ultraleftist 516 group. The 516's membership was never made explicitly clear. At one point it was said
to contain leftists such as Chen Boda, who was purged in 1970.
Later an attempt was made to link Lin Biao with this group, and
now we have been told that the Gang of Four were its real leaders.
The Imitation General and others like him thus turned out to be
pawns in a complicated power struggle directed from above.*

 *At the end of the Cultural Revolution, members of both
factions wound up in the same office working together as if
nothing had happened during those five years. The Imitation
General and those he had beaten and who had sworn revenge "if
it takes ten thousand years" were back side by side. But could
their relationship ever be the same again? One wonders what happened at the office when the "verdicts of the Cultural Revolution
were reversed" during the recent rehabilitations. Was the Imitation General again toppled from his post, and did Zhong win out
in the end? We will probably never know the answer to these
questions, and the conclusion of this particular story is left to the
imagination.*

I WAS BORN IN PEKING, went to university there, and then
was assigned in 1964 to a job in a bureau that was directly attached to the central government. We published materials in a
number of languages, and my assignment was to translate and
edit English-language materials. It was a good job by almost any
standards: a high salary, a creative post in an important organ in
the nation's capital. The bureau was located in the northwest
part of the city, in the so-called academic section of Peking, near
the zoo. The building had been built in stages. The older central
portion, made of red brick, had been put up after Liberation
with the help of Soviet experts. It was built in the well-known
Soviet style of that time, four stories with extra high ceilings,
lavish concrete ornamentation, and a flat roof. We sometimes
played badminton on the roof during our rest periods. The stair-
case was wide and gloomy. It went right up the middle of the
building, a colossal waste of space. We used to criticize the Soviet
architects for having designed the building to face the wrong way
—it was always dark and the fluorescent lights were never shut

off, in summer or winter. The newer Chinese-designed part of the building, which had been built in the early sixties, made the bureau into a more self-contained unit with eating, sleeping, and recreational facilities. Not everybody lived inside the high-walled compound, however: just bachelors like myself plus a few high-level cadres and their families. The rest were located in a special housing complex assigned to bureau personnel, about twenty minutes away by bicycle.

We were several hundred in the bureau, which was headed by a director and two deputy directors. They were cadres of high status, "old revolutionaries" [Party workers who had joined the Party early and had fought both the Kuomintang and the Japanese]. The director had a chauffeur-driven car and the high rank of a deputy minister, that is, of a Grade 10 or 11 cadre.[1] His rank entitled him to a beautiful old Peking-style four-corner courtyard house (*si he yuan*), with an inner garden complete with fruit trees. He had his own private telephone and his home was well furnished, with deep soft sofas and armchairs, rugs, even a refrigerator. Despite all this, Director Fu was actually a modest, hard-working man, who bore his privileges and rank with relative grace and humility. Thus, when the Cultural Revolution turned our bureau upside down, he was only moderately criticized because he had not used his rank unwisely and had not been arrogant with his subordinates, at least not as the deputy directors had.

The two deputy directors, Fang and Ma, were both struggled, set aside,[2] and sent to the countryside to be rehabilitated. They deserved what they got. Fang was an arrogant son of a bitch who took advantage of his rank as a Grade 12 cadre to lord it over his subordinates as if he were an official in some feudal dynasty. We used to call him Emperor Fang behind his back. Fang cultivated an ascetic image in public. He deliberately rode his wife's bicycle to work each day to show that he was a modest man. It looked ridiculous, this tall, gray-haired, well-dressed cadre riding on this woman's small bicycle. People outside the bureau never noticed the Omega Swiss watch that Emperor Fang flashed ostentatiously to his subordinates, and they never saw the inside of his lavishly furnished apartment. They didn't look closely at the fine cut of his woollen suits and didn't know that he owned several of those suits, all made to measure at a special tailor shop in Peking. He sent his children to an elite middle school for the children of high-ranking cadres,[3] and Emperor Fang's children quickly mirrored his ways. They used to come by the bureau, brash and proud, acting special and knowing they were elite, the sons and daughters of high cadres. Who else would have their own bicycles at the age of thirteen, when it costs about four months' wages for an average worker to buy a bicycle? Who else would come into our office with impunity and laugh at us, make noise and be rude? Later, when both Emperor Fang and his children had tasted the wrath of the masses and were shoveling shit in some rural area, I felt that there was indeed some justice in the act of revolution, regardless of its bloody consequences.

I liked my work because I could read a lot, especially foreign publications. We all read the *Reference News* and had access to the rarer *Reference Research Materials,* which was sent to the section head for his information.[4] That gave us a good idea of what was going on in the world and in China. Because I was trained as an English translator I also could read other foreign newspapers and magazines such as *Time, Newsweek,* the *New York Times,* and the *London Times.* We had quite a few foreign experts working at the bureau. They received a high salary and the best living conditions: extra food rations, extra clothing tickets, longer vacations, better housing. We even had a separate elevator for them at the bureau, with an attendant standing there to keep the regular Chinese away. That elevator was opened from 8 a.m. to 6 p.m., and the only other thing it ever carried besides foreign experts was freight. I got to know one or two of the experts and could get to read some of their books, occasionally smoke one of their foreign cigarettes, and listen to their stories of the outside world. We also caught a glimpse of that world in the foreign movies that were specially screened for us. Long after western films had been banned in Peking, we could see "reference screenings" of such films as "The Million-Pound Note" with Gregory Peck, "Camille" with Greta Garbo, along with a wide range of Soviet films, including the "Fall of Berlin" which showed how the world's leaders had been outwitted by Stalin.*

Most of our work was editing, translation, checking, typing, and proofreading. The rough draft of a translation was corrected in green ink. Then the foreign expert looked for language and idiomatic errors and made his corrections in red ink. Higher-level authorities, Chinese-born, then made the final decision on the text, using blue ink. Then the thrice-corrected text with its green, red, and blue markings was typed clean and three new copies were made. One went to the printer, one to the foreign expert, and the third to a Chinese-born expert. Again three kinds of ink were used. Meanwhile we used to get the proofs to read while waiting for the final corrections. Then the proof sheets were checked against the second round of corrections. Finally at the end of the process, which took five days, our section leader read the text in its foreign translation, without looking at the Chinese original. Then the presses, which were located in the same building, rolled. Despite all this checking and editing, the finished product invariably had mistakes, which often caused embarrassment to those in charge and to us as well. But too much checking was self-defeating because everyone assumed that the other person would catch the mistakes, so we didn't concentrate enough. One time we had a campaign to eliminate mistakes in the bureau. Some activists had the bright idea that a good solid campaign would do the trick and eliminate mistakes once and for all. Slogans were posted up all around us. "We can eliminate every technical and translating mistake!" They figured out how many mistakes we made in an hour, and how many words each person had translated. Performance charts were pasted on the walls.

In the next three weeks there were fewer mistakes, but immediately people began to relax and back came the mistakes, like an evil daughter-in-law's curse. We tried everything, but to no avail. By the time the "Eliminate Mistakes" campaign was over, we were making more errors than when it had started; at least that was the actual result of the campaign. However, we reported otherwise to the higher authorities, showing that our hourly rate of mistakes had declined and that the number of mistakes per total number of words also had declined. Everybody knew better, and the campaign to end mistakes was allowed to die a quiet death.

I had a good section leader, Old Zhou. He knew his job well

---

*Today they are again showing foreign films. Charlie Chaplin's "Modern Times," "The Great Dictator," and "Limelight," Olivier's "Hamlet," Anthony Quinn in "The Hunchback of Notre Dame," and some western science-fiction films have recently been shown to Peking and Shanghai audiences.

and also knew how to divide the work up among the thirty people in our section. A Party member, he was that type of middle-level cadre who appeared destined to spin out his life in the middle of things, not the best, not the worst, but doing his job. He suffered in the Cultural Revolution, however, because he came out on the wrong side and then, to cover himself, became involved with the ultraleftist group at the bureau. He hung on for a while but finally was sent down to the countryside in 1971 and didn't get back to the bureau until 1973. Old Zhou presided over the weekly work meeting in the section, usually in the afternoon from 2 p.m. to 6 p.m. Sometimes we had really good discussions regarding translation problems. We were mainly concerned with the quality of the translation, how cadres could be better trained for the work, how we could do more things ourselves in the section, and how we could learn more from the foreign experts. He handled these discussions crisply, made the right suggestions, and was clever at communicating higher-level decisions to us so that we almost thought we had made them ourselves. These weekly work sessions with Old Zhou were the most productive group meetings I attended. We felt like a real collective and always went back to work the next day with a genuine eagerness to improve our work results.

The same can't be said of the political study sessions, which took place on two afternoons and two evenings every week. They were also presided over by Old Zhou, at least until the Cultural Revolution. We were bored at these meetings, especially since we had spent all week reading and writing and translating these very same slogans. It was like the studied ritual of Peking Opera. We knew the main characters, the plot, and the conclusion; the problem was having to put on the play. So it went like this. A bell would ring at 2:00, and after the bell had sounded you picked up your chair and tea cup and went to a larger office and sat down. Then, when everyone in the section was assembled, Old Zhou would begin the meeting. Let's say the meeting was called to discuss the New Year's editorial that had just appeared in *People's Daily*. He would say, "All right, today, as you know, we are going to discuss the New Year's editorial. Let's reread the editorial and then we'll have a discussion. Now let's start reading." At this point each of us volunteered to read the editorial out loud. The idea uppermost in everyone's minds was that if you read it out loud first, then you wouldn't be called on later to analyze it. One lucky person was chosen and he read it out, loudly. Then Zhou would proclaim, "Fine, now let's start the discussion!" (*hao, dajia tan ba*). The room suddenly became silent because nobody wanted to be the first to risk saying the wrong thing. Zhou glared at us, pleaded, and finally became angry. "Come, come, speak up. Don't hold back!" (*sui bian tan*). Finally one who knew how to talk well under any circumstances, and had a good political sense, spoke a few carefully chosen words. He would start somewhat timorously (*wo lai tan ba*) and then the rest of us relaxed our tensed muscles. He invariably went on for about half an hour, cautiously repeating and embellishing but never straying from the editorial's meaning. The tenseness went out of the room. It became routine. Five or six began to doze in their chairs. The rest of us picked out a few choice phrases to repeat out loud if called upon later. The room was too hot; the voices droned on; cigarette smoke hung heavy in the air.

One person wrote it all down, every word, producing an accurate transcript of what was said. This transcript was given to the political department of the bureau Party committee whose function it was to ensure that we had followed the correct Party line. If the good talkers began to speak too quickly, the recorder would interrupt and say, "Don't talk so fast. I can't get it all down." After the first speaker had finished, it was easy to follow with a few well-chosen words. Even so, after four hours over half in the room still had not said anything and many simply said, "I agree with Comrade So-and-So's opinion, and so I won't repeat what has been just said, although one could add the following . . ." The bit he was adding might go on for five or ten minutes. Zhou would interrupt from time to time with comments and leading questions. There were a couple of other Party activists who also tried to keep the discussion going. If the editorial or policy document was really important, we might have to discuss it throughout the whole week. Sometimes if Zhou became exasperated with the results of the discussion, we stopped for dinner and then returned and went on into the night. Then you had to be especially careful because, after five or six hours, you were fatigued and hot, liable to say something stupid.

Most of us thought the political study sessions were a waste of time. We felt we already knew the correct political line; after all,

we were in the business of translating it for world-wide dissemi-
nation. Maybe that's why we had to endure so much of it, to ensure that it was drilled in so deeply that when we did make mistakes they were always "technical" ones and never "political"
ones. Still, in retrospect, all that political study didn't do us much
good when the Cultural Revolution came. Then you couldn't
hide or just spout back one of the Chairman's quotations. You
didn't always know what the new political line was going to be or
who would be in charge of interpreting and carrying it out.

I worked in a room with four others. It had large windows
and fluorescent lighting. We each had a desk, paper, ballpoint
pen, and wastebasket. It was hot in the summers and we often
worked in shorts and T-shirt. You could smoke as much as you
wanted and you could make your own tea. One of us was dele-
gated to fill the group's thermos jugs with hot water from a small
coal heater located in the courtyard behind the building. At
lunch some of us ate in the bureau dining hall; others unpacked
their lunch and ate at their desks, usually then just closing their
eyes and sleeping for two hours. Or we might play chess, ping-
pong, or badminton, chat with friends while going for a walk, or
take the opportunity to use the office telephone to call friends
and relatives in Peking. I used to read a lot, especially English
books that were lent to me by others. I also liked to flirt with some
of the women in my section. That, of course, was before the Cultural Revolution. There wasn't much opportunity between 1966
and 1971 for light relaxation.

Of my four office mates, I liked Big Gossip Wei the best. She
was in her mid-forties and had worked in the bureau for fifteen
years. She earned a good salary, approximately 80 yuan, and
since her husband made almost that much as a worker in a local
factory, she had a good living standard. She was able to employ a
full-time maid[5] for 35 yuan a month to take care of her three
children. Because Big Gossip had a two-bedroom apartment,
there was room for the maid to sleep with the children. The maid
made life a lot easier for her because she was not a well woman
and would not have otherwise been able to work and take care of
a family. She was only forty-three but had gray hair, looked
much older, and often was sick and unable to work. She suffered
from asthma and walked deliberately and slightly stooped over.
She was slow in her work (when she was at work), although she

always managed to do her assigned tasks. Big Gossip was in charge of the section's administrative work, which meant that she distributed stationery and materials to individuals when necessary, handed out the monthly salaries, distributed clothing coupons and ration tickets, and was in charge of the welfare fund.

I guess that gave her access to all kinds of information because she was the biggest gossip in the bureau. If there was a scandal to be told, she had all the details and she was always right. She was also the unofficial matchmaker in the bureau, so she knew more than anybody else about who was seeing whom, who was having an affair, and so on. We became good friends because she said she was on the lookout for a wife for me, even though I wasn't really interested. She would invite me over for dinner occasionally and would introduce me to various prospects. She knew all kinds of juicy stories—for example, that one of the top cadres in the bureau always went dancing on a Saturday night until midnight,[6] that he took a bureau official car to do this, and that his partner was the pretty dark-eyed girl from Section B. Dancing had been officially abolished in 1963, but it continued at the Friendship Hotel, where the foreign experts lived. Big Gossip knew lots of other stories too—say that so-and-so had a boyfriend who often came to her room at the dormitory when her roommate was away. "And," she laughed, "don't think they spend their time talking about the 'Eliminate Mistakes' campaign either!" After telling me the details of one such liaison she said, "Too bad. The girl would have been just right for you. Maybe you'll be interested when the affair is over? You now have proof that she is passionate and will help you stay warm during the cold Peking winter nights. Experience is worth something, you know."

She spent a lot of time with Wu, who was a bachelor in his mid-thirties and had worked in our section for seven years. He spoke a lot about finding a wife, so whenever he and Big Gossip got together they talked of nothing else. She would suggest names and he would reply, "She's not good-looking enough" or "Her family hasn't enough money to get me" or "The girl is too young and inexperienced" or, the opposite, "She's too old and I don't want second-hand goods!" It made for lively discussion in the office, and we used to tease Wu, asking him constantly, "Well, have they polished up the sedan chair for your wedding yet?"[7] He took all the joking in stride. As a matter of fact, he loved to play pranks and make jokes himself. Once I remember attending an important political meeting of our section. A girl in another office was there and it was always easy to make her laugh. So, in the middle of the most serious political discussion on dialectical materialism, Wu deliberately caught her attention and then slowly opened his mouth to smile at her. He had wrapped his teeth in silver cigarette paper and the effect was startling. He looked like one of those Soviet experts with their silver teeth. She started to giggle uncontrollably and quickly disrupted the whole meeting. Another time he was sitting at a meeting and suddenly asked loudly, "Who is Feng Zixiu? I always hear comrades criticizing this person, but I have never heard of him." (*Feng, zi,* and *xiu* are the Chinese characters that stand for feudalism, capitalism, and revisionism, not for anyone's name.) There was stunned silence and then the meeting burst into laughter. The section leader was trapped. He had to keep a straight face and could do nothing.

Wu was that kind of person. He wasn't very political, and he tried to avoid serious trouble by giving the impression that he was a light-hearted fellow. In fact, he bore a grudge against the bureau because, even after seven years of good work as a translator-editor, he still earned the same salary, 37½ yuan. He compared himself with two other colleagues who were university graduates (Wu had never attended university). He knew he was a better worker than either of them, but they both earned over 60 yuan a month and had received raises while working at the bureau. Wu felt that this was unfair, and thus he adopted a strategy of "work according to pay." To his trusted friends he said, "Let them work more because they earn more." He half-jokingly blamed his bachelor status on his low salary, saying, "Who would marry me? I'm not good-looking, I'm in my thirties and, most important, I have no money. If I earned 60 yuan like these other two, I'd surely be married by now."

When Bao came to the office in 1965, Wu was assigned to teach him the office routine. Even though Wu didn't exactly exert himself, Bao learned quickly. Bao liked to ask questions; he was not yet twenty-five years old and he was terribly eager to learn. A demobilized soldier, he was a bachelor and lived in the dormitory. He still retained his army life style and liked to wear his old army uniform, cap, and shoes to work. In the winter he wore a military overcoat and a military padded jacket. We used to kid him that he looked just like a general, and in fact during the Cultural Revolution he became known as the Imitation General. Then, however, it was no longer a joke because he had changed into a power-hungry individual who was terrorizing the bureau while claiming to follow Chairman Mao's line. But before the Cultural Revolution he led a simple life, eating inexpensive food, and doing considerable voluntary work—for example, he always offered to go down the three flights of stairs to get hot water for our tea, and he volunteered to clean the office even when it wasn't his turn. His roommate told me that Bao used to wash his shirts for him without asking. Bao was a regular Lei Feng[8] in those days. He was an active Party member, and during the political study sessions, when Big Gossip said nothing and Wu cracked jokes, Bao took an active part, along with Old Zhou and two or three others.

Bao learned quickly and was initially well liked by those in the office and the section. He worked hard and had that army and Party air of modesty about him. He got along with Wu because he respected Wu's skills and wanted to learn from him. He and I got on rather well because we were almost the same age. So we spent some time together. Bao, I think, respected me because I had been to university and was, in his opinion, "a high intellectual." He used to say, "You're a model for me to emulate. I want to do all the things you do and then I'll be a better person." I liked him then because in those days he tried to be a model Party member in his life and deeds, and because he was sincere in his relations with his co-workers. Big Gossip tried to interest him in finding a partner, but Bao kept putting her off saying, "I'm still busy learning my job and getting settled in. Besides, I'm too young." But she kept on with her sport and you could always tell what she was up to, by the embarrassed look on Bao's face.

I guess the one person that Bao never got along with, right from the beginning when things were relaxed and different, was Zhong, who came to the bureau around the same time. Zhong had been a Grade 17 cadre, a rank equal to that of a county magistrate, in the south before coming to Peking. He had been the head of the educational department in a large middle school. Zhong's wife also worked in the bureau, as a paramedic in the clinic, and between the two of them they had a good income, 95 yuan for him and 65 yuan for her. Zhong was in his mid-forties and somewhat set in his ways. He did his job well and was a responsible worker, but he showed no eagerness to advance in his work or to learn any more than what he was doing. We used to say of him then: "You see, that's what happens to a cadre from the provinces. In the provinces he was a big shot, but here in Peking he's just lost in the crowd, one of thousands upon thousands of similar small fry." I don't think he resented it in the least; as a matter of fact, he enjoyed Peking and seemed to be content doing his job, even though in the south he had always been in the center of things every day. Now he was on the periphery of power.

It also suited his nature, which was somewhat reflective. We used to call him the Theorist because he was a Party member who had a high level of knowledge in theory. He knew his Marxism-Leninism as well as anyone and could get up at our study meetings and talk on and on for hours without putting us to sleep. It was interesting to listen to him because he could bring life and meaning to the slogans that incessantly surrounded us. When the discussion lagged, we could count on him to revive it with a few well-placed phrases linking the discussion to Marxist-Leninist theory. Old Zhou especially liked Zhong. They were of a similar age and temperament, and they used to see each other a lot socially. The only person with whom he had a difficult relationship was Bao, the other Party member in our office. They never really hit it off. Maybe Bao resented Zhong's lack of initiative or maybe Zhong was irritated by Bao's excessive zeal. One was a doer (Bao) and the other was a thinker (Zhong). The three of us working in the small office could feel this conflict but, as good Party members, Bao and Zhong successfully masked their personal feelings toward each other outside the office. Even in the larger section, most people didn't know they disliked each other.

I wouldn't dwell on this so long except that during the Cultural Revolution many of the events that went on in our office and section were focused on the conflict between the Theorist and the Imitation General. They became engaged in a life-and-death struggle for political power at one point, and their conflict carried the rest of us along in its wake. We thought they were the monkeys, struggling for power; the rest of us were scrawny chickens, scurrying around to keep from getting caught in that struggle. Both of them went down, ultimately, but so did we. You know, it's like the proverb says, "Kill the chickens to scare the monkeys," although in this case the monkeys were also killed along with the chickens.

No one was prepared for the Cultural Revolution, that's for sure. As events unfolded in Peking we guessed that a big power struggle was underway, but no one dreamed that it would turn out to be that cataclysmic or that it would affect our personal lives so drastically. The seriousness of the whole affair only became evident to me when Peng Zhen[9] had been removed from his post, and when it was clear that "the person in high Party authority who was taking the capitalist road" had to be Liu Shaoqi himself. We never really had a chance to digest events because we were right in the midst of them, all the time. For example, we knew within an hour when Nie Yuanzi put up the first big character poster at Peking University. Because we were under central level jurisdiction, our bureau was the object of special attention for the next five years. At one point Zhou Enlai personally intervened in the political struggles that were going on in our building. When the ultraleftists stormed the Foreign Ministry in 1967, many people from our bureau were there. We went to the Great Hall of the People to listen to Zhou, Jiang Qing, and even to Liu Shaoqi. I was there when Liu stood up and admitted that the first work teams sent in the early summer of 1966 had been a mistake, although he labeled it a mistake of understanding (*renshi wenti*) and not the more fundamental error of incorrect class standpoint (*lichang wenti*).

The first wall posters appeared in our bureau at the end of May. They were initially cautious, and criticized the "bureaucratic work style" of leading cadres who acted like lords once they had become officials. This criticism was especially reserved for the two deputy directors, Fang and Ma. The posters began to ask questions such as, "Why are we publishing so few of Chairman Mao's works? Who is responsible for this? Why are we producing books that glorify the feudal past?" And so on. It was all very general, and the bureau's top cadres were still regarded as good cadres who only had made a few mistakes. But after the work teams had been discredited and it became clear that the real enemy was Liu Shaoqi and his supporters, the poster campaign heated up. Now we wanted to "drag out" Liu Shaoqi's agents in the bureau, and we began to speak of crimes and punishments:

"Chairman Mao's revolutionary line has not been carried out in the bureau's published work. The person responsible for this crime deserves ten thousand deaths." The walls were plastered with "facts" about the "towering crimes of those who are following the capitalist road at the bureau." We no longer called the director and deputy directors by the polite name of "comrade" — indeed, it wasn't long before the first banner went up saying, "Down with the Director," who was "Liu Shaoqi's agent," "his faithful running dog," "a daring warrior of the black headquarters." The director was accused of "having a deep hatred for Mao Zedong Thought"; "carrying out a revisionist and a counterrevolutionary line"; "obstructing the revolutionary masses." Dire warnings were given to those who had been criticized: "You will perish at the hands of the masses if you do not capitulate," or "If you remain stubborn to the end, it will be the end of you." At the height of the poster war, opposing factions covered the entire bureau with their posters. You couldn't eat in the dining room because it was full of posters hung from wires. The same was true of all the corridors and the walls. Every wall had its paper stories to tell, and even the sidewalks were filled with criticism. People took paint, crouched on their hands and knees, and denounced their targets.

The posters were imaginative and colorful, and required considerable skill in execution. Since we were a group of intellectuals who were gifted with words (and many of us were also skillful practitioners of ink and brush), we had some of the best posters in the city.[10] At the beginning, the poster writing seemed to be spontaneous, but as the Cultural Revolution developed, especially when two factions, the Red Flag and the Red Alliance, were locked in mortal combat, the poster war was well-planned and sophisticated. To write a good poster you first planned it out on typing paper. You decided the target and the tone of the poster. It was essential to decide the tone, how high to go. This was called *ding diaozi* (setting the tune). We'd compile a list of X's crimes and then decide what he should be: a "contradiction among the people," a "counterrevolutionary element," a "three anti-element," and so on. If the target was a cadre, we usually called him "a capitalist roader," but we also had other labels, such as "royalist," "opportunist," or "a refuge for ghosts, freaks and monsters." Two or three of us planned the poster, and then we got the best character writer to write out the text of the poster. Every faction had its own *xiucai,* a scholar who had great command of the Chinese language and of Mao's writings. We used Chinese brushes, paper and ink from the office, finished the poster, and then sought out the proper spot to paste it up. Some of the posters were true works of art, both in appearance to the eye and in content. Too bad they have all been destroyed.

In the beginning we criticized the top leaders in the bureau. That wasn't so difficult since Emperor Fang and Ma were universally disliked, and while Director Fu was all right for a high cadre, he still had his faults and it wasn't hard to find reasons for criticizing him. But once the outside work team came and took over the campaign, things began to change. It was clear that they were going to deflect criticism from the top Party people in the bureau. Indeed, it seemed that the targets of our criticism were actually colluding with the work team. Quite a few of us backed away at that point, saying, "It's another Hundred Flowers campaign designed to put us off our guard." I was one of those, and instead of hanging around the bureau I went out on the streets to learn what was going on in Peking. It was my way of doing *chuan lian* (exchanging revolutionary experience with the Red Guards). I went to the center of the city to Wangfujing and bought Red Guard newspapers for 2 cents a copy. They were publishing all sorts of stuff, including policy documents that had been stolen from government offices and the unpublished texts of Chairman Mao's speeches.[11] You could spend days reading these newspapers and the thousands of wall posters. You could also bump into victims of Red Guard zeal, young men with their stove-pipe pants cut off at the knees, girls with their braids chopped off, and half-bald young men who had received a "flying haircut" by a group of Red Guards. Later you would see groups of people wearing "hats" and "signs" being paraded around by the Red Guards. Things had changed on Peking's streets. My favorite restaurants had been shut down, as had the second-hand book stores. Chairman Mao's picture was everywhere, and his sayings blanketed Peking almost as deeply as the dust that blows in from the Gobi. People didn't linger on the sidewalks or in the shops, and now they always seemed to be on their way to some meeting. A rag-tag element had appeared, mainly young folk who were either Red Guards who had themselves come to Peking on *chuan lian* and didn't want to leave, or "black youth" (those who had earlier been sent down to live in the countryside but had returned illegally and were now hanging around Peking doing nothing except "making revolution").

In the bureau the political struggles began in earnest after the work teams had been repudiated by Chairman Mao. The bureau soon split into two factions—the more radical Red Flag and the larger Red Alliance. Both claimed to be true supporters of Chairman Mao's revolutionary line, and they fought for months before Red Flag finally took over the bureau. Then we had a "red terror" for over two years because the Red Flag faction wasn't content just to root out the true class enemies and those who had subverted Chairman Mao's line. Now the Red Flag became a bunch of extremists, attacking anybody who stood in their way—innocent and guilty, it didn't matter. It was a terrible time for those whom the Red Flag targeted as enemies and counter-revolutionaries. Of course, many deserved their fate—they deserved to be struggled, criticized, and sent down to do physical labor. There were basic ideological differences that had to be resolved, and not a few of us had been influenced by Liu Shaoqi's revisionist and bourgeois way of thinking. But a lot of the violence and the loss of life—for example, three cadres committed suicide because they couldn't endure the red terror of violent criticism and struggles—came not because the Red Flag faction was genuinely engaged in applying Chairman Mao's Thought, but because individual members of that group had become involved in power struggles while being misled by some clever conspiratorial elements. The notorious 516 group was behind all this. 516 was a national conspiracy against Mao by a group on the extreme left who used the revolution for acquiring personal power. They duped a lot of people and it took intervention from the very highest places, Zhou Enlai himself, to expose and crush them. Later, when the extremists had been removed from power, we realized how we had all been duped.[12]

Bao was one of those who got swept up in the political turmoil and became a top leader in the Red Flag faction. I now think that he was duped by the 516, but at the time we didn't know that. When the Liuist work teams had come, Bao and Zhong, being strong Party members, had worked with them in the mild, ritualistic criticism of Director Fu and his deputies.

Bao and Zhong were still friends then, but once the work teams were discredited, then everything changed. Bao realized that the tide had radically shifted and he quickly changed with it. He immediately denounced the work team, even though he had just played an important part in its work at the bureau. Bao soon became one of the top half-dozen leaders of the radical Red Flag group. He never made an individual self-criticism of his earlier cooperation with the now discredited work team. He became a radical activist, committed to the most extreme positions held during the Cultural Revolution. For example, he supported the incorrect theory of "revolutionary bloodlines," that only those who had a correct class background (workers, poor and lower-middle peasants) should be allowed to lead the Cultural Revolution. Since a number of workers at the bureau came from petit-bourgeois class backgrounds, this caused great conflict. Bao took little note of the enemies he was creating, and he changed his personality as well. He became conscious of his "superiority," being from a good class background, a Party member, and an ex-army man. In fact he became arrogant. He used to respect the intellectuals working at the bureau, but now he looked down with scorn upon them, calling them stinking counterrevolutionaries.

Bao became known as the Imitation General because he always wore his old army uniform and acted like a general. He rarely came to our office now, preferring to stay in one room on the fourth floor, where his faction had set up command headquarters. Bao no longer mixed with us, except in his recurring struggle with Zhong, who had become his mortal enemy. His way of life also changed. Although he called us all "stinking bourgeois elements who needed to be reformed," he himself lapsed into a bourgeois life style. Before the Cultural Revolution he used to send half his wages to his parents in the countryside, but now he kept his salary all for himself and bought a wrist watch and a bicycle. He began to play around with women, too, and was involved in a couple of messy affairs. One of the women became pregnant. He moved out of the dormitory into a larger apartment that had been confiscated from one of the deputy directors, Ma, who had been accused of being a royalist and had been sent down to the countryside to do manual labor. Bao thus lived a life of innate contradiction—in his politics he allegedly was the "purest of the pure," the "reddest," and "the true follower of Chairman

Mao's revolutionary line," but in his life style and work he had become bourgeois, grasping, and arrogant.

We were all caught up in the Imitation General's metamorphosis. He had long ago ceased to relate to us as friends and office mates, and he now dealt with us coldly and ruthlessly. He criticized Wu for his political vacillation, his passion for eating eggs ("a waste of state resources"), and his deliberate policy of "working to rule." Wu was the one who had been so bitter over his low salary. At first Bao had praised Wu for standing up to the "royalists" who had run the bureau, but soon he accused him of "having a reactionary attitude toward labor" because Wu had deliberately restricted his work output. Bao even criticized Big Gossip, the amateur matchmaker, for being a malicious gossip, revealing state secrets, and for "attempting to perpetuate a feudal practice" with her matchmaking. He personally supervised my own struggle and criticism at the hands of the Red Flag "masses." I was accused of the basic crime of belonging to the Red Alliance faction, and of being a royalist because I opposed the ruthless ultraleftism of the Red Flag faction. So I was frog-marched into the dining hall one day and given a verbal and physical beating. And my erstwhile friend, the Imitation General, was right there in the middle egging them on. But he reserved most of his energies for his conflict with Zhong. Compared to Zhong, we were just small fry in Bao's eyes. Zhong, however, was a formidable foe, a respected Party member who knew his Marxism-Leninism, a cadre who by no stretch of the imagination could be accused of having strayed from the Party line, at least not until the work teams had come to the bureau. That was when Zhong and Bao had their big falling out.

Zhong regarded Bao's political turnabout as rank opportunism. He argued that way to Bao's face: "You've twisted Marxism-Leninism for your own personal power." Bao replied that Zhong was like an "old cat too lazy to catch mice. You just want the easy way out. But there is no easy way now, except for bloody revolution." So they were poles apart, the older more theoretically inclined Zhong and the younger, more pragmatic, ex-army man Bao. They differed over the interpretation of Mao's teaching on class struggle. Zhong the theorist accused Bao of following the principle of "only revolutionary class bloodlines are good," a principle later explicitly rejected by Chairman Mao himself. At political study sessions the two openly criticized each other, sometimes violently. But Zhong was never as violent or active in his criticism of the established Party leadership as Bao was. So his tone toward others was essentially mild. When the tide shifted in favor of the Red Flag, and when the army work teams came down on the side of Red Flag, Zhong's position became tenuous. He and Bao had long stopped talking with each other, although they hurled epithets and accusations at each other through posters and by means of intermediaries. Zhong had such a mastery of theory and Marxism-Leninism that for a long time he could battle the more inexperienced Bao in a "war of characters." But Zhong was handicapped ultimately by his past, because even though he was a Grade 17 cadre and Party member, he had a petit-bourgeois class background and he once had awkward affairs with two different women. Both these facts were used by Bao in a lurid poster war, followed by Zhong's being humiliated and forced to write endless self-confessions. Then came a gigantic struggle meeting in which Zhong along with Old Zhou, the section head, and others were paraded in front of a packed hall of Red Flag supporters during the "Purify Class Ranks" campaign. Soon afterwards Zhong was sent down to the countryside to be reeducated. Before he left, he told me: "It won't be long now; the Red Flag is about to fall and the Imitation General will be one of the first. They knocked me down, called me a class enemy, and trampled on my faith in Chairman Mao. But I will wait ten thousand years for my revenge. I can wait!"

His revenge came quickly. A few months later, with direct supervision from the highest levels, a top team of military investigators entered our bureau. Bao's days as the Imitation General were numbered. He was accused of being an ultraleftist element, a member of the 516 group that was secretly opposed to Chairman Mao and was plotting to take away his leadership. Now all the methods that he had used on his enemies were applied to him. Bao was the real class enemy now, and so we set up a study group with Bao as the object. Several persons were assigned to interrogate and denounce him. He was kept in a room and constantly watched when he went to the bathroom or to eat. One of the interrogators used to say, "None of those suicides for you, Bao. We will watch you very carefully because we want to have our revenge and wouldn't want to see you escape the people's wrath. Maybe after we've struggled you properly and found out all we want to know—maybe then we'll arrange a special 'accident' for you, a phoney suicide like you arranged for Old Shao."* We took turns supervising and struggling Bao. I was puzzled by his initial reluctance to confess and admit his crimes. He was sullen and said little, even though the extent of his crimes was formidable: being linked to a conspiratorial group that had actually tried to destroy the Chairman himself! Bao finally confessed to crimes of ultra-leftism, but it was never proved he was a 516 element. Indeed, he apparently was never consciously part of the bigger conspiracy. It was clear that he was only a tool used by those directing the struggle from above. It turned out that we were all puppets being manipulated by others and they had used Bao's desire for personal power as a way of getting their policies applied in the bureau. That much became clear. In the end he was just another dupe, just another "chicken" like the rest of us.

They killed the chickens, but did they really scare the monkeys? Well, that's hard to answer and depends on who the monkeys really were. I thought that Bao and Zhong were the monkeys, but they turned out to be chickens like us. Director Fu came back to his old position and, though he had been roundly criticized at the outset, by 1973 he was back in his career almost as if the Cultural Revolution had never happened. Fang and Ma, the two deputy directors, shoveled shit for two years in the countryside, but they are back too and, to be truthful, I wonder if deep down inside they changed their old ways. Old Zhou, the section leader, died of natural causes, and maybe the Cultural Revolution speeded him on his journey to another world, but in any case, he was a chicken like the rest of us. So were Wu, Big Gossip, and myself. Eventually we all wound up back at the bureau. Bao came back to the bureau and wound up working again in the very same room with Zhong, at the desk beside him. We speak again with each other now, somewhat guardedly but almost as if the past eight years hadn't happened. Of course, what each of us holds in his heart is another matter. Can Zhong ever forgive

---

*Old Shao worked in another section and was an important member of the Red Alliance. Bao and his Red Flag supporters had him locked in a room on the third floor under guard. Shao supposedly jumped out the window to his death, although everyone was convinced he had been pushed by Bao and his followers.

how he was treated when Bao was in command? Zhong swore revenge, even if it took ten thousand years. How many of us sit quietly with revenge burning inside our hearts, wanting to settle old scores? Some of us also feel betrayed by events; the Cultural Revolution degenerated into a secret conspiracy run by the 516 group at the top, using the rest of us for their own nefarious ends. In the final analysis, the real monkeys weren't even in our bureau, but in the top echelons, right around Chairman Mao. So you couldn't help thinking to yourself, What did it really accomplish? Was it worth it?

Yes, on balance I suppose it was worth it, even though good blood was shed unnecessarily and real enemies went unpunished as the innocent were knocked down. Surprisingly, work output at the bureau improved during all the confusion. We were actually making fewer technical mistakes in our work, so maybe all that political struggle had cleared our minds and made us better workers in the end. The top cadres became a little less arrogant, and were more concerned about their relationship to the rest of us working in the bureau. So the Cultural Revolution at our bureau did have its good results, although the cost was high and afterward you could never really know what lay buried in people's hearts.

The One Whose Girlfriend Turned Him In

IN 1957, for reasons that even today are not altogether clear, Chairman Mao launched the campaign "To Let a Hundred Flowers Bloom and Let a Hundred Schools of Thought Contend." Everyone was asked to offer criticisms of what had been achieved since Liberation in 1949, including criticism of the role and actions of the Party itself. The intensity of the criticism that emerged was a rude shock to Chairman Mao and the Party, and they quickly moved to stem the tide by branding those who had publicly expressed criticism as "rightists." Many were struggled and lost their jobs. Some were sent to languish in prison. Others were dispatched to be reeducated and then reassigned to lower-level jobs, still wearing their "rightist hats," which confirmed their status as politically unreliable persons. Wherever a new campaign emerged thereafter, there would always be a ready-made group of handy targets. During the Cultural Revolution old rightists served as a convenient first target until more attractive enemies were found.

In this story a hard-working young economist-planner who was somewhat politically naive gets caught up in the Hundred Flowers campaign and voices his personal criticism of the Party to another individual who later accuses him of being a rightist. He is publicly struggled and made to wear the rightist hat. His budding career as an economist-planner came promptly to an end, and he spent the next fifteen years in China shuffling around from labor camp to agricultural work. Luckily he was able to spend a part of that time in Peking, and later he returned to his home village in the south prior to leaving China.

Recently the Chinese have moved to rehabilitate people like this economist-planner, who had their careers permanently destroyed by being unjustly branded as rightists back in the fifties. It is claimed that hundreds of thousands of ex-rightists are being released from prisons and labor camps, given state pensions, and even being returned to their former jobs, with payment of all wages lost over the past twenty years. The implications of this rehabilitation are significant because it not only suggests that the Party has tacitly admitted it overreacted to criticism in 1957, but that it will encourage criticism once more in the future. The criticism of elitism in decision making appearing on the so-called Xidan Democracy Wall in Peking in 1978 and 1979 indicates that a few daring Chinese citizens are willing once again to risk their careers, regardless of the lessons of the Hundred Flowers campaign. Indeed, some of those who actively led this criticism have been arrested, tried, and are now in prison. These few individuals are the exception. Undoubtedly the vast majority of Chinese plan to follow the advice of Black-Face Meng in "Chairman Mao's Letter to Li," to keep quiet until absolutely certain which way the political winds are blowing.

I AM A SOUTHERNER, born in Mei county, of Hakka parents, but I lived most of my adult life in the north.[1] Maybe that was my mistake. If I had stayed closer to home, perhaps my life would have turned out better and today I'd be near my home village, working as an ordinary cadre, raising a family, and getting my share of the fruits of revolution. But I got caught up in politics just as I was making a big career for myself in Peking. One mistake and I was branded a political misfit for the rest of my life. No matter how you struggle, no matter how you try to make amends and attempt to build a new career, once the Party has decided your fate you can't do much. There is an old saying: "The Monkey King can somersault all he wants, but he can't get off Buddha's palm." They had me tight in their fists for fifteen years until, when the breath of my life was almost squeezed out, I finally fled, with the rightist curse still hanging over my head.

Things had been quite different after Liberation. After

getting a basic arts education at Zhongshan University in Canton, I went on to do graduate studies in 1951 at the Northeast Planning and Statistics Academy in Harbin. For a southerner this was quite a contrast — going so far away from home, to a cold and sometimes bitter climate, to live among the unwashed northerners, trying to shed my southern accent, and filling my rice bowl with millet and sorghum. Still, I was young and romantic and the Party had encouraged us to go to the northeast to help rebuild Manchuria. We were going to learn all about economics, statistics, and planning, and this interested an eighteen-year-old young man who believed that China's salvation lay in a planned socialist economy. I fancied myself graduating from the academy, as one of China's new specialists, then being sent to Peking where I would sit consulting with our leading specialists on the economy and with our Soviet brothers, deciding what would be produced where and when. Perhaps that was my mistake, thinking in terms of a personal career without really understanding the political consequences of my dreams. There is a saying that "the higher a sparrow flies, the farther he falls." I was too ambitious, too naive, too careless, and paid a heavy price.

I spent two years at the academy studying economics and statistics. I learned a great deal and stood near the top of my class. They even asked me to stay on as a teaching assistant. But I wanted to leave, to do something more practical and also see more of the northeast. After two years I was beginning to get used to the place, especially to the hustle of industrial cities like Shenyang, Harbin, and Changchun. I was assigned to work for the Northeast Forestry Department Planning Group, developing reforestation schemes and coordinating wood production.[2] The Party liked my work, and I was sent to the department's cadres school in Harbin as deputy director for three years. Now I was important enough to be teaching other cadres basic principles of economics and planning. My status rose and there I was, not yet twenty-five and already getting special housing, food, and travel privileges. I went all over the northeast, to places like Jiamusi and Yichun near the Soviet border and to the Daqing oilfield when it was just a bunch of villages.

Those were good days, the best for me. I worked hard and enjoyed my job. I was a responsible person, doing useful work. Several times various Party officials mentioned that the Party was pleased with my progress and that I would soon be asked to join the Party. Lin, the Party secretary in the cadres school, spoke with me several times about joining the Party, saying, "We need people like you to join us. The Party becomes strong when it can add members like you."

I was flattered by the prospect of becoming a Party member. That would be a big step toward that job in Peking, helping plan the national economy. It seemed that an irresistible tide was propelling me to the top, and I figured in a few months I'd be a member. Lin, once he had broached the subject, then began to give me advice: "Do you think you have spent enough time on political study? Shouldn't you think a bit more about relating Mao's writings to your work with other cadres? Yesterday when you were explaining economics to the students, why didn't you refer to Mao's writings on class struggle?" As the Gao-Rao purge[3] unfolded before our eyes he wondered out loud: "We need some strong opinions from you here. If you are to be a leader of men, you must know what the political line is, be able to explain it to others, and in your heart believe in the Party!"

I had a girlfriend and we were planning to get married in the near future. She was also a cadre in the school and came from a good family in Shanghai. We spent a lot of time together, and I guess she was the only person in whom I really confided. When I told her what Lin had said, she replied, "Of course you will soon be a Party member — a person of your ability deserves it. And you work well with others." We talked a lot about the school and about our profession, and I would occasionally ask her advice about various problems at work.

Then, disaster struck. It was 1957 and the Party launched the Hundred Flowers campaign, which was supposed to provide an open forum to discuss and evaluate the Party's performance and policies since Liberation. It was a good idea in theory: get criticism out in the open so that mistakes could be corrected, so that inadequate Party members and cadres would be rooted out and Party policy would be reaffirmed after a period of criticism. In my naiveté and through political miscalculation, I made the blunder of my life. I wasn't careful enough and acted recklessly. What happened was that I actually had believed the Party wanted honest criticism of its policies. And I had plenty of criticisms. Several times over the years we economists and planners had found ourselves restricted in our work by Party officials who mindlessly applied Marxist-Leninist theory to situations way beyond their understanding. Not every Party member had good character and only a few possessed enough expertise to understand our work. Often while we were trying to work out complicated statistical or planning concepts and policies, we would have to listen to endless political talk and empty phrases about the correct political line. I suppose that was one reason why I had hesitated from making a strong bid up till then to become a Party member. A part of me had always resisted the prospect of having to become a political organizer. Old Lin knew I felt this way, although we never talked about it openly. I figured he was my weathervane. I'd follow his actions whatever the campaign, since he would always know what to do.

Well, I followed old Lin, right to my doom. Here's what happened. At the beginning of the campaign we all kept our mouths shut to see what it was all about. Even a political amateur like myself knew that was the thing to do. But then, as public criticism of the Party and of particular Party members mounted in intensity, we let up our guard and plunged into the fray. Lin himself led the attack on Party cadres in the ministry who had been arrogant in dealing with lower-level Party cadres and who had tried to substitute the wrong political line for correct knowledge. Lin gave a speech denouncing three of these officials, calling them remnants of the Gao-Rao clique and people in need of serious reeducation by the masses. The gist of his criticism spilled out into the press, and suddenly our school was awash with debate and wall posters. Most of them repeated Lin's attack: "Down with the evil clique that has betrayed the Party line." Meetings were held to discuss the criticisms, and Lin encouraged me to let myself follow the correct political line.

So I did, but only privately to my girlfriend. We talked about the campaign and what it meant. I said that I agreed with Lin's criticism. The Party secretary was right in exposing arrogant and corrupt Party members. The Party was not perfect; it had made countless mistakes. Why should Party members not be called into account just like ordinary citizens? Some Party policies needed changing, and why not seize the chance now? Even the Party was involved in this criticism. If the Party leads such criticism of itself, then should we not follow? To hold back and say nothing when we were expected to join in the campaign might be seen as a lack of faith in the Party. We talked a lot about these things, but only to each other. We both hesitated to take a public stance, even though our own Party secretary, Lin, had committed himself on behalf of the school.

Well, the tide suddenly changed and she turned me in. It was the blackest time of my life. She turned me in without blinking an eye and we never spoke to each other again.

It happened like this. Lin had been spearheading the attack when a small item appeared in the press warning about "those who cover up their own errors by attacking others." A few days later a poster appeared at the school: "All Party members must undergo self-criticism. It is not enough to criticize others." Then there were more and they were more specific. Lin was accused of being "a fox who could no longer hide his tail"; "a white-eyed wolf"; and "a cat who weeps over the death of a rat" (that is, one who doesn't say what he means).

Give sly old Lin credit for cunning. As soon as he saw what was happening, he changed course and began to admit all his mistakes. This saved his neck because somehow he managed to deflect the attack on himself to others. I was one of them. Lin admitted that he had made mistakes and that he had not criticized himself for his own arrogance and failings. But no one knocked him down for what he had said about the Party cadres. He wriggled off the hook without suffering a damning blow to his career. But others like myself weren't so lucky. If the big fish get away, then you settle for shrimp. So it was with me. The old Chinese proverb "Beat the mule to terrify the horse" fit my case perfectly. Old Lin jumped to the attack and suddenly there was earnest talk about "those rightists who presume to destroy the Party by their words and deeds." Who was the next target? I wondered, and there I was walking along the corridors when I saw my name on the wall, along with four others, accused of being "secret counterrevolutionaries in their hearts and deeds," "stinking fish who must not be allowed to pollute our school any more."

It was like a stab of ice in my heart. How could it be? Why me? What had I done? The answers came swiftly enough at a general meeting in which I had to stand at attention and hear my girlfriend in a clear, confident voice tell the whole school how I had secretly opposed the Party and had tried to enlist her co-operation in this effort. She said I had spoken maliciously of specific individuals, including Lin, and was plotting to restore the old pre-Communist government. She said that at first she thought she could persuade me to come forward and admit my mistakes, but now she realized I was too dangerous and had to be exposed. She looked straight ahead while reciting these lies. Her accusation, together with Lin's testimony that I was a secret rightist, sealed my fate.

They struggled and criticized me for several weeks. At first I just denied their accusations and refused to say anything else. I was enraged at her perfidy, at Lin's slippery behavior, and at all the rest of them who unhesitatingly joined the hue and cry against me. It wasn't fair and I had become a convenient target, a handy scapegoat to get the rest off the hook. They dragged out my past and accused me of having a reactionary class background because my father had been a landlord under the KMT. I said that I hadn't seen my family for eight years and that I came north to serve the revolution as a good cadre. But Lin and his toadies fabricated all kinds of accusations and my girlfriend sealed my fate. True, I had been politically naive, but I never consciously opposed the Party. I had assumed that the Party's request for criticism was legitimate and had confided my innermost thoughts to someone I had trusted. Now my career was in ashes. Try as I might, I could not prevent them from putting the rightist hat on my head.[4] The more I protested, the worse it became.

For several weeks I stayed at the school, took meals by myself, and underwent struggle and criticism. I was forced to confess to a number of rightist crimes, which included "trying to hide my counterrevolutionary class background"; "secretly trying to undermine the Party's authority at the school"; and "plotting with others to restore KMT supremacy." I wrote a confession that took weeks to finish, and then they sent me to Hulin, an isolated farm for cadres in the northeast, 100 kilometers from the Soviet border. There must have been a thousand of us there. Conditions were primitive, the work harsh. We spent most of our time in the forests, planting, tending, and cutting trees. It was tough work and when we weren't on the job we would be in political study sessions. All of us were being reeducated, and some had been at Hulin from before the Hundred Flowers campaign. What a group we were! Some had been high-level cadres in Peking; many were Party members; all had stumbled and fallen at a critical time in their careers; all of us felt the injustice of what happened and our own powerlessness in the face of Party policy.

Most of my time at Hulin was spent outdoors or in rewording my confession. You see, they had trouble with this confession because, except for my father's landlord status, there was no other concrete flaw in my record. So they made me invent conspiracies and put words in my mouth.[5] I finally just wrote what they told me to, and then things began to get better. Within a few months I was told "your political attitude has improved," and then I was released after having spent nearly two years there. Actually the last year wasn't so bad. The work had toughened me up, and I had grown used to the political reeducation sessions. They taught me a lot. I was no longer a political simpleton. I had learned how to mask my true feelings and how to repeat the correct phrases when required. Still I was a "broken reed," someone who had a black mark on his record, and I knew that I could never expect much for my career again.

They sent me to a suburban farm belonging to the Central Offices Cadres School, where I labored for three more years until they finally took off my rightist hat in late 1962.[6] Now I no longer had to perform manual labor and was sent to Peking where I was reinstated as a cadre in the Central Offices Cadres School. They let me do administrative work but did not allow me to teach. Although I had worn my rightist hat for five years, I was considered by most to be "a pretty good guy." The work was routine and I had a decent income, but I knew my dreams of being at the top had been permanently shattered. I had made it to Peking but was branded as a political misfit. I would never be trusted with a responsible job.

I was luckier than some, however. Of the five of us that had been sent for reeducation, two had committed suicide. One had been sent with his entire family to the northwest. I didn't know where the other two were, but it's clear they never got back their old jobs. Old Lin had died, apparently without suffering from his two-faced behavior. My ex-girlfriend was in Nanking married to a cadre with a safe class background. I hope for his sake he keeps his mouth shut when she's around.

I suppose that being in Peking took the place of a dashed

career. Living in Peking is a privilege for most Chinese. We all try
to get a permit (*hukou*) to live in the city, because it's the center
(*zhongyang*) of everything. Shanghai may be more worldly and
Shanghai goods may be of better quality. Kunming may have the
best climate. But if given a choice everybody would choose to live
in Peking. I loved the city, even though it's a tense place and the
weather isn't so good. The seasons of the year run into one another so that autumn slips into winter without warning. Not like
in Harbin. In Peking it's windy and hot in the summers. You
went to the bathhouse whenever possible. Being a southerner I
was used to keeping myself clean, whereas northerners bathed
only once or twice a year. When the March dust storms came,
however, even the bathhouses didn't help to keep me clean.

I lived in dormitory housing provided by the school. At first I
shared a room 100 feet square with three others. Each of us had a
single bed and a desk. It was very cheap, costing 70 cents a month
for rent, water, and electricity. We had a 25-watt lightbulb, but
we didn't use it much since we worked in our offices on most
nights. Offices were five minutes away. The area in the Hepingli
district had been a large cemetery before Liberation. In 1954
they began to move the cemetery to another place—I can't recall
where. When I first visited the district in 1957 while on a business
trip to Peking just before the Hundred Flowers campaign, it was
bare, with only a few five-storey buildings scattered about. Now
it is a prosperous area with attractive buildings and plenty of
trees. In fact, Hepingli has become a model district to which
foreigners are often taken. In the early days they used coal for
cooking and heat. Later gas pipes were brought in, and each
kitchen had three gas stoves that individuals and families used in
turn. In winter most people had small coal heaters in their rooms.
Our building was fancier and we had central heating. It was a
good place to live in. In the older parts of Peking, floors were
made of mud and when it rained people got soaking wet. Most of
the city's roads were not paved till 1954, when they began to cover
them with tar. Most Peking housing had no indoor plumbing and
you used the public watertap outside, on the street. But in Hepingli we had indoor plumbing, asphalt roads, and concrete
floors.

Every unit wanted to control its own housing and wanted to
use its housing allocation as a way of gaining status and keeping

its employees. Housing wasn't supposed to cost more than 50 to 70 yuan per square meter of space to build, but many dormitories cost over 100-120 yuan per square meter. I used to visit friends in other buildings where they had spent far more than they should have on housing materials and frills. One housing area had deliberately been constructed with extra large halls and smooth floors on which people could dance. These dances were really something until they were ordered stopped in the early sixties. They tried to halt this misuse of state funds by setting up a National Offices Management Administration, which was to work together with the Peking City Planning Bureau. But the special buildings with frills kept going up. When an important ministry claps its hands, everybody dances to its command. That's the way it always was in Peking all those years. Nothing ever really changes.

When other parts of China had food shortages we were better off in Peking, probably because the Party wanted Peking to be well stocked to show foreigners that all was well. Also, many high-level cadres live in the city and they always demand special privileges. I heard that when food rationing started in 1954, Peking residents received an even larger share than they now get. We had the best cultural events, and I went to any performance that was playing. I'd trade off food and clothing coupons for hard-to-get tickets. I probably saw every film shown in Peking. I remember seeing lots of foreign films, especially Soviet, but also English, French, and Japanese. Some of them I saw six or seven times just because they were something different to see and do. On days off, I walked a lot, did some shopping, or rode my bicycle. I liked to see friends who worked in the city's many research institutes, and we would spend time together, sometimes just walking and talking. The Summer Palace was one of my favorite spots and it was good to get away to relax there. I never had a serious girlfriend. My experience in Harbin had left scars. Also, as a rightist I wasn't a good match. Any girl who had political sense would avoid getting entangled with me. In Peking there were plenty of cadres who were good prospects, with clean class backgrounds. I was an outsider, still a southerner, with a broken career and a bad class background.

At work it was much the same. I was shut out from the mainstream. The odd jobs without political risk were left to me, and I

was never again allowed to teach what I knew on a formal basis.
Informally it was different. The instructors would discuss economics, statistics, and planning problems with me, and they
recognized my experience and knowledge. But many books and
documents were closed to my eyes, and I knew that there was a
thick dossier about me sitting in the Public Security Bureau. It
was a funny feeling. You felt as if at any moment someone could
jump up and stick a dunce cap on your head. No room for error;
no chance to breathe. Even if you stayed on your very best behavior you knew that at a moment's notice the Party could pull
the string and dangle your rightist status in front of the masses.
So, whenever a campaign emerged in Peking, you sucked in your
breath, studied political events closely, and hoped that the storm
clouds would pass.

It was interesting to watch the rise of Peng Zhen, mayor of
Peking. He was also the city's first secretary and eventually became one of the three or four most powerful men in China. Peng
Zhen made a big point of saying how he would make Peking a
model city for the peoples of the East. He said he would make Peking as clean as a mirror. One of the projects he directed was the
famous filling in of Dragon's Beard Ditch near the Temple of
Heaven. This disease-ridden stinking ditch had been a symbol of
the backwardness and exploitation of the old days. Peng wanted
to make Peking the most beautiful city in China. He wanted to
use only the best materials, for example, bringing marble all the
way from Yunnan province. Later, when he was toppled during
the Cultural Revolution, he was accused of using his power to
accomplish selfish personal goals for Peking at the expense of the
national interest.

But Peng was determined to make Peking a showcase. To
achieve this, he pushed forward a number of key projects. He
made the Peking railroad station the largest in Asia — at least
that's what he claimed when it was built. I've never been to all the
big Asian cities so I can't tell if it really is the biggest, but it certainly is impressive. Peng was in charge of constructing the
famous "triple ten" buildings in Peking in 1958 [ten buildings in
ten months to celebrate ten years of Liberation]. These included
the railway station, TV center, Great Hall of the People, the
Workers' Stadium, the Cultural Palace of the Minorities, the
Agricultural Exhibition Hall, the Museums of Chinese History

and of the Chinese Revolution, the National Art Gallery, the Military Museum of the Chinese Revolution, and the Peking airport. These are the buildings that today are Peking's most famous new buildings. Peng also extended Changan, the main street, for 10 kilometers in both directions and widened it to 150 meters from 50 meters.

Peng had all kinds of ideas. He wanted to tear down the old residential buildings and replace them with a totally new city.[7] But Chairman Mao objected, saying it was too expensive to tear down the hutongs, and he also asked where the money would be found to compensate those who had to be relocated. In the struggle between Mao and Peng, Liu Shaoqi was on Peng's side.[8] Peng wanted to build a new Zhongnanhai, the elite residential area, for top Chinese leaders such as Mao, Peng, and Liu. Peng wanted to make it something special, like an emperor's palace, but Mao opposed this. Liu sided with Peng because Liu always thought that after Mao's death he could "inherit the emperor's throne." You may think this sounds like a lot of gossip, but in those days, those of us involved in planning and economic development had a pretty good sense of what was going on in the city. I first heard those rumors even before I was branded a rightist, and they were common knowledge in Peking.

After Mao opposed his grandiose schemes, Peng had to be content with more modest plans. He still wanted Peking to be a special place, but then so did most of the top Party leaders. The idea was to make Peking even better than Moscow, with greenery, wide streets, and monumental buildings. We decided to build a subway modeled after Moscow's, which we knew was the best in the world, even though we didn't need a subway for Peking's transportation needs. Still, when you think about it, Peking is the best-planned city in China. It is way ahead of Shanghai, Wuhan, or Canton. Maybe Peng wasn't all that wrong. He started the subway-planning process in 1958, with Liu's support and over Mao's objections. Design and survey work was slowed because of the problems of the Great Leap Forward and the Three Difficult Years, but by 1965 construction had begun in earnest. Peng was also largely responsible for the redevelopment of Tiananmen, the huge central square, despite opposition. In the end he was right in expanding the square even though Mao had disagreed. Also the people living around Tiananmen didn't want to leave their

homes in the surrounding hutongs, even if Peking's urban reconstruction was a good example of "socialist progress."

When the Cultural Revolution came, it quickly washed me
out to suburban Peking where I went back to work in our office's
farm unit. Fortunately, even though old rightists were a choice
target for Red Guards and nervous Party officials, I managed to
avoid most of the struggling and lay low, only 85 kilometers from
the heart of China's power struggle. The times were by no means
easy for me, and I had to get involved in many unpleasant political intrigues to avoid another disaster. This time I was careful
and managed to tie in with the right faction, at the right time.
My hat was not put back on my head, and I was left to labor on
the farm for three years until, at the beginning of 1970, they gave
me permission to return to my native village in Guangdong
province.

[*This was the one part of the interview where the narrator
was evasive and avoided giving any details. I suspect he had a
harder time of it during the Cultural Revolution than he cared
to mention. As a former rightist, he undoubtedly was a prime
target for struggle by Red Guards and by those Party officials
who were looking for targets to escape being "unhorsed"
themselves. Later, when ex-rightists were no longer a primary
target, he didn't have to endure political struggles, but farm work
was difficult and his life deteriorated.*]

When 1970 came, I was forty years old, a man without career or hopes. At a time when I should have been in my prime,
with sons already old enough to contribute to my household,
there I was alone and, as the saying goes, "like a man with three
nostrils, two of them shedding tears." I had thought of suicide
several times, but my personal pride was strong enough to keep
me going. The pride that had blinded me a dozen years ago and
had robbed me of a career now preserved my life. Others around
me succumbed to the violence and despair of the times, deciding
that self-inflicted death was better than endless personal indigni-
ties and hopelessness. Sometimes, however, I never was sure
whether they had committed suicide or had been murdered.[9]

For no apparent reason, the farm's cadres abruptly called
me in one day and asked me about my home village in Guang-

dong. "Have you been back since 1950?" "No," I replied, "I have not." "Do you ever write to your family?" "Only twice in all the years," I replied, "and that was only when I was sent to Hulin in 1957, and later when my father died in 1963." "Do you have any relatives there?" "Yes, two sisters and a brother, but I haven't heard from them for eight years."

It was an odd conversation. After all those years to start talking about my home village! But they had something in mind, that's for sure, and I had begun to hear rumors about people being sent from Peking back to their villages.[10] Especially discredited cadres like myself. Maybe they would send me back, and maybe this would be a chance to find some personal security away from all the turmoil. My Peking office job was a dead end. I had no family obligations and was homesick for the south. My accent had always stamped me as "inferior" in northern eyes, although I had always felt it was the other way around. Anyway, within a very short time I found myself on a train bound for Canton. There had been no tearful goodbyes when I left. One or two friends had seen me off and that was all. My belongings were stuffed into one bag. I had my special grain coupons allowing me to eat in other parts of China during the two-day train ride. My Peking residence permit had been officially canceled, and I could never again legally live in Peking. I gave away some warm underwear and heavy clothing to my friends, since there would be no more harsh winters to endure.

I was going home, but I didn't really have any feeling for "home." I was being sent back because I had no other place to go. When I returned, my family made an effort to make me feel welcome. My older brother had taken over my father's house, and even though he had jammed it full of children (five), chickens, and pigs, he found a spot for me. My two sisters were living with their husbands' families, so I saw them only occasionally. My younger sister's husband was a brigade cadre, and it was politically unwise for him to invite me, a rightist, into his house. I think I was a real embarrassment to him, a walking career setback. My brother, though, was understanding and helped me settle in, introduced me to his friends, and was sympathetic when listening to my story. "You should have written to us, little brother," he said. "You know we often wondered about your fate when we were riding out the political storms here. Our father did not have an easy time of it. This hut is all that remains of his prosperous estate. But he managed to survive all the struggles, and in ill health he finally died. We've fitted in well with the new system. My two eldest sons are team cadres, and we're politically clean."

They put me to work in the brigade accounting office, even though I had volunteered to go out and work in the fields. I complained: "You treat me like a cadre but, remember, I've labored in the fields for a half-dozen years since I left here." In the accounting office I worked with Pang, whom I remembered from the old days. Pang had worked hard, raised a family, had a good job, and was a Party member. He liked to lecture me about the correct political line, but he did it in a good-natured way, well aware of the fine line that separated good and bad cadres, especially here in the south.[11]

It was interesting to live once more in a southern village and see the differences between peasants in north and south. Peasants around Peking had only a primary education or even less than that, maybe two or three years of primary education altogether. Older peasants in the north were usually illiterate. Northerners weren't as concerned about education as we are in the south. In Mei county we had several middle schools, and even before Liberation many peasants in my home village had gone to middle school. Of course, a lot of us were Hakka and had a tradition of being more interested in education than most Han Chinese. Even our women could sometimes get a middle school education. Peasant girls in the north hardly ever went more than a few years to primary school. I can't remember meeting many northern peasant girls with an education, but in my home county almost every girl went to junior middle school. We really prized education there, and I think the reason is that we've been exposed to the ideas of the West concerning the value of education. The majority of Chinese living outside China come from the south, and we're influenced by ideas on education which we get from our relatives living abroad.*

For a while life settled into a typical village routine. My work

---

*It is interesting to note that in the whole of Guangdong province there is only one nationally known middle school. It is located in Mei county and not in the city of Canton. Ye Jianying, one of China's top leaders, graduated from this school. (I am indebted to Martin K. Whyte for this observation.)

was easy and I relaxed. Thoughts turned to finding me a wife. Pang and my brother approached me one day about a widow in the next village ("she's from the same clan and a good worker"). It seemed that the time was ripe to start a family. She had two children who were almost grown up. It was not too late for me to raise some sons. We had a matchmaker discuss marriage details. Her family wasn't too anxious for her to marry someone with a bad class background. But she and I had met and actually liked each other. It looked at last as if I would finally settle down and raise a family, the most natural thing to do back in my home village.

Then came the campaign "To Criticize Confucius and Lin Biao." The new Party secretary had taken over in our commune, and he went after people like myself, who "never reform their ideas and live among us spreading their class poison and undermining the masses." By early 1974 I was back in the old routine of being a target, getting struggled, and under daily supervision. Even Pang's good nature hardened and we talked in slogans rather than from the heart. As always happens in such campaigns, people try to stay away from obvious trouble. Few people talked with me unless they chose to repeat the slogans and clichés of the campaign. My brother remained faithful, saying, "You're not the only one to blame. Everybody's face has a smudge on it. All pots have some black on them." Still, there were major consequences. My intended bride's family decided that I was too much of a risk and called the marriage off. I found myself completely isolated again, this time in my own village. At the age of forty-three, alone in my home village, there were precious few options left. I had an uncle in Hong Kong and decided to start a fresh life. Escaping isn't that hard. You have to know the escape routes and either swim or find a boat. I decided that swimming was easier and safer, since I didn't have to rely on anybody. Thus it was at the end of 1974 that I dragged myself up on dry land in Hong Kong, leaving behind a life of ups and downs—more downs than ups actually. I became a factory worker in Hong Kong and now earn a good living. I haven't married and I guess I never will.

Sometimes I find life in Hong Kong just too frantic and too hard to swallow. The crime and the dirt are worse than I had imagined. Yet I do feel freer than I have felt for nearly twenty years. It's a chance to live my life a second time, without a big black mark beside my name. I feel somehow that I have failed China. I should still be in Peking, helping to build a socialist economy and not here working for a capitalist factory owner. All that training, all the knowledge — it vanished like an April Peking snowfall. I had puffed myself up like a dragon who was so big he couldn't find his tail. It was my rightist tail that tripped me up, and it was my own fault. I had a great future and wasn't careful enough. It's tough when you wind up in a foreign place, without any sons to feed you when you're old and with a failed career. I didn't deserve such a fate, but at least I'm alive and healthy.

[*The narrator left China because he felt that his rightist status was too great a burden to bear for the rest of his life. As with most refugees, he had mixed feelings about this choice. It is irrevocable and almost nobody goes back. Hong Kong life is tough, and for many the capitalist world is a big shock. He managed to get a factory job through his uncle's connections. In 1975 he was slowly getting used to the pace of capitalist life, and he may yet even find a woman and raise a family, despite his gloomy predictions. Most refugees integrate rather quickly into Hong Kong's socioeconomic setting, and he seemed to be someone who would be able to adjust. After all, he adjusted to living far from home, in the north of China; he survived three major political crises (1957, 1966-1970, 1973-74); he worked both as a cadre and as a farm laborer.*

It is interesting to note that, in 1978, the Chinese began to restore full rights to others like him who were accused of being rightists over twenty years ago. Hundreds of thousands have apparently been rehabilitated. Based on recent Party decisions, former rightists will get a full pardon and may resume their old jobs with the stigma of "rightist" removed from their official dossiers. Had the narrator stayed in China, he might well have received his old job back. He might now even be able to resume his career as teacher of cadres and as economist-planner, perhaps not in Peking and not as a Party member, but with a chance for at least a decent career with a white-washed political record behind him. However, one recalls the official in Prisoner of Mao *who compared rehabilitated prisoners to cracked dishes: "If you drop a plate on the floor, Bao, there will always be cracks no matter how carefully you glue it back together again."*[12]]

Rubber Man

THE CHINESE ARMY, aside from its main task of guaranteeing the security of China's borders, performs many other tasks. As a political decision maker, it helped govern China during the chaos of the Cultural Revolution, and it still exerts an important influence on central-level politics. As administrators, army men have provided the organizational structure and discipline to maintain order where civil authority is absent or inadequate. As a socializer, the three-million-member army recruits youth from one part of China and sends them to another part of the nation, in a process that invariably breaks down localist tendencies and develops a greater awareness of national goals and policies. As an employer, the army runs its own farms on the borders, performs public works projects, and teaches specialized skills to many peasant recruits who otherwise would remain in the villages, performing routine agricultural labor. Finally, the army serves as a model to be emulated by China's youth. It is essentially a volunteer army—only one out of every ten volunteers is accepted—and the standards are relatively high. Those accepted acquire status, mobility, and the prospect of better job opportunities after demobilization, but they must conform to an official image of an organization that "serves the people" in a selfless fashion, emphasizing close contact with the masses.

Sometimes it is not easy to live up to this image. The following story in part illustrates the problems that the army faces in fulfilling its many functions. In this case, the army was ordered in the late sixties to step in and take over the administration of rubber plantations on the island of Hainan off China's southern coast. Hainan, because of its location, posed security dangers to the Chinese. Moreover, continued production of rubber was of strategic importance to China, which must import rubber from Southeast Asia to satisfy its current needs. Hainan was also a volatile place, with large numbers of sent-down youth, demobilized soldiers, and the presence of Li and Miao minority nationality groups. The latter were generally hostile to the Han Chinese, who in turn thought of the Li and Miao as backward savages. Many sent-down youth yearned to return to Canton and other cities from which they had been "exiled," and their lukewarm feelings about their new home in Hainan were reflected in low labor productivity. The soldiers harbored grudges against the army because few had chosen to settle in Hainan and they had been ordered demobilized there against their wishes.

Commander Pang and his subordinates do their best, but rubber production under their administration declines sharply and everyone is pleased to see them go. Even the army is relieved when it hands the farm back to the civilian administration in 1972. Now the business of rubber tapping could resume as before, and production rose significantly. The army is gone, although the problems of the sent-down youth, the Li and the Miao, and the demobilized soldiers remain unchanged.

I WORKED ON A RUBBER PLANTATION for seven years. We got up at 5 a.m., had a quick breakfast, and went out to tap trees for the precious latex. The best time is just after sunrise, when the latex flows most easily. We made a diagonal cut on the tree extending a third or even a half the distance around the base at a 30-degree angle. We tried to be very careful not to injure the tree during tapping, because damaged bark and latex vessels take several years to regenerate. By the way latex, unlike sap, comes from the bark. The latex ran into cups we attached to the trees, and then the cups were emptied into pails and taken away to be processed at the battalion rubber factory, where we made crude-rubber sheets for shipment to the rest of China. Our company was responsible for 30 rubber-tree units, each containing 200 to 300 trees. There were one hundred of us in the company, of whom sixty were classified as able-bodied rubber workers. The others were either dependents or people working at other assigned tasks. Thus sixty of us were responsible for between 6000 and 9000 trees, and a person had to tend, on the average, over 100 trees.

That was quite a responsibility, especially since many of us had come to Hainan having never worked in the countryside, let alone at growing rubber, and most of us had not volunteered to come to this hot, sticky, tropical island. Of the one hundred in our company, forty-five were demobilized soldiers who had been recruited to come to Hainan by means of a generous demobilization allowance. Another fifteen were sent-down youth who had been given an ultimatum: "Either go to Hainan or to the Yingde labor camps."[1] The remaining forty were local peasants who had lived in the area for some time, from the plantation's beginnings a few years earlier. The local peasants taught us techniques that they, in turn, had learned painfully through experience. It wasn't easy to grow rubber trees, especially in an area of relatively new cultivation. It took seven to ten years for the rubber trees to be ready for tapping, and the young saplings constantly needed protection from disease, especially from a local fungus that destroyed the leaves and buds of young trees. We also had to keep cutting away the scrub and weeds that quickly grew back around the newly planted trees, to prevent them from being choked by underbrush. We were always clearing land to plant new rubber trees. In reclaiming this virgin land we first planted sweet potatoes and then peanuts. This kept the scrub and weeds from growing back so rapidly. Then we planted the rubber saplings while continuing to plant sweet potatoes, peanuts, or vegetables around the trees. When the rubber trees had grown high enough, we stopped interspersing other crops, and then we considered the land permanently cleared.

We were always experimenting with our plantation because rubber was in scarce supply, and we were always being asked to produce more. When you enter the gates of our plantation there's a large faded red and white sign with the characters "Vigorously Develop Rubber Production in Order To Satisfy the Nation's Needs." The army and the Party organizations tried their hardest to raise production, but even Chairman Mao's best quotations can't make latex flow any faster. We tried bud grafting, where a dormant bud from a high-yielding tree is grafted onto a one- or two-year-old rubber seedling, and also artificial pollination. Most important, we conducted experiments to determine the best rates of tapping; for example, some trees did not get tapped daily because they produced more latex when only tapped three times a week. Others yielded the largest and steadiest amounts of latex if tapped daily. We found the best yields came during the dry season, and we stopped tapping during the rainy season. We never tapped in December or January. From time to time we rested our trees, especially the ones that had only just begun to produce latex. Experiments had shown that too much tapping early in a tree's development stunted its capacity to produce large amounts of latex. We rested the trees periodically, even though we were under constant pressure to raise production. When the army took over the rubber farm in 1970, we were told: "Forget about those stupid experiments. Just get us more rubber out of those trees. The state needs rubber right away." Those were the words of the battalion commander who had been sent from Guangdong to take over the farm. Later, when yields dropped and trees had been seriously damaged, some of them permanently, he sang a different tune: "We must preserve China's wealth and learn to use our resources effectively." By that time the army was pulling out anyway, so he probably didn't care anymore about setting production records.

I lived in Hainan from 1968 to 1975. In November 1968 I was sent down to the rubber farm. There was never any thought in my mind of volunteering to go there. In the first place, who wants to leave Canton? And Hainan had a reputation as a dead-end place, just far enough from Canton to make it difficult to return home easily. I was sixteen years old and had just graduated from Junior Middle School No. 2, in Canton. There were eight hundred of us, junior and senior graduates awaiting assignments to the countryside. Fifty lucky ones stayed on at the school to become instructors. The rest were sent away either to Hainan or to Boluo county in Guangdong. They put me in the Hainan group and, no matter how I resisted, I couldn't escape my fate. I tried to hide out in Canton, but they caught me. Then I disappeared a second time and they put pressure on my family to make me go. Finally I was told bluntly that it was either Hainan or Yingde, although they did say that I wouldn't stay forever. Well, I stayed for seven years, maybe not forever but certainly a long, long time for a sixteen-year-old on his way to being twenty-three.

So I wasn't "chosen," I was ordered to go, and under those circumstances you'd expect that I wouldn't like it. Yet after the first few months I did grow to like it and might easily have settled down there forever. There was a group of us, all sent-down youth, and we became good friends, living together and enjoying one another's company. Because it was a state farm, we received a fixed salary and were in a better position economically than our Canton classmates who had been sent to Boluo communes, where they practically starved to death on the work-point system.[2] We got a fixed income, day in and day out, and it was enough to live on. I loved sugar cane and the island was full of it—nothing better than sucking at stalks of broken sugar cane while working in the fields. Hainan was rich with fruits and vegetables, and there were bananas, even pineapples and grapefruit. I didn't mind the tropical climate in the least. Most of all, I liked to grow rubber. I had never seen rubber trees before and, until I arrived in Hainan, had never realized how rubber was made. Here was a whole island devoted to making rubber by sticking cups in trees and then heating the liquid to make a thick spongy substance that was airtight, waterproof, and resilient. At the age of sixteen, I was truly amazed. Then, as I stayed on, caught up in the task of serving China, and as our production kept rising, I became involved in being a "rubber man." I began to listen to those peasants who had been there the longest and who knew how to raise and take care of the trees. I could see the possibilities of better scientific techniques and better ways to increase latex yields. They made me a team leader, and then at the age of twenty-two I was appointed to a position at the next highest level, the company level. So I guess you could say I was like one of those reluctant brides who is pushed into an arranged marriage and then truly falls in love with her husband. If I hadn't left China, I bet I'd still be at the rubber farm right now, a Party member, in a top position, maybe in charge of scientific techniques or something like that.

I left for personal reasons. My girlfriend had returned to Canton and I applied to go there, partly to be with her and also to attend higher agricultural school. When I got back, I found my mother seriously ill and this kept me occupied with family affairs. Then two events occurred that permanently altered my life. My application for agricultural school was turned down, for no apparent reason. I was heartbroken because I wanted to pursue a career in agriculture, perhaps to return to Hainan as a skilled specialist who could make a real contribution. But they turned me down saying, "You can go back to Hainan and do what you have been doing there already." The other thing that happened was that my girlfriend had gone to Hong Kong (legally) to visit relatives and did not return. Through a third person I learned she intended to stay and wanted me to join her. At first I couldn't think of leaving, but my rejection as an applicant to agricultural school had given me second thoughts about returning to agricultural work. At the age of sixteen I had already started one new life; maybe, at age twenty-three, it was time to start another. So I swam across the bay with ease — all those years in agricultural work had made me strong enough.

I can't really speak for the other sent-down youth, because each individual has his own reasons for staying or leaving the countryside, personal reasons that he'll probably never divulge to anybody, even to a close friend. At our farm many sent-down youth did leave, some of them illegally. They just would go home on vacation and then disappear, usually in Canton. Others who had influential parents were able to get their stay shortened to less than two years. Because I was so young and hadn't been thinking of a career, unlike many of the twenty-year-olds, maybe I was less disappointed at going there. Then again, there were a few who genuinely liked Hainan, worked hard, and quickly moved into responsible jobs. They usually found a woman and thought of settling down. Some are still there, even though they could probably have left by now if they really wanted to.

When I arrived in 1968, the plantation was a state farm with a population of 15,000, of which approximately 9000 were able-bodied workers and the rest dependents. It was a fairly large farm, measuring over 15 kilometers from north to south and 50 kilometers from east to west, in all, about 750 square kilometers. The farm had been established in the later fifties, but the bulk of the trees had been planted in the past decade. Rubber was the main crop, although we also planted subsidiary crops for our own consumption. The farm was divided into eight subfarms and each subfarm was again divided into teams. The whole farm was under the jurisdiction of the Bureau of State Farms of Guangdong province, which set the annual production plans and targets for rubber production. The farm director, together with the Party secretary, reported directly to the bureau and needed its approval for all major decisions affecting rubber production. On smaller matters not directly affecting the farm's main cash crop, we could make our own decisions—for example, how many peanuts to plant or how much land to devote to vegetables. Until late 1969 when the army took over, therefore, the farm was run like any other state farm in China.[3]

In late 1969 the state farm was taken over by the military, as was the case with most of the other hundred state farms on the island. Now we fell under the management of the Canton Military Region Production and Construction Army Corps head-quartered in Haikou, the island's largest city. The reasons for the military takeover were never made clear, but presumably it had to do with political struggles during the Cultural Revolution. We assumed that the military farms were formed mainly in border regions for security purposes and, given our proximity to Taiwan, it made sense to strengthen the military presence on the island. Later, however, when these military farms were being phased out in 1974, we were told that the military takeover had just been "one of Lin Biao's schemes to set up a revisionist reserve army" that would be loyal to him when Lin tried to take over from Chairman Mao. In 1969, we had no inkling of any schemes or plots—we just assumed it was part of the ongoing political strug-gle in Guangdong and in Peking. Since our rubber was vital, re-gardless of whose line was in command, we knew we would expe-rience minimal disruption of production during the transition. The civilian cadres were not dismissed; they merely became the deputies of the military personnel that had been sent to the farm. The farm was reclassified administratively along military lines, and thus it was now called a regiment rather than a farm. The subfarm became a battalion, the production brigades became companies, and teams became squads. The farm director now became the assistant or deputy to the regiment commander; the old Party secretary now was the deputy to the political commissar of the regiment. The army placed its personnel in all key admin-istrative and production levels so that any important decision would have to be made by a military man. In all, about sixty army men became cadres of the new military farm, a small number but enough to take the farm over completely. None of the civilian cadres was ever purged, and it was almost as if the

political struggles of the Cultural Revolution had been deliberately excluded from our plantation. The army went out of its way
to work with the old cadres and to utilize their experience. As
Commander Pang himself reportedly once said, "What do we
know about rubber? Our job is just to carry out Chairman Mao's
instructions. We came here to help you, not to cause any
trouble."

Most of the cadres and farm workers breathed a sigh of relief
when they realized that the military's role really was administrative rather than political. However, tensions and problems inevitably developed. The military had its own ideas about how to
organize 15,000 people, and it didn't know that much about
farming. Commander Pang wasn't there to preside over any political purges, but he still politicized our lives at the farm because
he took the slogan "politics in command" to heart. Consequently,
the early months of military administration were quite confusing.
For the first half of 1970 we only worked on the plantation in the
mornings. The rest of the day we had to read Chairman Mao's
Thoughts and participate in political study sessions. The army
had its own newspaper, and one day it announced that the slogan
at our plantation gate ("vigorously develop rubber production in
order to satisfy the nation's needs") had actually been first said by
Lin Biao ten years ago. Lin, the head of the armed forces, reportedly also had said at that time, "Vigorously develop tropical
crops." We were told that Liu Shaoqi had suppressed these two
quotations of Lin Biao's and only now, once the counterrevolutionary nature of Liu's revisionist thought had been exposed,
were we finally able to see the correctness of Lin's thought. We
studied these two quotations, as well as all the usual selections
from the daily press and from the Chairman's works. Commander
Pang used to say, "Politics is the spirit and the decisive factor in
all our work. Once we all think in a proletarian way, our production will rise like a rocket."

Unfortunately, the results of so much political study were
contrary to Commander Pang's expectations. Because we had
spent so much time away from the fields, we didn't have enough
time to do our farm work. Rubber production began to decrease,
and so did subsidiary production. Not only were we not meeting
our quotas, but we couldn't grow enough paddy rice, sweet potatoes, and peanuts for personal consumption. The military farm

had become an economic drain on the state instead of a prized asset. So after six months the commander one day announced that political study sessions would cease because "the army and the Party are pleased with the great rise in political consciousness that has taken place." Now the reverse occurred — all work and no study. We worked like hell, day after day, sometimes for several months at a time without a day off. We accelerated our tree-tapping frequency so much that I remember being forced against my better judgment to tap the same tree 38 times in one month (common practice for such a tree was 20 times a month). For a whole year we abused our trees in this fashion. Production rose significantly, but the long-term cost in exhausted trees was incalculable. From mid-1970 to the beginning of 1972 we lived as if it were another Great Leap Forward. Individual households were not allowed to cook their own meals and families had to eat in the company dining halls. Older peasants grumbled, saying, "It's like those ridiculous days of the public dining halls back in 1959." Farm members were forbidden to raise a few chickens or to grow vegetables for personal use. It was impossible to leave the farm even to visit sick family members. If you were genuinely ill, as sworn to by a doctor's certificate, you could get no more than ten days off at full pay. On the eleventh day, they started deducting a full day's pay if you were absent, regardless of the reasons. Needless to say, there were no raises in pay during those eighteen months.

Abruptly in 1972 everything returned to normal again. All excesses, both of too much stress on politics and the subsequent reversal to overemphasis on production, were condemned by the army and the Party. The blame was placed on Lin Biao because he "had deliberately tried to sabotage the national economy" in his mistaken plot to overthrow the Party and Chairman Mao. The army abruptly stopped referring to Lin Biao's two slogans about rubber production and tropical agriculture. Commander Pang was arrested and replaced soon after Lin Biao was purged. A new commander arrived and immediately announced that he knew nothing about farming and expected the old farm director (his deputy) actively to help him run the farm. About a year or so later, in June 1974, we learned of a central government document circulating around the island. The document suggested that the army should leave the farms, turning them back into state farms under civilian administration. It gave several reasons for this decision. First, the military farms had been formed by Lin Biao as part of his plot to undermine the Party. Now that Lin Biao was discredited, they could be eliminated. Second, state farms operating under military control were a real burden on the national economy, since they all cost the state money. Thus, while labor was well organized under military control, productivity as a whole remained low because military management was not as capable as civilian cadres. Third, the state farms had run well before the military takeover so they could easily run that way again if put back in civilian hands. Attached to this central government document was another from the Guangdong Provincial Party Committee, recommending approval of the suggestion that the military hand back the state farm to the civilians.

It was clear that the army was about to pull out. We were soon asked to comment on these documents, and of course most of us agreed that we were better off in civilian hands. Even the large group of demobilized soldiers who had settled in at the state farm preferred civilian administrators. The sent-down youth were ambivalent because, while they knew the military lacked the appropriate skills to manage the farm, the military had also been fair, had worked hard, and indeed had measured up to its official image as a group of modest, dedicated servants of Party and people. The third group, the local peasants who had worked on the state farm since its creation, were happy to see the army go because its departure meant better management and higher productivity. They wanted the farm back in familiar hands. And so in 1974 the deed was done. In a few days the last trucks left with our commanders, commissars, and captains. The regiments, battalions, companies, and squads were replaced by farms, subfarms, brigades, and teams. The old slogan exhorting us to produce more rubber remained intact at the front gate — only now it wasn't attributed to Lin Biao (if in fact he had ever really said it).

Let me tell you about the various groups on the farm and how they got along with each other. The demobilized soldiers were a real problem for the military. Demobilized soldiers had been settling in Hainan for some time, and some of the older personnel at the farm had been demobilized soldiers as far back as the late fifties and early sixties. According to local gossip, in 1960 a group of demobilized soldiers staged a minor rebellion in

Haikou because they didn't want to go to the rubber plantations, but they were suppressed and sent to the farms. At that time the rebellious demobilized soldiers complained that they had a bad deal in comparison with other demobilized soldiers who had been sent to the cities and received higher pay for less arduous labor and a far better life style. That was a decade previously. During the sixties these resentments gradually faded as the number of demobilized-soldier settlers dropped sharply. But at the beginning of the seventies a new group arrived, and the same old grumblings arose again; only this time there were added complications. First, the new group of demobilized soldiers hoped to get preferential treatment, now that the army was running the farm. To their disappointment this was not the case—indeed, feelings of strong antagonism developed between the ex-soldiers and their army bosses. Second, the new demobilized soldiers found out that even after a decade of resettlement, the economic position of the old demobilized soldiers was relatively poor. So the new group didn't see any long-range prospects for their own relative economic betterment.

Ugly incidents occurred in which frustrated demobilized soldiers were the main participants. For example, we were under martial law from late 1969 to 1974, and during that time there were several instances of insubordination and even assaulting of superior officers. A regimental chief staff officer was beaten up by an ex-army farm worker. When soldiers came to his assistance they were also beaten up, one so seriously that he was in Haikou hospital for months. Several ex-army men were accused of raping sent-down women, and I recall one series of rapes that resulted in court martials for six ex-soldiers. Whenever there was crime or violence in the area, it was more than likely that dissatisfied demobilized soldiers were at the root of the trouble. Their main quarrel was with the military authorities. They didn't relate much to the sent-down youth, whom they considered to be a "bourgeois lot" (except for the girls, of course). Sent-down youth, especially those who arrived in the early seventies, were at the bottom of the pecking order because they were less productive economically than the other groups, and were more likely to leave after two or three years.

The sent-down youth associated with one another almost exclusively. Indeed, one of my jobs at the team and later at the

company level was to break down the barrier of clannishness that
the sent-down youth erected around themselves. At times they
were so clannish they deliberately talked to each other in their
local dialects so that the demobilized soldiers, peasants, or army
men could not understand them. It was partly because the sent-
down youth felt superior owing to their city background and
better educational training, and partly because they felt discriminated against since they could not work as well. Still, the
problems of the sent-down youth weren't nearly so serious in our
state farm as in most of the communes where other youth had
been sent. We experienced tension and lots of grumbling, and
many youth drifted off and disappeared, but by and large it was
better in Hainan than elsewhere in Guangdong. I'd say that at
least one out of every three sent-down youths was fairly happy on
our farm and many married and settled there permanently.

The local minority nationalities, the Li and the Miao, also
created special problems. To begin with, they disliked Han Chinese and wanted to have as little to do with us as possible. Less
than 10 percent of the state farm population were Li or Miao, but
the nearby villages were inhabited exclusively by them. As a
matter of fact, the nearest commune had no Han Chinese members. Even the cadres were minority people. The top cadres in
that commune were all Li, and their deputies were Miao. The Li
were more civilized than the Miao. Many of the latter remain in
the mountains and refuse to come to settle in the plains. I have
heard several people say that the Miao practice a form of black
magic and that their enemies mysteriously fall under evil spells.
Even Han cadres spread those stories. The Miao refuse to intermarry with other groups and have a primitive marriage custom in
which the man stays with the woman for three years at her place.
If during this time she produces a child, he then takes the woman
(and child) as his wife to his place. If there is no child, the marriage is nullified. The Li are a bit more civilized. When a Li girl
wants to marry, she asks her parents to build a hut for her and she
moves alone into that hut. Suitors competing for her hand in
marriage make daily visits to her hut and, when she decides upon
her partner, her parents contact the prospective husband's family
to arrange the marriage. Then they have a wedding feast and the
whole village is invited. The Li dislike the Han—maybe the word
"hate" is a better description of their feelings toward us, probably

because of the history of Han-Li relations.[4] So it was best not to enter a Li village if you didn't know someone because you stood a good chance of being beaten up. If you couldn't speak Li they'd never talk with you, since they didn't speak any other languages.

The minority groups were a problem for the army. In the first place, relations between the state farm and the neighboring communes had always been difficult, ever since the rubber plantation had expanded in the sixties. This usually boiled over into disputes about land because commune and state farm land was interspersed in some areas and the exact boundaries were always disputed. Sometimes if you planted crops too close to a disputed piece of land, you might find water buffalo tracks in the morning and the crops crushed. If your pigs and chickens strayed onto commune fields, you stood a good chance of never seeing them again. When our vegetables and fruits were ripening, even a hundred armed guards couldn't stop the Li from stealing them. Most of the state farm workers were angry at the way the Li treated us, and at the preferential treatment the state insisted on giving the Li, even though the Li were so hostile and uncooperative. The Li never fulfilled their production quotas; they didn't try to improve themselves; and they supplemented their meager incomes by engaging in the illegal selling of surplus cloth coupons to state farm members. They used most of this extra money to buy grain alcohol, which they drank in large amounts. Once we had a meeting, I recall, at which an angry team member complained about the Li and said, "It isn't right that we give preferential treatment to such a group of thieves and sluggards." At that point the Party secretary interrupted him: "It is Chairman Mao's policy to protect and nurture minority groups. Once they see how improved their lot has become under the Party's benign rule, they will shake off their feudal ways and develop their potential as a people. You must be patient. We all must be patient with our little children, the Li and the Miao." That was the official Party line and we were ordered to follow it, although we often wondered if it was worth it because our crops kept getting trampled and our chickens and pigs stolen, while the Li and Miao remained as implacably hostile and remote as ever.

At the farm we lived fairly simply, in brick dormitories, four bachelors to a room. There was no electricity and we used public lavatories located nearby in the compound. We ate our meals in the dining hall. Those who had families lived in a room and usually ate at home. My rice ration was 40 catties a month, enough to keep me going. I was also entitled to one catty of sugar per month which I could buy for 78 cents per catty. I also could buy one piece of soap each month costing 36 cents. My monthly food costs were about 10 yuan, and since my total salary was 28 yuan, this left me with 18 yuan for things like soap, clothing, and all other essentials. My needs were simple so I managed on this meager salary, but others could not and they devised ways to beat the system. For example, they would not use up their monthly rice ration at the dining hall, and then they had their surplus rice coupons changed into food coupons. With these food coupons you could go to eat at the regiment's restaurant, which had better-quality food since mainly cadres and army officers ate there. Sometimes the sent-down youth would buy extra soap and sugar from the local peasants who didn't need them and were willing to sell them for about 30 percent more than the official state price.

On Sundays I usually spent time with my friends. Sometimes I went on bicycle rides with a girlfriend; other times I visited friends on a nearby state farm. Often a group of us just got together and organized a feast, cooking up special foods and inviting friends to come and join us. I also spent my spare time in studying Marxism-Leninism Mao Zedong Thought, because I was active in the local Red Guard movement and hoped one day to join the Party. Some Sundays I did propaganda work, hanging up slogans and pasting up signs. A few times I went with friends to the army store located at regiment headquarters. It normally only served the military, but on Sundays it was open to the public. They had things there that weren't even available in Haikou, the main city, things such as canned food, synthetic cloth, good cigarettes, and so on. You could also shop there without coupons. I used to buy a few cookies and eat them bit by bit each day. The army was very nervous about nonmilitary use of its store and placed limits on what you could buy. We also were invited sometimes to regiment headquarters to see the latest movies. Occasionally the army invited us to compete with them in basketball or football. I liked that a lot, since I was good at basketball. These games were held at regiment headquarters, and afterwards everybody was invited to a free meal in the dining hall.

The contrast in my life then and now is striking but, you know, there are many days that I take a deep breath and wish I were back there. Life may have been austere and even boring, but Hainan was a secure place and we were doing something useful for China's economy, for the rest of the people. Here in Hong Kong everybody is really out for himself and no one cares about what the other person does. You don't have to care about others if you're rich enough to take care of yourself. The richer people are, the less they worry about their neighbors. I've not yet adjusted to the life in Hong Kong. It's too fast and undisciplined. But I'll learn—after all, there's no place else for me to go now. I work in a warehouse and I make more money than I ever dreamed I could make. The rubber plantation is far away now, in the sense that I know I can never go back; yet it is also still very close to me, a way of life that I had for seven years and haven't yet learned to forget. Except for a strange twist of fate, I'd probably still be there right now, applying Chairman Mao's Thoughts in my daily practice instead of sitting in this room with a foreigner, drinking Coca-Cola.[5]

The One Who Loved Dog Meat

THERE ARE ALWAYS THOSE who live by their wits on the fringes of the system. Most eventually get caught. This is the story of one such individual, a southerner who spent over two decades trying to "beat the system" and managed to do that for most of his life in China. Yet he was also caught several times, and spent three years in a forced labor camp at Yingde. It was remarkable how he was always able to bounce back from adversity, to a new and better position in the system, despite the many controls and barriers that are allegedly designed to filter out "bad elements."

Perhaps this tells us something about the nature of the Chinese system, especially in Guangdong province. Bribery, corruption, promiscuity, illegal speculation, use of the backdoor, still go on behind the scenes. An enterprising individual can build himself a "small empire," especially in a county town or in a key production unit, where this individual may be in a position to distribute a scarce resource to others who are willing to go around the system to pay for the exchange. When the narrator was headmaster of a local school, he used his control over grades and over teachers' careers to enhance his own career. Later, when he had become a doctor, he used his control over medicines and over the writing of sick-leave permits to further his own interests.

The first time he was really caught, the authorities sent him to a forced labor camp, accused of being a bad element. There are many prisons in China, and Yingde is one of the better known. Some 25,000 people lived there, growing their own food, providing their own entertainment, and producing large quan-

210

tities of sulfur and tea for export. The camp had its own schools, farms, repair workshops, and factories, and a large buffer population comprised of ex-prisoners surrounded the area. The narrator's experiences there are typical of most descriptions of Chinese prison life, only he was lucky to have been released after three years.

Are there many others like this man, living on the edges of the system and on the edges of criminality? We have been led to believe that China is relatively crime-free and that the Communists have really "cleaned up" China. Unquestionably they have drastically reduced the opportunities for criminal activity, especially with the almost complete elimination of opium trafficking. Still China has prisons and labor camps and they contain their share of murderers, rapists, thieves, prostitutes, and speculators. Compared with pre-1949 conditions, these problems have been greatly reduced although, as we can see from this story and from current reports in the Chinese press, they have not been eliminated.

AM ONLY FORTY YEARS OLD and I have gone through so many dramatic events, it's like a novel. I started to write one once, but I didn't finish. I've been a teacher, a doctor, and a prison-camp inmate. I've lived in many places and have left wives and children in some of them. I came from a bad class background, but at the time of Liberation they classified me as a "revolutionary cadre" because I helped the guerrillas fight the Japanese. My personal life always caused me more trouble than my politics. For more than three years I sat in the Yingde labor camp because of a love affair I had with a classmate of mine. But more about that later on.

My biggest weakness, besides women, is dog meat. I'll do anything for some dog meat, and often got into trouble over that craving. The small black dogs are the tastiest. They shouldn't be killed right away, but when they're several months or a year old. I used to have an arrangement to get a whole dog at a time from a team member in a commune near Hengli, but he was caught one day transporting a carcass and I never saw him again.[1] Sometimes I could find someone willing to sell a piece of dog meat on the streets, but it was terribly expensive, especially in the winter months when you like to eat dog meat "to thicken the blood" and

make it "hot" again. Later, when I was a doctor, I could sometimes get dog meat in exchange for medicines or for certificates
which said that "Patient Wang is suffering from such-and-such
disease and should be excused from work for a period of X days."
With that certificate in hand, people didn't have to go to work
but still were paid. All the doctors did it, and I was as guilty as
anyone. We received not just dog meat but all kinds of favors in
exchange, ranging from money to hard-to-get tickets for operas
and plays.

At the time of Liberation things looked pretty good for me. I
had been a young revolutionary fighting the Japanese, and this
seemingly canceled out my parents' bad class background. In
1948 at the age of sixteen, I was married to the daughter of a
prosperous local family in an arranged marriage that brought a
large dowry with it. I was doing very well in school and had expectations of getting a higher education after graduation. As a
matter of fact, as soon as the wedding was over, I went off to Huizhou to attend middle school there. I never had met my future
bride before the wedding and left her right afterward. She was
only twelve years old. I didn't sleep with her on the wedding
night, never saw her again after that day, and can't even remember what she looked like. All I recall is that we were there because
our parents had arranged our union. It was assumed that when I
returned from middle school she would live with me in our family's house.

Meanwhile I went to Huizhou, and there I fell in love with a
classmate of mine from a nearby village. We started living together and our affair lasted six months. My mistress was beautiful
and I wasn't the only young man captivated by her charms. An
older man with a responsible position in the city also fell in love
with her, and I guess she didn't exactly discourage his attentions,
although she swore she would love me forever. He decided that if
he could get rid of me he could get her, and so he accused me of
adultery, saying that I had a wife back home. This wasn't so bad,
even in Huizhou, because in those days there was a great deal of
confusion due to the war and also because the new marriage law
had been enacted. The old-style arranged marriages were now
illegal, and people like me could ask to have our arranged marriages dissolved. When I was accused of adultery, I went before
the authorities and said that because of the new marriage law my

first marriage was not legal: so how could I be accused of adultery? I thought that this would stop his attack, but he then produced witnesses who claimed I had consummated the marriage and that I had been home several times in the past few months to visit my "legal" wife. Things became unpleasant, and finally my mistress and I decided to run away. We had heard that they were going to arrest me and that my rival was saying I was an "American Chiang Kai-shek spy." We ran from Huizhou in different directions so they wouldn't catch us together. I was caught, but she escaped.

I didn't see her for seventeen years, when we accidentally ran into each other in Pingdan on the street. It was in the midst of the Cultural Revolution and I was in trouble, having been sent down to Pingdan from Canton. She was visiting friends and told me she had married and had several children. "As a matter of fact," she told me, "I was pregnant with your child when we ran away in 1950. I gave birth to a boy, a few months later, and when I met my future husband in Canton I told him that my first husband had died at the end of the war, fighting the remnants of the KMT. The boy and my husband didn't get along, and finally I had to leave the boy in Canton with friends. I haven't seen him for four years, but I think he's all right."

So I guess I have one son in Canton somewhere today. As for my mistress, she wanted to help me out during the Cultural Revolution. She had a connection with the Red Flag faction[2] and tried to reverse my status as a rightist. It was no good, however. She was unable to help me and I never heard from her again.

When I was caught back in 1950, it was a strange business. The cadre who had hounded me into running away thirsted for revenge. He had lost the woman, and much face. He tried to get the Party to step in to deal with me, but with the new marriage law it wasn't that easy. My arranged marriage could be dissolved; as a matter of fact, my bride's parents had asked to have it dissolved probably because my parents had been accused of being KMT landlords. It was politically expedient for my bride's family to withdraw from a marriage to a class enemy. Somehow they had managed to cling to middle-peasant status,[3] I guess by some luck and heavy bribery, because they had been on top just before Liberation. Anyway, he couldn't really do much to me because of my love affair, so he shifted the attack to my class background and accused me of being from a landlord family. The Party took this accusation seriously, even though I had a revolutionary cadre status. It was an awkward moment, but I squeezed through. I recall being told by the Party committee: "Li, you acquired revolutionary status by a stroke of luck. But remember that what was granted in haste can be taken back at leisure. Everything about your life and actions stinks of your being a bad element and a reactionary. We have decided to let you go, but all this has been entered on your dossier. The next time the Party won't be so forgiving. You are young and can still change your ways."

To save embarrassment to the cadre who accused me, I was sent to Hengli to help in land reform. This was clever of the Party because it got me out of the way. In any case, I decided to work as hard as possible, to win their confidence and get a foothold on a new career. I wasn't worried about the love affair, but many people around me were getting chopped back because of their class background. I worked hard and performed so well I was made headmaster of a primary school, and then a year later was promoted to be deputy headmaster of the middle school. I found a woman and we married in 1953. She had only a primary education but came from a good class background. It wasn't much of a wedding, only a few gifts were given. She's ok, I guess. She's been my wife all these years and we have five children. I was lonely then and needed a woman; she was available. I wouldn't have married someone with such a low education under normal circumstances.

Living in Hengli was ok because it had the only middle school in the area. Students came from all over the country to attend my school. Most of them were from the countryside and there was strong competition to get in. They paid me 76 yuan a month as deputy headmaster, but I made a lot more than that on the side. It was said that I was one of the richest people in town, probably because I had so much extra income I couldn't spend it —even for all the dog meat in Huizhou. The cost of living was low and we lived rent-free and ate in the school dining room. I had to live in the school dormitory because it was stipulated in the regulations, but on weekends I could get away and I'd visit friends in other towns or try to get to Canton. My wife stayed behind when I went away. She was busy with the children and I really didn't want her along. It was better that way.

We gave away our daughter to friends in another town. They were childless and wanted to adopt her. I didn't really care for her anyway and, besides, she was a girl. Actually they paid us for her but we couldn't admit this because it's against the law. In any case, I kept the other four children, three of them boys.

A small county town can get boring and I soon tried to find a way to get to Canton. I pulled some strings and lined up a position in Canton at a suburban school. I had trouble with my legal residence but used some of my surplus income to "persuade" people that they should give me the permit. I was just making plans to go to Canton when I was swept up by the anti-rightist campaign. If I had gotten out of Hengli a few weeks sooner, everything might have been different, but once again I was unjustly accused and this time the punishment was severe, three and a half years at the Yingde labor camp in Guangdong province. My bad luck had returned and this time I was the target of two jealous teachers in my school who were out to get me for personal reasons. They had the ear of the Party and I still had that black mark on my dossier. Nobody had forgotten who my parents were. So I had to endure more than three years of prison-camp life for nothing.

[*Li was not truthful about what happened. According to him, the reasons for his downfall were personal (the jealousy of a few people in a small town) and political (as the son of a landlord he was a natural target). In fact, another respondent who came from the same area knew Li and observed the following: "Li was denounced because of his moral and criminal corruption at school. He had managed to entrench himself so well in the school that he had a powerful influence on admissions policies and on grading. If you wanted to get your son admitted to our school, you paid Li a visit and made sure you left there 'lighter than when you came.' If you were concerned about grades, you could invite Li for tea and make an 'arrangement' with him. That's why he was always hopping about our county. He bribed the local Party committee to look the other way, and it was only when a new man was sent to the area in early 1958 that he became vulnerable. He also dominated the teachers, especially the young women, with whom he had several affairs, threatening to blackmail them or to ruin their careers if they protested. A friend*

*of mine told me that one teacher became pregnant with his child
and left to get an abortion. He was also accused of raping a female student, but this was never proved because the girl left the
area and her family did not let her return to accuse him. Pay no
mind to what Li says now about personal jealousy or about his
parents' class background. In fact, what tripped him up was that
he is an out-and-out bad element, someone who has, as the saying
goes, 'a head fit for execution.' We all knew that he was sent to
Yingde not as a rightist, but as a bad element. Of course in those
days they were almost always called rightists because the anti-
rightist campaign was in full swing. Because of his landlord past,
he was a reactionary deep down inside, as the saying goes, like an
onion hanging out to dry under the eaves with its skin and roots
shriveled but still alive inside! No one in our town felt the least bit
sorry when they sent him away."*]

I was taken in a boxcar to Yingde, a huge forced labor camp
located 120 kilometers north of Canton. What a place Yingde
was, like a miniature country of 25,000 people, all of them prisoners or ex-prisoners! We grew our own food, provided our own
entertainment, and produced large quantities of goods for export. I'm sure the state made a big profit from our work. Sulfur
and tea were the big exports. The sulfur mine employs nearly
20,000 people and Yingde "Big Leaf" tea is famous throughout
China. We also produced sugar, bamboo, and other forestry
products. We had our own schools, farms, repair shops, and
small factories. Contact with outsiders was almost nonexistent,
and many of our neighbors were ex-prisoners who had been asked
to stay on after their sentences had been completed. These people
couldn't leave, even though they had served their sentences. The
whole area was fenced off by barbed wire and guarded by the
Guangdong Province Security Bureau, which operated Yingde in
conjunction with the various economic agencies involved in its
production enterprises.[4]

They issued me a metal mug which served to hold my food at
meal times and also for washing myself. We used a small wooden
barrel in the corner of the room for night soil, but we had to piss
outside. I was given a vest, shorts, cotton padded tunic, trousers,
rubber shoes, bed sheet, and thin blanket. There were forty of us
in a brick room with wooden bunks side by side. At night the

guards locked the doors from the outside. We got about six
ounces of rice per meal, often with pickles and bean curd. Once a
month we received a small piece of meat. You began work in the
fields at 6:00 a.m. and you worked all day till 6:30 p.m. Each of
us had to pick 50 pounds of tea leaves daily, and this required
backbreaking work on the steep hillsides. In the evenings we had
to attend political study sessions, usually outside our barracks on
the basketball court. A large blackboard was placed on one side
and we listened to lectures on politics, on the Party, and on how
even prisoners could better serve the Motherland.

I was put in a tea plantation within Yingde, which turned
out to be a lucky break. It was a small farm of only 300 people
and conditions there were pretty good. Once you learned how to
pick tea in a squatting position, and once you mastered the techniques of political reeducation, then it was easy to survive. We
had enough food, even during the Three Difficult Years when the
rest of China was starving.[5] Of course, you had to have your wits
about you. If you questioned authority, or if you brooded too
much about the injustice of your fate, you could suffer a horrible
end. I remember Liao, who had been sentenced to five years for
profiteering. He had been repairing a few electric engines on the
side for communes. One day a commune refused to pay him and
the next thing he knew he was in Yingde. "They never paid me
any money," Liao kept saying, "and I was only doing what everybody else was doing." He appealed his sentence even though
everyone said that was a waste of time, since the state never admits it made a mistake. "No one gets a reduced sentence," said
old Wang who had been at Yingde for four years. "If you appeal
then it merely means that you need still more reeducation and
obviously need a longer sentence!" But Liao was stubborn and
sure he would be proved innocent. One day they told him the bad
news: the appeal was over and he had been given an extra five
years. So he hanged himself from a hook in the drying shed with a
rope made of torn-up cloth strips.

There weren't any other "successful" suicides I can recall.
Two prisoners once escaped by smuggling themselves out in a
truck. One of them was brought back ten days later, dirty and
exhausted. He had managed to reach Canton but no one there
would dare help him and he couldn't get food because he had no
money or ration tickets. They caught him stealing food, brought

him back to camp, and invited us a week later to watch his execution. The other prisoner never came back, but local gossip said he had been killed in a fight, trying to escape his guards. It was foolish to try to escape because the camp was too isolated and, even if you did get out, it was almost impossible to survive.

So the best solution was to flow like water. That's what you had to do to stay alive. I saw that I had to become a model prisoner, because then you get a little leverage and some privileges. I stayed out of trouble, worked hard, watched carefully, and always kept my thoughts well hidden. The trick was to make a full confession of your "sins" and then become an activist in the political studies group. I plunged into politics with a vengeance, surprising even myself with my ability to talk convincingly about the correct political line, fundamental principles of Marxism-Leninism, the Party's role in leading the masses, and so on. Soon Zhang, the cadre responsible for our sessions, came and praised me for my improved thought. "We've been watching you," he said, "and we think you're making progress." This was encouraging. Within a few weeks I was asked to lead some of the political study sessions and there I was, next to the basketball hoop, explaining Party policies to my co-prisoners. It was an easy game to play and, since I had confided in no one, my co-prisoners never knew for certain whether I was serious. Some figured rightly that I was an opportunist and others thought I was an informer.

It wasn't long before the authorities made me a trusty. With this status I could win favors from the guards and could help prisoners get certain things. The guards would do almost anything to have a woman, and many of the prisoners were willing former prostitutes and actresses. Some were just lonely. Others figured they could get extra food, blankets, and other privileges. I knew just about everything that was going on and could use this information to make life easier for myself. My biggest break came when Zhang, the cadre, got me involved in his affair with one of the prisoners. After that I practically had the run of the camp — extra food, easier workload, and free time with my own girlfriend, an actress from Canton who had been sent to Yingde because she spurned the advances of the big-shot political boss in charge of her troupe's activities.

All in all, prison wasn't that bad. You had to learn to accept the permanent smell of piss lingering in the air, the ever-present dirt, and the constant duplicity. No one could be trusted—but then why should a labor camp be any different than the rest of China? Actually in some ways we were better off than many "free" workers. While parts of China were desperately short of food and people were starving, we had food in our rice bowls even in the blackest months. We didn't have to worry about making any political mistakes because we had already been branded (most of us) as political misfits. So we could relax and not worry so much about politics as those on the outside. For me, life at Yingde taught me how to play the game of politics, so that in the future I wouldn't again blunder and get caught unawares.[6]

It wasn't that hard for me to leave the camp. I had been a trusty and managed to walk that tightrope so carefully that I was considered to have been politically reeducated. Zhang had been transferred, but my file now indicated that I had made a remarkable shift in my attitude. In 1961 a few prisoners were released and I somehow got on the list, after just over three years. I left Yingde suddenly one morning, without any tears, along with thirty others. We were given a certificate of release stamped by the authorities, 50 yuan, and were allowed to keep our prison clothes. I was then taken to the train station to begin the trip back to Huizhou. I was told I would be put under three years of surveillance back in Huizhou, which meant I had to report regularly to the local Public Security Office, but in fact nobody bothered with this once I came home.

I went to join my wife and children, and we got reacquainted. I had only seen my wife twice while I was at Yingde and we had a lot of catching up to do. Life had been harsh for them and I had to find a new livelihood. I had a plan, however, that had come to me while I was in Yingde. The most privileged person at the labor camp was the doctor, who was also a prisoner. He had all kinds of advantages and made a tidy income on the side— better, it was said, than the director himself. I decided that I would become a doctor.

This was one of the luckier parts of my life. You see, when I was a middle school student in Huizhou I had symptoms of appendicitis and went to several doctors. They told me that it was only a stomachache. I didn't believe them and went to have a checkup in the Huiyang district hospital. There the doctors diagnosed an infected appendix and operated immediately. I could have caused those Huizhou doctors a lot of trouble for their mistake, but in those days I wasn't interested in such things. They didn't forget me, however, and when I returned from the labor camp I went to see them. This time I wasn't so forgiving and suggested that they help me. So they recommended me for a study at the Canton Chinese Traditional Medicine School, stating that I had some training already in Chinese medicine. Actually that was true, because at Yingde I had helped the doctor and had learned about acupuncture and the use of local herbs and medicines. Even before Yingde I had read avidly about Chinese medicine and knew a lot about diagnosing diseases. That's how I had been so sure my appendix was infected.

I passed a peaceful four years in Canton, from 1962 to 1966. My superiors at the school knew of my past, but nobody else did. As a matter of fact some thought I was a real political activist since I continued to express the correct political line publicly at every opportunity. If the game worked so well in prison, why not try it on the outside? I worked hard at my studies and did well enough to graduate near the top of my class. Life in Canton was ok, though it's not what it's cracked up to be. It's too big and there are too many rules and regulations, too many obstacles, and too many temptations. You always had to hustle in Canton and never could be sure of things. In smaller towns life is more predictable. So I was glad when they assigned me to work in the Pingdan town clinic in Huiyang county. I was now a full-time doctor with a salary of 48 yuan a month. But I made much more than that on the side, closer to 100 yuan a month when you added it all up. So it was a comfortable life there.

The clinic had fourteen doctors, all with some knowledge of western medicine (I had learned some western medicine at school in Canton). We were not divided into "western" and "Chinese," but into two other categories: one for herbs and one for manufactured or refined medicine (pills and so on). Compared with Canton, the medical facilities in Pingdan were quite primitive. The doctors were pretty good and it was fine by small-town standards, but often we didn't have penicillin and our motto was, "A patient's feet should not leave the floor until he's out the door" — meaning that we didn't want to keep a patient in the clinic even overnight unless we had to. Two days was our desired maximum, and then on to the district or county hospital. By every conceivable means, carrying the sick on one's back, by motorcycle, by cart, as fast as possible, we shoved those patients out of the clinic and into someone else's hands.

People in Pingdan like to see doctors because it's so cheap. Medical care was practically free. The registration fee was only 15 cents, an injection was 20 cents, and a large operation cost no more than 10 yuan. At first medicine was free, but this proved too costly and patients had to pay for their drugs. Still it was cheap, and 100,000 units of penicillin only cost 30 cents. Quite a few residents had relatives overseas who sent drugs. They brought the foreign medicine to the clinic and would ask me or a nurse to administer it. We had no X-ray equipment, but had two operating rooms and two sets of abortion equipment. There were forty-two beds in the clinic and we could perform basic operations such as male and female sterilization, abortion, appendectomies, childbirth, bone setting, and so on.

I made a lot of money in Pingdan because many people would go to a doctor to ask for a certificate indicating they were sick and could not work. Then they could stay at home or work in the family private plots and still get paid. The idea was to give the doctor something in exchange for the certificate. I used to get dog meat that way. I had one patient who would come from time to time for his certificate, and in exchange I'd find a fresh piece of dog meat hanging on a string by my door. That was the easiest way to get extra income. Another way was to steal medicines and equipment and rearrange the record so it showed that the medicines were given to patients and the equipment had been lost or never received. All the medical personnel were involved in this operation, and we took about 25 percent off the top of every shipment of drugs for ourselves. Then we sold the stuff or traded it for food or other favors. Still another shady practice was giving out birth control pills to unmarried women—it was illegal to do so—and giving abortions on the side to unmarried girls without informing the authorities. We would just let it be known that what we were doing was a "special favor" and you would then get something extra in your pocket. So it was a good life in 1966 in Pingdan, lots of money, good status, and a past that seemed to be forgotten. Then came the Cultural Revolution, and once more they took my past and beat me down with it.

Even though I thought I had tucked my rightist tail out of

sight and had mouthed all the correct slogans, they showed me no mercy. I was accused of being a member of the "seven kinds of black"[7] and was dismissed from my post as a doctor. It didn't help that there had been a scandal at the hospital involving one of the doctors who was accused of molesting and raping several women patients who had been examined by him. In the course of investigating these charges, the local authorities uncovered shortages and evidence of "general moral decay" among the doctors and nurses. So they sent most of us down to the countryside as barefoot doctors.[8] I was sent to a small village 60 kilometers away. My family stayed in Pingdan and I went off in the back of a truck, listening to the jeers of Red Guards and a chorus of curses and epithets.

Once again my life had taken another abrupt turn. I spent most of my time as a barefoot doctor going around from village to village, curing minor ailments, and propagandizing birth control. There were five of us who regularly visited rural production brigades, explaining state policy and disseminating birth control devices. We weren't very successful, I would say. The further you go from Canton, the larger the household; it's almost a basic rule. We came in and talked about postponing marriage, about IUDs, oral contraceptives, spacing children, and sterilization — but still the babies kept popping out of Guangdong stomachs. Peasants just didn't believe that the collective would provide for them in their old age and they surrounded themselves with as many children as possible. "Our children are our insurance against poverty in our old age. How can we be expected not to have them?" Nor could you keep young warm-blooded peasants from sexual intercourse when they were so eager and willing. In spite of all our education, contraception was not well understood, especially in the male-dominated rural parts of Guangdong where females had little to say in such matters. If you issued contraceptive pills to unmarried women you incurred the wrath of the entire community, including the cadres. Thus we made little progress here. Some of the villages I visited were so backward that they still practiced female infanticide. In Pingdan I had never seen bodies of girl babies killed at birth, although there was always such talk. But now I actually saw one floating in an irrigation canal, a tiny corpse that showed how powerful a hold the past still could have on people's lives.[9]

By 1970 things were rather bleak for me. I was barely sur-
viving as a barefoot doctor in a backward rural part of China. I
had run out of tricks to play—there seemed no golden key that
could unlock the door to some urban hospital. My rightist status
was just too great a burden to bear. I was an outsider stuck in the
middle of nowhere. My family was back in Pingdan, but I had
lost interest in them over the years. So I tried to escape across the
frontier to Hong Kong with a woman friend. She wasn't strong
enough and she held me back. Then we were both caught. I was
taken back to the village and deprived of my job as a barefoot
doctor. With the last bit of my status gone, there was no point in
trying to hang on. So I tried again to escape without success. Finally on the third try, I made it to Hong Kong in 1973. It's a
dirty, noisy place but I'm at ease here, something that eluded me
in China for the last twenty years of my life.

[*Li has settled in Kowloon with a woman he met soon after
his arrival. He refuses to say what he is doing, other than working
in a factory. One suspects he has slipped into the shady side of life
in Hong Kong. With his medical background, one wouldn't be
surprised if it were into drug dealing of some kind. Li has completely abandoned his wife and children back in China, in contrast to most other refugees who continue to send money to their
families, a practice that has been maintained by generations of
overseas Chinese. He admits that he sends them no money and
hasn't told them where he is: "I feel no obligation whatsoever and
I couldn't care less what happens to them. Let the state that
stripped me of my career support them now."*]

My Neighborhood

*CLOSE CONTROL over community organization and neigh-
borhood life has been a characteristic of the Communists' urban
policy. Building on a pre-1949 legacy of small-group control (the
bao jia system), the Chinese have tried simultaneously to monitor
the activities of residents while developing socialist urban com-
munities. The residents' committee serves as an ideal expression
of these goals because at the grass roots it is an arm of higher-
level political control and yet a means by which the community
can administer itself, solving small day-to-day problems on the
spot. In large cities such as Peking and Shanghai resident's
committees have become fairly effective in the solution of selected
problems of daily life, and foreigners are frequently taken to
visit urban neighborhoods to see how these committees function.*

*In this story we learn about the structure and functions of a
residents' committee in Shanghai, and the various problems it
encounters in its daily work. The narrator, a middle-aged
woman, typifies the average member of a residents' committee:
female, unpaid, middle-aged, and no longer in the work force.
She is usually not a Party member, but she has a good record of
community work and relates well to her neighbors. As is evident
from this story, committee work is the equivalent of a full-time
job. She is always on the go, organizing people, checking on
them, solving their problems. She is a combination of building
superintendent, PTA leader, and off-duty policeman, a multi-
plicity of roles that can be exceptionally taxing at times. When
the unexpected occurs, such as Widow Wang's defiance of the*

housing authorities, the residents' committee can exert little influence and has to turn to higher authorities. Even the combined pressure of the police, Party, and the district housing authorities fails to move the determined widow, who successfully defies the bureaucrats by "squatting" in an empty apartment. The residents' committee mediates but cannot solve this problem, mainly because it is such an unusual defiance of authority. The committee is better equipped to settle disputes among the residents, such as the quarrel between Country Bumpkin and Two-Face, although here too the committee ultimately fails in its goal, that of trying to bring the unhappy couple back together.

The story only briefly touches upon the economic activities of large city neighborhoods. These are organized by the neighborhood or street committees, the basic local level of government, of which the residents' committees are a smaller part. Unemployed youth, housewives, and pensioners in the past have often been employed in small workshops located in the neighborhood and under neighborhood jurisdiction. The production of these workshops usually feeds larger economic enterprises in the city. As China now pushes its industrialization campaign, neighborhoods may be encouraged to expand their economic functions, along with the tasks of political control and of fostering socialist community consciousness.

I AM FIFTY-TWO YEARS OLD and have three children, all of them married. My husband is a machine tool operator and makes a good salary, 78 yuan a month. I used to work in a textile factory when I was younger, but I stopped in 1963 because of my health. I suffer from high blood pressure and got dizzy while working at the machines. Also the noise was affecting my hearing. Luckily my two eldest children were already working, so the loss of my income wasn't a burden on the household. Only one of them was still living with us. The others had their own families, and my number-one son lived far away in Xian, where he was a teacher. After I retired from work (I had been working since I was twelve years old), the Party decided to recommend me for membership in our local residents' committee. I'm not a Party member, but that doesn't matter a bit. Actually most members of the residents' committee are just housewives like myself or pensioners.

I guess they chose me because I had lived in that neighborhood, in the same building, since 1956. I knew most of the people in our building by name and all about their personal backgrounds and problems. Not that I'm a snoop or gossip, mind you, but I like to talk with people and find out about them. When the Party first asked me about becoming a member of the residents' committee, I was hesitant; I replied that I wanted to wait a while to see about my blood pressure and also to catch up on a few household matters. I also expressed concern that I was almost illiterate—I really could only read a few slogans that I knew by heart and could only draw a few simple characters. "Never mind," the Party cadre said, "it's not your fault that you can't read and write very well. You've worked hard for thirty years and when you were little, you didn't have the chance. Now that you've retired, the Party will help you, so don't worry." His words were reassuring because I was embarrassed about my illiteracy. The Party cadre did ask me to make up my mind soon, because the woman now responsible for our building was in bad health and couldn't continue much longer. Well, after three months I decided I wanted the job, and within a month it was mine.

For the next nine years I was a member of that residents' committee, and it was like a full-time job. There were eighteen members on the committee and I was responsible for my building, containing forty-seven households and totaling over two hundred people. You can imagine that with this many people there were always things to do and problems to settle—there were many days where I was so busy that I didn't have time to take care of my own household. Fortunately my husband was a modern man and was willing to help out. Many days after his shift ended at 4:00, he did the afternoon shopping and helped prepare the evening meal. My daughter-in-law (second son's wife) also helped occasionally, but she worked the evening shift at her factory and slept in the dormitory there. So she usually only stayed with us one or two nights a week. It wasn't so bad, really, and I loved my new work. At the beginning I wasn't sure whether my friends in the building would change their feelings toward me, now that I was a member of the residents' committee. It was no secret that the people didn't always welcome our presence. We had called my predecessor Old Snoop, Meddler, and other such nicknames behind her back. Most residents felt that the committee spent more time poking its nose into personal business and prying into people's lives than in acting on behalf of the residents. One of my neighbors asked me bluntly before I took the job, "Do you really want to do this? Your relations with your friends won't be the same anymore. They'll never speak their minds when you're around. They'll always think of you as someone who is going to cause them trouble. You know how people feel about the residents' committee: it's like a little policeman always checking up on us."

Actually the job turned out better than I had expected. True, my neighbor was right: my relations with old friends had changed. Nothing I could point to with any certainty, mind you, but they were more reserved in my presence now and we didn't do much gossiping together anymore. On the other hand, I was so busy that I didn't have much time to bring out my little wooden stool and sit around gossiping. Now I was either at meetings, organizing some sort of activity, or solving a problem. With over two hundred people in one building, I just couldn't keep an eye on everything, and I had help from four activists who were each responsible for one of the entranceways into which the building was subdivided. These activists weren't members of the residents' committee, but they were our eyes and ears in each of the entranceways. You know that in Shanghai, as in other large cities, the four-storey apartment building built in the fifties is really a separate housing unit with four separate entrances and staircases. People don't just have an address such as "No. 10 building, such and such neighborhood," but you must add, "No. 10 building, No. 2 entranceway" as well as the neighborhood and street. Each entranceway has twelve apartments, divided into one, two, and three bedrooms (the three-bedroom apartments are only on the ground floor, and they are the most desirable). The activist in each of these entranceways was an older woman, who was either widowed or retired and who enjoyed organizing and checking on residents. Three times a week I met with my activists at my place to discuss problems and to assign them their duties. I got on well with them, although I knew that the residents didn't care for them because one of their main duties was to check up on illegal residents and to settle household arguments. The activists were the ones who showed up at night with the local police, not me, so the residents didn't like them. I had some problems for a while with the residents of No. 3 entranceway because the activist there, a retired worker, was too zealous in her job. But eventually she was right: through her vigilance we caught two illegal residents, one of them a bad element, and during the Cultural Revolution she was one of the leaders in the neighborhood struggle against revisionism and class enemies.

In fact most of the work of the residents' committee had little to do with snooping on other people's affairs or with looking for class enemies. We devoted a large part of our time to public health and sanitation. For example, we conducted campaigns to get rid of flies, cockroaches, rats, and mice. In June and July we gave everybody powder to burn in their apartments. I think it was called 666. This smoked up the apartment and killed all the pests. We made sure people did it properly and that they stayed out of their apartments for six hours afterwards. We ran campaigns to tell parents to get their children vaccinated against chicken pox, small pox, measles, and scarlet fever. Sometimes it took a lot of persuasion—many parents were still reluctant to trust vaccinations and others simply had no time to spare. So we knocked on doors and held special meetings and hung up posters that told residents about vaccinations. In the summer we warned everybody about encephalitis, what its symptoms were and how you could catch it from mosquitoes. We urged people to report any serious sickness like that at once so it wouldn't spread. Once we had three cases of encephalitis in one entranceway. We sprayed the place with disinfectant and got rid of all the mosquitoes. Then we inoculated all the children at the local clinic with a special encephalitis vaccine.

In 1964 we began a major birth control program, holding meetings in which we talked about the need to plan family growth. Actually it wasn't much of a problem in our neighborhood, since families weren't that large. Mine was one of the largest, but then I had my children before Liberation. We were mainly trying to get younger couples to postpone having children for a while, so that the wife could work longer and there would be fewer children per household. This wasn't difficult to do in Shanghai because families weren't as large as in some other cities, and certainly much smaller than in the countryside. We talked to the women and gave information about contraception, what devices to use and how to use them. During the Cultural

Revolution, we dispensed birth control pills free of charge to all married women. First we held a mass meeting, usually of all women in a building, to explain about birth control and the possibilities involved. Then the entranceway activists visited individual families to talk with them, especially with the husbands who, though fairly enlightened, didn't pay much attention to our efforts. We often brought along the doctor from the local clinic to explain birth control methods. We didn't talk much about vasectomies because the men didn't want to listen. Abortion was available on demand, however. Also, for 5 yuan you could get fitted with an IUD. We persuaded one woman to have her tubes tied after she had her fourth child, despite preventive methods. I think our efforts were successful because over the next decade the number of children in our neighborhood did drop.

The residents' committee kept the neighborhood clean and secure, and that was an important duty. I went around personally from time to time on inspection trips or on special clean-up campaigns. Each entranceway had to be swept up, and any garbage had to be put away daily. We checked for fire hazards and in the winter made sure residents remembered to keep a supply of fresh air coming into their rooms while they had the stove on. Each year hundreds of careless people in China are asphyxiated because of the fumes from their coal stoves. We tried our best to make the neighborhood look nice and clean; that wasn't always so easy, however, because the city Housing Administration was responsible for maintaining and repairing the buildings and they wouldn't give us any money for painting or repairing. Sometimes we used extra supplies from political campaigns to do some painting or patching. When there was a real emergency and the Housing Administration refused to come (for example, if a ceiling had fallen down), we put pressure on the street committee to get the Housing Administration to do something. We weren't always successful, but at least we tried.

We also kept a sharp eye out for unwelcome strangers lurking around our neighborhood. If you didn't do that, you'd find sooner or later that something important was missing. I remember that in 1969 a bicycle was taken from the courtyard. It just happened that the activist who normally kept an eye on that courtyard was at a meeting. Someone had seen a young man passing through from the street entrance. It was probably a "black youth" who stole the bike for cash so he could survive a bit longer in the city.[1] That bike wouldn't stay for long in Shanghai; it would quickly be sold to a gang of thieves, who would then re-sell it in the countryside where second-hand bikes didn't have to be licensed.

We locked our doors when we were away and at night cleared the courtyard of personal belongings. The activist on duty always called out around 10:00: "Come and take in your bicycles. It's ten o'clock." Only a fool would leave anything out after that. When we were at home around the building, however, we didn't lock our doors and even left them wide open while we were outside talking, doing the laundry, or eating on the stoop. We wouldn't steal from each other, but you had to be on guard against "outsiders," and I don't mean class enemies either, but just ordinary thieves and bad people (*huai ren*). During the Cul-tural Revolution you had to be particularly vigilant because you couldn't be sure that a so-called revolutionary wasn't simply a thief in disguise. Between 1966 and 1971 we were especially care-ful about people coming into the neighborhood from outside. Once a group of Red Guards burst in looking for trouble, but we managed to send them on their way since we didn't have any class enemies living in our building and most of us were factory work-ers or pensioners. So after we read each other quotations from Chairman Mao's Thought, we sent them on their way to continue "raising high the banner of revolution."

During the Cultural Revolution I had plenty to do. The residents' committee was constantly relaying the latest instruc-tions to the neighborhood, mobilizing people in support of new policies, and organizing political study sessions, sometimes two or three a day. So much political pressure soon took its toll: my health deteriorated and I had to stay in the hospital for several weeks. Luckily my daughter-in-law had given up her dormitory room and was now living with us, so she helped out with the cook-ing and shopping. I recovered quickly, however, and was soon back at my job. What I especially remember about those days were two events: the institution of the *qingshi* and the episode of the "substitute class enemy."

The qingshi ceremony began in 1967 and lasted for several months. We called it "qingshi" (asking for instructions), but its full name was *xiang Mao zhuxi qingshi* (asking Chairman Mao

for instructions). Each day at 9:00 a.m. and at 6:00 p.m. we assembled the residents together in front of their respective entranceways and we "confessed" our thoughts to Chairman Mao —
or, more precisely, to his color portrait, propped up on a window
sill outside the building. Each entranceway activist was responsible
for her picture of the Chairman which she kept in her apartment
for safekeeping. Some decorated the portrait with ribbons and
flowers. The activist from No. 2 entranceway always had three
red paper carnations pinned to the Chairman's portrait. Qingshi
was run by the activists, and it was their job to get people to read
quotations from the little Red Book and to confess their thoughts
about politics. In this way we could all memorize the contents of
the Red Book while purifying our own class standpoint. A few
took the thing seriously and earnestly searched their hearts each
morning to see if they had followed the Chairman's teachings
since the day before. These people would confess such sins as: "I
didn't sweep up the entranceway last night because I thought I
was too tired. Actually I was just too lazy"; or "Yesterday I
shouted at my children and even hit them. I must learn to be more
patient and reasonable"; or "I was too busy to help Old Li with
his bundles. That is not the way to serve the people. I promise to
follow the Chairman's teachings more closely in the future." And
so on. Most of the assembled housewives and pensioners didn't
volunteer any confession. They sang the revolutionary songs and
repeated the quotations, but that was all. The activists were
happy if three or four confessed each time, and if everybody at
least turned up for qingshi. It was a useful device at the time: it
gave housewives and pensioners, many of whom were not too politically active, a sense of what was going on in the factories, bureaus, and other units throughout China. Some residents complained that they felt funny confessing to a picture, and the older
residents said it was too tiring to stand around for such a long
period (thirty to forty minutes). Sometimes there was so much
noise from children running around, or machines nearby, that
you couldn't hear what was going on. Still the local Party unit was
pleased and so was the residents' committee. Our building managed to get almost full attendance every time, and we even won
an award as the most active in confessing to the Chairman.

In 1968 we had a bit of a problem. The authorities were
concerned that people weren't getting involved in class struggle,

especially at the neighborhood level. So they instructed us to hold a public struggle session on a Sunday in front of all the local residents. The problem was that at the start of the Cultural Revolution we had a few genuine "landlord/KMT" types, but they had either died, moved away, or were too sick. Efforts to find a genuine class enemy in our midst were not too successful. We had one fellow in mind—he wasn't really a class enemy, and as a matter of fact his father had been a worker and he himself had been a sailor. But he had become mentally unbalanced and used to go around talking about all the foreign places he'd visited in his younger days and how he'd like to go again. He used to sing "Sailing the Seas Depends on the Great Helmsman" all day long, and he'd change the verses around so that he and Chairman Mao were sailing around the world together, making revolution in all the foreign ports he'd once visited. At first the residents' committee decided to make him our choice to be struggled, but then we had second thoughts because he was too old and silly for something like that. What if he had a heart attack in the middle of the event? Or if he started singing and wouldn't stop? We decided to find someone else but didn't have a suitable candidate. Finally, the chairman of our committee said, "Why not borrow a class enemy from the adjoining neighborhood? It doesn't really matter if he lives here or not, just as long as he's a genuine class enemy. We can have a first-rate struggle session, everybody can participate, and the leadership will be pleased."

So we "borrowed" a class enemy from next door and had our struggle session. He was a veteran of such struggle sessions, about fifty years old, a known collaborator with the KMT. We built a platform, assembled the masses, denounced him for his crimes, and shouted revolutionary slogans for most of a Sunday afternoon. Then we returned our borrowed class enemy, none the worse for wear (we had promised we would avoid any physical violence and would return him unharmed), and everybody was satisfied.

Life in our neighborhood settled down after the Cultural Revolution. Less of my time was spent on political campaigns and we all gratefully forgot about such ceremonies as qingshi. The residents' committee again was doing a lot of public hygiene and sanitation work, as well as maintaining the security of the neighborhood. We also spent a great deal of time in settling disputes among residents. As a matter of fact, it seemed as if our building was always erupting into quarrels and arguments. I remember two such incidents in which I was closely involved, since they both took place in my entranceway, and I confess that I didn't resolve either of them very well.

One of the disputes concerned the illegal occupation of an empty apartment in our entranceway by Widow Wang, who lived on the second floor in a one-bedroom apartment, with her son, daughter-in-law, and grandson. What happened was very embarrassing to the authorities. Widow Wang had applied for a larger apartment to the Housing Administration two years previously, after her son had married and was living with his new wife together with Widow Wang in her one-bedroom apartment. Widow Wang had to give up her bedroom and she slept outside on the balcony in summer and in the kitchen in the winter. She didn't seem to mind this until the grandchild was born, but then she became impatient and kept after the housing authorities to get her a larger apartment. Their reply was always the same: "Sorry, comrade, we have no empty apartments and there is a long line of people ahead of you; you'll just have to wait your turn." She asked the residents' committee to put in a good word for her, but there was little we could do because we had no power in this matter, and the Housing Administration heard all kinds of pleas from countless residents' committees all the time. Well, it was just one of those situations where a deserving citizen had to suffer until things could change. At least that's what we thought, but Widow Wang had other ideas. One day she went across the hall to the empty two-bedroom apartment right opposite to hers, ripped off the seals, broke open the door, and moved herself in, with all her furniture and possessions. We didn't even know it had happened at first, but there she was and we couldn't get her out. She refused to leave, saying that her family would not budge until she had been given a larger apartment. Her argument was that the apartment had been empty for five months and why shouldn't it be occupied by someone who was in need of it? She said she'd refuse to move unless the Housing Administration found her another apartment. Otherwise she would squat in the apartment forever.

As soon as I found out about it, I hurried back home to persuade Widow Wang to move back to her old apartment. But when I tried to talk with her, she wouldn't let me in. Her son had already fixed the broken door and put in a new lock. The activist in my entranceway, Elder Sister Chao, was nearly in tears, wringing her hands in despair. She had tried to reason with Widow Wang through the door, but after an hour the Widow seemed even more determined to stay in the apartment. I tried to tell Widow Wang that it was wrong to occupy that empty apartment, that she had violated socialist laws and established procedures. What would happen if citizens did whatever they pleased all the time? Life would be quite impossible. Where was the Widow's political consciousness? Didn't she know that her action was against the interests of the collective and in violation of socialist principles? I told her that I would do my utmost to help her get better housing — but first she had to move back into her old apartment.

The Widow refused to leave. She said she didn't care any more about procedures and the interests of the collective. She had her own family and herself to think about. "I'm a widow who has served the revolution well. For many years I worked in a factory. Then after my husband died, I've been doing embroidery and home sewing. No one can say that I haven't done my share. For two years I've been waiting patiently while others get more space and I get nothing. I've been to the Housing Administration countless times. They don't bother about me because I'm not important — just an old widow who complains. But when I sleep in the kitchen, I can't close the door and my feet stick out into the hall, and in the summer when I sleep on the balcony there's hardly any room either. I know others suffer too, but when there's an empty apartment right across the hall, three meters away, and it's been there empty for several months and the Housing Administration keeps saying they need to keep that apartment in reserve for an emergency — well, after five months, where's the emergency? It's just a bunch of people sitting in an office making rules and shuffling papers without regard to the people's needs. You talk of being a good citizen and respecting the collective — well, Chairman Mao also says we should fight against bureaucrats and injustices, and that's what I'm doing. I won't budge and neither will my family until they agree to solve my housing problem. So leave me alone!"

It was clear to me after listening to Widow Wang that no

mere words could move her now. I told the entranceway activist to keep a close eye on things and especially to settle down the other residents while I went to report to the head of the residents' committee. There wasn't very much the residents' committee could do. We decided to send the policeman over that night, together with the entranceway activist, to tell the Widow that her occupation of the apartment was illegal. We also got the street committee to contact the Housing Administration to see what could be done. The head of the residents' committee said he would get the local Party organization to work on the problem. Meanwhile, I was told not to use force or threats of any kind to dislodge Widow Wang from her stronghold.

We had to be careful because the majority of residents were in sympathy with the Widow's case. Any harsh reprisal against her would be sure to create ill will in the building and neighborhood. Secretly (and even not so secretly) many residents applauded her courage in standing up to the local housing authorities and the entire system of housing distribution. Many others had been waiting years for better space and had seen others pass them by or, as in Widow Wang's case, watched as certain apartments stayed empty for months without adequate explanation. To use force against the Widow would be a serious error on the part of the authorities, and the Widow knew this all too well. She had even told me through the locked door that she could stay there as long as she liked, because no one would dare to use force to get her out. The residents in our entranceway actually organized themselves informally to help the Widow in her "fight against bureaucracy." They volunteered to keep an eye out for the police and any strangers that might come around, and they helped her daughter-in-law with the shopping and other chores so that the Widow wouldn't have to stay alone in the apartment too long. One neighbor even took her place from time to time so she could get outside to the local workshop to pick up and deliver her sewing. They seemed to relish the idea of confronting the housing authorities; everyone seemed to have a grievance and here was a chance to sympathize.

I was put in an awkward position because it was my job to organize residents to do what was correct. Furthermore here I was, having a rebellion against authority in my very own entranceway and I couldn't do much to stop it. I tried to persuade

residents that what the Widow had done was not outright defiance, but a theoretical violation of socialist laws and procedures;
most people just smiled and nodded at me. One woman told
me: "Never mind. I know you have to say the Widow is wrong
because of your position. But in your heart I know you sympathize with her, only you can't reveal your true feelings to the
people." Maybe I did, secretly, feel admiration for the Widow's
actions, although I never admitted it to myself at the time. It was
somehow gratifying to see someone challenge the people in the
Housing Administration, which had always given us trouble,
never providing enough money to maintain our buildings and
always acting in an arrogant manner.

But we had to do something to get her out. First the police
arrived together with Elder Sister Chao and tried to persuade the
Widow, but she wouldn't even let them in. For most of us, a visit
from the policeman was a threatening experience, since the local
police had control over our dossiers and when anybody got into
serious trouble it was the policeman who always came and took
you away. The Widow, however, just ignored them and the policeman went away shaking his head. Then the Party sent activists
around to try to pry her out, but she just kept replying that Chairman Mao had said we had to fight against injustice and bureaucratic arrogance and that was what she was doing. The Party
activist reminded her that she hadn't been that zealous in following the Party's line in the past—indeed, she used to fall asleep at
political meetings, never talked about politics, and never quoted
the Chairman's words before. The Widow replied: "That was
before I became politically conscious. Now I understand what the
Party has been trying to teach me for years—as the Chairman
once said, 'It's time to stand up and fight for revolutionary principles.' "

The Party put pressure on her son through the Party organization where he worked, but he just replied, "Look, it's my mother's apartment. There's nothing I can do. It's a problem of the
residents' committee and not this factory committee. I can talk
with her but, as you can see, she's a stubborn woman and won't
listen to your arguments anymore." I received much the same
answer from her daughter-in-law, whom I took aside one day for
a heart-to-heart chat. She agreed that the situation was awkward
and that no one liked to live that way. They were getting tired of

the pressure and wanted this matter settled. She said, however, she would support whatever her husband and mother-in-law decided, and that she had no influence over their decision except to support them in their defiance, "because at least now we can live like human beings, not all squashed together like beans in a *doufu* pan." The Housing Administration finally sent someone over to persuade the Widow to leave. He was a young man, slightly bewildered by all the fuss. He just refused to believe that the Widow would continue to defy the authorities. We explained to him that she had no intention of leaving, and that her case was a popular one. He told us that their office was getting pressured from all sides to kick her out. "She's setting a bad example for the rest of Shanghai," he said. "Who knows where it will stop — people will just break down doors and take over state property. The longer she stays there, the worse it will get."

Finally, after an "occupation" of two months, the Housing Administration gave in or, more precisely, the district Party organization put pressure on them to settle the matter in favor of the Widow. One day at a residents' committee meeting, I was told that the matter had been settled, that the Widow and her family would be allowed to stay in the occupied apartment, which would become legally hers. By this time the hubbub had died down, and even the entranceway residents had turned to other matters. Widow Wang had long ceased locking the door to the occupied apartment. As a matter of fact, the apartment often was empty and unlocked as members of her family went about their normal daily affairs. The Widow had won and the Housing Administration had lost much face, although they made it clear that this did not constitute a precedent and that Widow Wang was "responsible for properly fixing the broken door." In the future, it would be unlikely that the Housing Administration would allow a flat to be unoccupied for long, and I noticed after the Widow incident that a special large, thick wooden sheet was being nailed over the doors of other empty apartments, making it unlikely that another squatting episode could occur so quickly.

Not long after the Widow Wang matter had been settled, a second problem arose that involved our entranceway. This was a simmering quarrel between husband and wife that suddenly erupted into days and nights of shouting, upsetting everyone in the entranceway because it went on for hours at a time. The

yelling, easily heard by everyone, became so intense that people
began to take sides with the quarreling parties—the men with
the husband and the women with the wife. Frankly, neither
was a prize citizen. The wife was fresh from the countryside
and had no idea of city life—we nicknamed her the Country
Bumpkin. The husband was one of those types who treated his
women as if they were still in feudal times. When the Country
Bumpkin no longer suited him, he simply found a girlfriend
nearby. He thought no one knew, but we all did and we called
him Two-Face. They were a mismatched couple, one that should
never have married in the first place. He had gone to the countryside (to a suburban commune, actually) where he was temporarily "implanted" in her village. At that time Two-Face was very
attentive to the Country Bumpkin and her family. He hauled
water for them and swept their courtyard, and her family decided
that since he was a citydweller he'd be a fine catch for their young
daughter. The Country Bumpkin was pretty and she liked him.
She knew that he liked her and it wasn't long before they were
married. It was a cheap wedding for Two-Face. He didn't give
any gifts to his wife's parents because everyone knew that when a
peasant girl marries a city youth, it's like getting ten bride prices
in return. So everyone was happy, including the young couple—
and every young couple is happy at the beginning.

   Through her husband's family, a way was found to switch
her suburban residence permit to Shanghai, and her husband got
a good job in an iron works factory. They were assigned an apartment in my entranceway and moved in without fuss. All went
well, it seems, for two years and then the problems started. The
Country Bumpkin was slow to adjust to city ways and had kept
most of her country habits, such as talking too loudly or eating
her meals outside on the stoop while squatting. She had become
sloppy in her personal habits, regularly wore dirty clothes, and
their apartment was always a mess. With two babies to look after,
she was just not able to cope with her duties. Back home she had
a grandmother who could do many of these things, or at least
share in the burden. Here she had to do it herself, and her husband no longer seemed as attracted to her as he was earlier. She
wanted to "get out of this concrete prison" in which she felt en-
tombed, if only for a few minutes each night. He wanted a pretty,
young wife who provided a meal every night and with whom
he could talk about "city affairs." She was always surrounded by

babies or duties so it was hard for her to do all these things. Sometimes she was so eager to get outside that she would go downstairs to talk with the other housewives, leaving him alone in the dirty apartment. She would come out into the courtyard, squat down, and let her kids run around the courtyard. She didn't seem to care that her two-year-old son was rolling around in the dirt and was filthy, and if the baby started crying, she'd just open her blouse and stuff her breast into its mouth, no matter who was around. She did that because that's how they did it back home.

We figured that our Country Bumpkin would eventually get used to city ways, and we didn't go out of our way to reeducate her, although we did constantly try to improve her attitude concerning public hygiene. But it was slow going. She never seemed to have the time to listen, and no one knew how to get her to be less sloppy at home and in her appearance. She never attended political study meetings, saying that she was only an ignorant country girl and wouldn't understand what was going on. We told her she should just come and listen but she was always busy, it seemed, with her children. The only thing she took a special interest in was in learning how to ride a bicycle. Whenever she had time she would take her husband's bike and wobble around the courtyard trying to master the knack of riding. She was a slow learner and kept falling down, even after many weeks. It was a man's bike, too high for her, and she was always off balance.

Anyway, the quarreling began to build up over one long summer. The husband, self-righteous in his complaint that she didn't always have his food ready when he came home and that the flat was a mess, began to shout at her more and more. She replied that he didn't care at all about her and was only interested in food and sex. She wanted to get out of the place—see the city and go to the parks, to a movie, or to visit people. He just wanted to stay at home after a long day's work. I guess it's a familiar story to most of us, but in this case the argument got out of hand. He began to go out after supper without her, saying that he couldn't stand the nagging and complaining. She shrieked and cried and ran after him cursing, waving the baby nursing at her breast like a stick with which to beat him. The more he complained the less she did, and often he'd come home and find no supper at all. So he took to staying away even more, and that's when he found a girlfriend in another neighborhood not far from ours. She was a worker in his factory and he began to have an affair with her.

This made him all the more irritated and angry when he came home, because he was guilty about having begun a secret liaison.

So they quarreled all the time, and it began to create serious problems in the entranceway. As I said, people had taken sides in the quarrel—the men supporting Two-Face and the women siding with the Country Bumpkin. Then, too, the racket was getting on our nerves. On those nights that Two-Face came home for supper, all would be quiet for awhile. Then you'd hear voices rising, doors slamming, and finally a few thuds and smacks. There was no doubt that he hit her, although you never saw marks and she denied it. But they'd spend hours yelling and cursing at each other. The activist would run up and try to get them to stop, but they always locked the door and you couldn't get in to quiet them down. Neighbors would come into the hall muttering and cursing, and it used to end with the husband suddenly bursting through the door and out the building, with his wife's shrieks and curses following behind.

We tried everything to stop the quarreling. During the day when her husband was away, I and other activists talked with her and tried to get her to change her ways, but she wouldn't listen. She just said she was tired of being locked up at home with never a chance of getting out. She was ready to go home to her parents, but she didn't want to take the chance of losing her precious Shanghai legal residence. She'd make him pay for his treatment of her, and she would make life for him as miserable as he was making it for her. The Party tried to reason with both of them, especially with the husband. He was told to stay away from his new girlfriend and to uphold the principles of socialist morality. He said he would try, but after a few days of vicious yelling and screaming, off he went to see his mistress. There was little we could do, and other neighbors fared no better. One woman, a transport worker, lived next door and tried very hard to help the Country Bumpkin. She told her that she needed to free herself from the past and try to become a modern woman. She said, "Look at me. No one dares to yell and shout at me or to beat me. My husband helps with the household and I have an equal relationship with him. You can do the same if you wish." The Country Bumpkin, surrounded by her squalling children and her messy household, replied: "If you'll lend me your mother to look after my children as well as yours, and if you'll lend me your husband too, then maybe I could become like you. Right now, it's impossible for me to hold up half the sky,[2] as you suggest. There's too much here that keeps me down."

The outcome of the affair was no testament to the work of the residents' committee or to the ability of the people in the entranceway to settle their own problems. Two-Face and the Country Bumpkin stopped quarreling, but only after he had given her a real beating one day, which led us to convene a special meeting to warn him that he would be brought before the authorities the next time it happened. After that the quarreling stopped, but that's because he didn't spend much time at home anymore. He was always at his mistress' place and sometimes even spent the night there. It wasn't long before it was clear that the only solution to our unhappy couple's problems was a divorce, and that's where they were heading when I left the neighborhood in 1974. So that's one time where we failed to solve a problem that we should have been able to settle. Maybe we should have worked harder with her at the beginning. I don't know, but it just shows you that where people's lives are concerned, you don't always know what to do even if you live so closely together.

In thinking about my work as a member of the residents' committee, I would say that I enjoyed it a lot. What I lost because my former friends no longer trusted me, I gained in understanding how different people behave and how they respond to authority. I left China feeling that we try too hard to control people's lives and we keep too tight a rein on what they do after work in their homes. Here in Hong Kong, however, neighborhood life is so impersonal that I wonder if my Shanghai experience couldn't somehow be applied here. Maybe we should try to organize some type of Hong Kong residents' committee—not to snoop on people or to mobilize them politically, but just to help them keep the place clean, to take pride in their surroundings, or simply to get them to know one another. What's missing in Hong Kong is people in the neighborhood feeling part of some group. In Hong Kong almost everyone is a stranger. As a result there is dirt and chaos, and people don't care about each other. In China there's too much control and in Hong Kong there's not enough; at least that's how I feel right now after a year of living in Hong Kong.

The Apprentice

WHILE THERE ARE ONLY about 50 million workers in China's modern industrial sector (compared with some 500 million peasants doing full-time work in agriculture), this group wields a great deal of economic and ideological influence. If China is to "modernize" itself, the industrial proletariat will have to bear a large share of the load by working harder and on a higher technological level. Much of China's industrial capacity, however, needs replacement and large doses of new technology. Workers have been told repeatedly that they are the advanced class, but their efforts to win salaries commensurate with this advanced status proved relatively ineffective over the past fifteen years as China's leaders attempted to "build up the countryside," "reduce wage differentials," and "avoid emulating the mistakes made by Soviet elder brother" (excessive central-ization, high wage differentials, reliance on material incentives). During the Cultural Revolution many workers expressed their dissatisfaction with the consequences of these policies by turning to "economism" (emphasis on production and its rewards) rather than to politics. In the seventies there have even been major strikes in such cities as Zhengzhou, Hangzhou, and Wuhan. Now, in the post-Mao era, workers' salaries have finally been raised and material incentives reintroduced to encourage better productivity and to reduce worker dissatisfaction.

In this story, which describes how a young factory worker adapts to his new job, many of these issues are expressed in the reaction of workers to a 1975 campaign which sought to "restrict bourgeois rights." Most workers perceived the campaign as a threat to their incomes, and the factory leaders were put in a dilemma because they realized that production was suffering. In a classic confrontation between politics and production, factory morale declines and the campaign fails to meet its goals. The factory leadership finally makes its own compromise between the realities of production and the wishes of the ideologues. An uneasy calm finally settles over the Wuhan factory. Bullethead, the political leader of the small group, is happy because he does not have to force an unpopular policy upon his fellow workers. The Old Craftsman can again expect a higher income because his work performance is superior to anyone else's.

Today China's factories are once more stressing material incentives, based on individual work performance, rather than on collectively focused incentives. There is little talk of replacing material rewards with moral incentives (praising people instead of rewarding them with bonuses and higher income). Wage differentials have been maintained, and they may even be widening. For better or worse, in these areas the Chinese industrial system once again resembles that of Soviet elder brother.

MY UNCLE, who had connections, helped me to get assigned as an apprentice to the Wuhan No. 2 Machine Tool Factory. It was early 1974 and I was nineteen years old at the time, already a veteran of two years of life in the Hubei countryside. My parents were both dead and my elder brother had gone to work in an office in another city. It was good to get back to Wuhan, however, even if only to a low-status job in a factory. The job didn't really matter; what counted was that I was back safe and sound in the big city, with a legal right to be there and with a chance to build a decent life for myself. Being an apprentice wasn't much to start with, but I figured I could work hard and eventually get a better education, and maybe the factory might train me to be some sort of a technician. I was grateful for having been rescued from a bleak future in the countryside, and determined to use the opportunity to the best of advantage.

The factory wasn't much to look at from the outside. It was located in the grimy industrial section of the city and had its own dormitory nearby. The factory had been built in the mid-1950s and consisted of half a dozen buildings grouped together and surrounded by a large fenced-in area. The central building was two storeys high and contained the administrative offices and meeting rooms. Behind it was the cafeteria and behind it, like ducklings following their mother, a series of large one-storey hangars in which the bulk of the 1500 employees worked. A five-minute bicycle ride away was the dormitory, in which about half the workers lived. The rest lived at home with their families in various parts of the city. I was given a bed in a room with four other young workers and couldn't have been happier with my new accommodations. It only cost 40 cents a month rent and was the first decent place I'd slept in for over two years. My roommates were all in their twenties and had been working in that factory for several years. They had been apprentices once themselves, and it was clear they were going to keep an eye on me until I settled in.

The factory specialized in making precision tool parts and was divided into six workshops (*chejian*). One was a foundry in which the parts were cast in rough steel; two workshops specialized in large and in small tool parts, respectively; a fourth was responsible for notching, filing, and polishing gears for precision drills; a fifth specialized in the assembly of small parts made in the factory; and the sixth workshop did repair and construction work for the machinery and equipment of the other five. It was the smallest of all the workshops but, as it always turns out, by far the most important. Machines were always breaking down and, if it wasn't for the heroic efforts of the skilled workers in the repair workshop, the factory would never have fulfilled its plans. Time and again we would be rescued as we stood in front of our dead and dying machines, waiting for the repair squad to nurse them back to life. Much of the equipment needed major repairing, since it had been in continuous use since the mid-fifties. We were replacing as much as possible, but some of the lathes and drills were foreign-made (Soviet and British) and couldn't be changed so quickly. Sometimes it wasn't the fault of the machine but of some foolish mistake by a careless worker who wasn't paying attention and jammed up the machine. That's why at the outset they never let apprentices work on any of the machines. For a long time we had to stand around and watch, sit on a bench and do filing, or haul boxes and carts of stuff around the factory. It was several months before I finally got to use a lathe or even a

simple machine like a drill press, although I had worked in the
agricultural machinery repair shop back in the commune. I knew
a bit about machines and knew I could operate those simple
lathes and drills—we had a punch press on the commune and I
used to run it in the off-season. But the factory foremen just
smiled at me and one old skilled worker said, "This is the city, my
boy. Here we are real workers and not dumb peasants pretending
to be workers. So just watch and listen and maybe you'll learn
how to do it the right way."

After that I never mentioned my experience in the commune
repair workshop again. No, it was clear that in Wuhan the workers didn't like to be compared with "half-baked workers" out in
the villages. "We are the vanguard," the political leader of my
work group told me one day. "We are the class on which socialism
is based. We are the true builders of socialism in China. The
future of China is in our hands, and you should be proud to be a
worker."

Well, it was better than working in the commune, but I
wasn't too enthusiastic. Being an apprentice was often boring and
frustrating. For the first few months I only did menial jobs,
watched other workers use the machines, and listened to endless
lectures and speeches. I filled up boxes with heavy metal stamp-
ings and pushed them in carts from one workshop to the other;
swept floors and brought hot water to the various work groups;
went around with the repair team watching them fix broken
equipment; sat in a corner sorting out nuts and bolts and screws;
listened to the political leader of my small group (*xiao zu*) tell me
about how I could become a model worker, why I should follow
the leadership of Chairman Mao and the Party and why I should
work my hardest for socialism. Gradually I began to be trusted
with the machines—first it was the drill press, a simple machine
in which the inside of the gears was notched on four sides, like a
cross superimposed on a circle. That was easy. Then they let me
use the small lathe to work on the outside teeth of the little 3 inch
gears. Much later I was allowed to work on the big lathe, used for
the 5-6 inch gears with their complex beveled teeth. That was
when I had already been at the factory for more than a year, and
it was during the campaign against bourgeois rights in the early
spring of 1975. But more of that later.

My small group had eight workers in it including myself,

located in one corner of the big hangar-like building. Two rooms had been constructed and in them were five machines—drill presses and lathes of varying size. I was the youngest of the workers there, the only apprentice among them. Of the eight of us, three were women. One had been there three years and had just become a Grade 2 worker. She was called the Little Listener because she rarely talked to anyone but always knew what was going on. Another woman had been in the factory for twelve years. She used to be in the assembly workshop, where most of the women worked because they were better skilled at putting the small precision machinery together than men. She was a model worker and had asked to be transferred to more challenging work where she could actually make the parts. So she joined our group two years before. The third woman was in her thirties and a steady worker. Trouble was she talked incessantly, and in those small rooms her voice was more annoying than the din of the machines. We called her Auntie Chatterbox.

The oldest and most skilled worker was the Old Craftsman (the *shifu*). He was around fifty, with a steady gaze and a strong back. He didn't seem to be afraid of anything, and almost nothing bothered him except when Bullethead, the political leader, would begin to lecture us about our work habits and political ideas. We called him Bullethead because he looked like a bullet on top. He was getting bald and, when he got excited, his head shone with perspiration. Most of the time he wore his worker's hat so people wouldn't notice his bald spot. The other two workers were young men in their late twenties. One was nicknamed Earthquake Mu, because when he came to the workshop he thoroughly messed up his first job and broke one of the tools. He knew he was going to be criticized for this but couldn't find an excuse for his sloppiness. So he told the Old Craftsman that something made his hand shake and that's why he broke the tool. The Old Craftsman winked and smiled his crooked smile: "I guess it was one of our local earthquakes," he said. "They always seem to happen to clumsy young workers like you." That's how he became known as Earthquake Mu.

The other worker was about the same age as Earthquake, but a much better worker. He helped me a lot at the beginning and I grew to like him very much. He had a large, round smiling face—I guess that's why he was nicknamed Moonface by the rest of us. His character was in keeping with his peaceful expression, so he got along with everyone, even during political disputes. He had been at the factory for ten years and was a Grade 4 worker making 55 yuan plus a supplement of 5 yuan per month. It was just an average wage, but he was happy and always smiling. You could spot his round moon head from far away, and I never saw him frown, even when he thought nobody was looking his way. He was just that kind of person—pleasant and unassuming, a solid worker.

The Old Craftsman was also a solid worker, but of a different generation. He had been a worker for nearly forty years, through civil war and revolution. Nothing seemed to bother or surprise him. He liked to observe what people were saying or doing around him, suck on his pipe, and then make a comment that was usually based on some old Chinese saying. When he was teaching me how to grind gears and make the notches the correct depth, he always found the right proverb. If in his opinion I worked too slowly, he would say: "You'd better speed it up; there won't be any waves if there's no wind." If I had poorly set up the machine or made a sloppy first grinding, he would say: "Come on, now. Once you start badly you can't change things later on. Remember, if you plant melons, you'll get only melons, nothing better." When I complained about the repetitive work and that I was spending almost all my time on the simple tasks such as filing and polishing, while others were doing more complicated machine work, he would wink and say: "Little Apprentice, you're like a young colt and you know that a colt has to gallop a lot before he can become a horse."

The Old Craftsman thought that most political campaigns were a waste of time, but he usually kept his mouth shut and ignored them. I knew he disliked Bullethead, the political activist in our group. The Old Craftsman thought that Bullethead was wasting our time with endless meetings and words when we should be making gears. Whenever Bullethead began a political speech, if you sat next to him you could hear the Old Craftsman muttering such phrases as: "He never stops talking. He's living proof of the saying, 'Those who know much talk little; those who know little, talk much.'" Or he might comment that "it is deeds and not words that produce gears in this workshop." Once he openly complained that a new policy Bullethead and other acti-

vists were advocating made no sense at all. It was "like pulling up
the beans to make room for seedlings." When Bullethead objected, the Old Craftsman fixed him with a stare and added: "I'm
only agreeing with Chairman Mao. It's like the Chairman once
said, you're selling a carp in order to buy fish."

The factory leadership left the Old Craftsman alone because
he had the best possible class background. He was the son of a
poor laborer and had served China well in his forty years as a
worker. Politics wasn't his interest, and the factory leaders also
knew that many other workers in the factory felt as he did, especially the older ones who were tired of all the politics and just
wanted to do their jobs. They didn't like the younger, more politically motivated workers who, in their opinion, were less concerned with quality and hard work than with advancing their
own selfish interests. The Old Craftsman felt that way about
Bullethead and even about the Model Worker. He didn't think
much about Earthquake Mu who, in the Old Craftsman's opinion, "is as greedy and opportunistic as the others but, thank
Heaven, he's too stupid to do much about it."

The workshop had been recently converted to the system of
Five Leaderships, the *wuge dayuan* system. The Old Craftsman
was the nominal head of the workshop by virtue of his age and
skill, but Bullethead was our real leader because he was the Party
activist in charge of propaganda and political work. Moonface
was responsible for economic accounting, which meant that he
had to make sure how much we produced and get receipts for
what we finished and sent off to the other workshops or outside
the plant. The three women had typical women's jobs. The
Model Worker was in charge of materials and supplies which, as
it turned out, was a fairly responsible task. She checked off the
materials we received and made sure there were no shortages.
That was essential because there always were shortages and a box
of 100 gears could easily shrink to 98 in the shortest of journeys,
around one small corner. Workers stole materials and sneaked
back into their workshops to make spare parts for bicycles or
stoves when no one was around. The other two women were in
charge of safety and of "daily life and health." The latter was a
useless job and so we gave it to Auntie Chatterbox. She was responsible for telling us once in a while about public health campaigns and things like that. The Little Listener was responsible

for safety, but that was an equally useless job, since no one bothered about safety rules. We didn't wear goggles and we all stood too close to the machines. We smoked on the job and no one said anything. The Old Craftsman had lost part of his finger in the machines a long time ago, and he didn't care in the least about safety precautions. We did make sure, however, that we didn't have any scarves or long sleeves dangling too close to the spinning gears and lathes. Otherwise you could strangle to death in a second, and that had happened once in a neighboring workshop.

The Five Leaderships System, and the nominal leadership of the Old Craftsman, meant that only two of us didn't have any special job, myself and Earthquake Mu. I was too young and inexperienced, and Earthquake was too stupid. Anyway, he didn't seem to want to have any responsibility and was content, he said, "to let the women do those things." When we had a major meeting, Bullethead usually was in charge and the Model Worker wouldn't hesitate to make her opinion known. Moonface always smiled and said good things, and you had to watch out that Auntie Chatterbox didn't get going on some useless subject. Earthquake, the Little Listener, and I hardly said anything. When it came to production, and how to make things, we all shut up and let the Old Craftsman talk. He explained everything quickly and clearly, and we all listened to him because he was the expert among us when it came to making gears. Bullethead and the Model Worker weren't bad workers, but no one could produce better high-quality finished steel than the Old Craftsman.

Things went along pretty well the first few months and I began to fit into the workshop routine, slowly getting to work on all the machines. Factory life was alright, certainly better than the countryside. You put in your time, and then you were free to do what you wanted after work. In the countryside you could never plan your time like that. As an apprentice I got a pretty low salary, 18 yuan per month, and that would climb to only 21 yuan after three years. Even so it was enough to live on since I didn't need much clothing and my food and rent were cheap. There wasn't much else to spend money on, just a few smokes, maybe a movie, a bit of wine or beer. Every year the factory issued me a new set of work clothes, so I didn't have to wear out my own clothes and didn't have to buy new ones for a long time. Trade union membership cost me 5 cents a month, and in exchange I got coupons for free haircuts and a free bath once a week. Once a month they issued me a bar of yellow soap. There was plenty of soap left over, and a smart worker could take the extra soap home to his family and keep them in soap forever. I also got a monthly transportation allowance of 2.5 yuan in cash. It was like a wage supplement actually, since I walked to the workshop from the dormitory every day.

Now I began to think of a long-term career in precision tool-making. I wasn't doing too badly and was beginning to pull my weight in the workshop. We had been notching and polishing 5 inch gears and each person was supposed to finish four gears an hour. At first I could never get past two and, when I did, they were flawed and couldn't pass inspection the first time around. Then the Old Craftsman showed me a couple of tricks: how to stand more comfortably at the machine so as not to be too tired; how to line up the gears more quickly for notching; how to polish them so they'd pass inspection more quickly. Soon I was doing three an hour and, after a few weeks, I hit four and stayed there. You couldn't go faster because then the quality would be unacceptable. Four was the limit, the highest one could attain, and I had done it in only six months! My experience in the agricultural machinery repair workshop may have proved more useful than those city workers realized. The factory leadership took notice of my achievement, and my name was prominently displayed on the factory bulletin board. Bullethead came over especially from the other room to congratulate me on behalf of the Party. What was more important, however, was that I was told that starting in 1975 I would be assigned to take courses two days a week in the factory's July 21 School for upgrading precision metalworkers and teaching workers to become technicians. I was told that I had been selected along with twenty others, out of a hundred and fifty potential applicants. Competition for such an assignment was keen; not only was it an opportunity to advance your career, but it would get you out of two days of work for well over a year. So my life as an apprentice was working out far better than I could have hoped.

In the midst of all this, the central authorities began the campaign to "Study the Theory of the Dictatorship of the Proletariat."[1] We were expecting some kind of a national campaign after the meeting of the Fourth National Peoples Congress in

January and the publication of the new Chinese constitution at that time. We had been studying the documents of the National Peoples Congress and the new constitution in our daily study session—for example, discussing the significance of the right to strike, to put up wall posters, and to farm private plots. So the new campaign hardly was a surprise. We had already been reading editorials and articles from the February issues of the *People's Daily* when Yao Wenyuan's article, "On the Social Base of Lin Biao's Anti-Party Clique," appeared on March 1st.* Now the old "Criticize Confucius and Criticize Lin Biao" campaign was linked to the new movement. For the next few months we were kept busy by the factory leadership and by Bullethead, studying Yao's speech, reading what Marx, Engels, and Lenin had to say about the dictatorship of the proletariat, and trying to apply the new campaign in our daily work.

It wasn't that easy, for several reasons. First, the local factory leadership wasn't clear exactly how to proceed and was hoping for further instructions from Peking. To many cadres it seemed as if the new campaign was the result of yet another phase in the struggle between factions in Peking. The local cadres wanted to be sure about the durability of this new line before committing themselves to it. Second, a large part of the new campaign had to do with restricting bourgeois rights, and for factory workers this apparently meant the elimination of overtime pay, the end of the piecework method of payment for work, and the reduction of the eight-grade wage scale so that the gap between older, more experienced workers and people like myself would be reasonably

---

*I was living in Peking when the "Study the Theory of the Dictatorship of the Proletariat" campaign emerged. The Apprentice's account of the sequence of events is basically correct, although his emphasis is slightly different. Foreign residents focused on the results of the National Peoples Congress and on the new constitution, whereas it is apparent that in the Apprentice's factory what counted most was the campaign that followed these events. Once Yao's article had appeared, many workers and cadres concluded that China remained locked in a major factional struggle at the center and that Yao's radical position on restricting bourgeois rights had more than canceled out the "bourgeois concessions" (private plots, the right to strike and to put up wall posters) that had been granted in the new constitution. In retrospect, Yao's article represented one of the last attempts to paper over differences in Peking between the factions still struggling for power. The Tiananmen incident (when thousands of demonstrators, apparently mourning the death of Zhou Enlai, clashed with government troops and security forces in Peking's central square) took place only a year later. Not long after that, Yao and the rest of the Gang of Four were discredited.

reduced. Each of these was a big issue in our factory and in our daily lives, so the leadership had to figure out how best to establish a clear policy to deal with them. Almost no one in our factory, from cadres down to the lowliest apprentice, wanted the abolition of overtime, and as far as piecework was concerned, even though we had a grade wage system it seemed that we really were operating on the piecework principle. Finally, it was evident that we were expected to immerse ourselves in Marx, Engels, and Lenin. Few of us had read more than a couple of lines, and that included cadres and Party members. Now we were faced with the alarming prospect of spending long hours working through *Anti-Dühring, State and Revolution,* and so on. So, as you can imagine, at the outset the campaign in our factory moved rather slowly.

Bullethead was caught up in the critical uncertainty over the campaign. He had a weak background in Marx and Lenin, and Yao's article at the outset was difficult for him to understand, let alone to have to explain to such political simpletons as Auntie Chatterbox or Earthquake Mu. Nor did Bullethead want to argue with the Old Craftsman, who was already angry that his salary had barely changed in twelve years. The Old Craftsman wasn't interested in ideological implications; all he saw was a possible reduction in his income if overtime were abolished, or if the eight grades of wages were to be reduced by raising the lower ranks while reducing the top ranks. Moonface, as usual, just kept smiling, but surely he too, with a growing young family, must have had some sober hidden thoughts about how he could feed them if his income were reduced.

Bullethead was in a real dilemma, one that actually wasn't of his making and hadn't been solved since before the Cultural Revolution. As an ambitious young Party member he had to support the Party line that emphasized politics over production. The Cultural Revolution had been fought over that line, and who would dare oppose it? Yet in his heart Bullethead knew that not only his small group but most of the factory opposed the new campaign. I was still too young to understand the workers' silent anger, but they saw the campaign as an attack on their livelihood, if overtime and piecework were really going to be abolished and if the older workers would once again be denied the raise in pay they had been waiting for since 1966.

When it came time to discuss concrete ways in which the factory was implementing the new campaign, especially with respect to restricting bourgeois rights, Bullethead and his Party superiors had a difficult task. Most of us had figured out that we were going to lose out economically and we were a sullen bunch. At a meeting of all six workshops, the factory director anticipated our unhappiness in part by pointing out that in working to reduce the gap between the highest-paid and lowest-paid worker, "no worker in this factory will see his present salary and wage supplement reduced."[2] He emphasized that the policy was designed to "stop the rich from getting richer." He also made it clear that technicians and cadres who made more than most workers might have their inflated salaries reduced. "This is in keeping with the Party's policy of emphasizing the role of the proletariat, of the working class, while reducing the pernicious influence of bureaucrats and so-called experts." Finally he hinted that there might be a way to "maintain the moral incentive of overtime as a *collective* task." In other words, if individuals could not directly get the extra cash from their efforts on the machines after hours, then maybe a clever small group could get this cash through a collective type of accounting. As the director reminded us, "The extra cash has not been taken away from our hands. We just have to find a more acceptable way to get it into our pockets."

The result of the director's speech was a bit of optimism, although the Old Craftsman was not impressed. "Take that business about collective overtime as an example," he said to me during our lunch break. "It is easy to say that the collective will get the extra cash and then distribute it to its members. Does he really think it will work? If it hasn't worked all these years, why should it be a good thing now? Is it fair that my forty years of experience should be rewarded in the same way as what that dumb Earthquake does? What happens if Bullethead continues to spend two thirds of his time away at political meetings? Should he still get his share? Do we have to put in extra work so he can study Marx and Lenin? Seems to me it's just another stupid idea that will come to no good. Look around. You see that the older workers are angry and they won't work as hard anymore. Production is starting to go down, you'll see. When that happens, we all suffer."

Well, production did drop over the next few months and it

was a difficult time for all of us. It seemed as if we were looking over our shoulders, waiting for something big to happen. "Collective overtime" was established in April but it wasn't working out too well. In our small group, for example, the good workers like the Old Craftsman just weren't producing as much. Also there seemed to be a general letdown in the factory's internal supply system. We weren't, for one thing, getting enough turnings from the other workshop. So there were times when we had nothing to do. Machines lay idle. Bullethead used that extra time to get us to study Yao's speech and to read Marx, Engels, and Lenin. Then there was grumbling in the workshops that so much time was being spent on politics that we weren't keeping up to our production quotas. Rumors were flying around that workers in other cities had actually refused to work unless overtime and piecework were restored on an individual basis. There was talk of strikes among the railway workers, of unrest in Hangzhou and in Zhengzhou too. We knew that workers in many other Wuhan factories were getting restless. The Old Craftsman said to me one day: "They gave us the right to strike. And then they gave us something to strike for. What stupidity! When will they realize that you can't turn the machines on and off just to please the politicians in Peking?"

One rumor amused him. It concerned the reduction of wages from eight ranks downward. At first there was talk that within a year everybody would earn the same wage—I think the figure was 60 or 65 yuan. This was dismissed as preposterous. But then gossip had it that China's most famous mathematician was at Peking University right now, working on a plan to reduce the eight grades to four. He had it almost all worked out, and it meant that some of the top earners would have to give up some of their salary, while the bottom ranks would be boosted up. The four new ranks would be 45 yuan apart, ranging from 90 yuan to 45 yuan. This was a ratio of 2:1 between highest and lowest, compared with the current ratio of over 6:1 in a range from 120 yuan to 18 yuan. Of course those earning less than 45 yuan thought this was a great idea, and those who were Grade 7 or 8 earning over 90 yuan were rather upset. Yet all of us knew the idea was absurd, that some great mathematician sitting at a computer could actually find the magic solution to a problem no one had ever solved before.[3]

The criticism of the piecework system was more or less ignored, since even though we were paid in time wages, by grades, the factory depended on piecework accounting. Our small group's production targets were based on how many pieces of various gears or turnings could be produced in a given period of time. Everybody in the factory was always counting: so many pieces in, so many out, over a specified period of time. That was the system and that's why we had the Model Worker and Moonface in our own small group counting very carefully how much came in and how much went out. That was the system and who would dare change it? What the factory finally did was to abolish individual piecework as a way to get overtime business. Once we switched to collective overtime, this could be done by incorporating a former piecework task (say, a turning job that paid 10 cents per gear) into a collective task that still paid the same money per piece but with the money now being credited to the collective. This, it seemed, was ideologically acceptable, although of course production went down.

By the end of the summer we had become accustomed to the latest campaign. Like all other campaigns, it promised far more than it actually delivered. The eight-grade wage system had survived all the rumors and was still intact with its 6:1 ratio. Furthermore, factory cadres and technicians were still making 120 yuan at the top. Collective overtime had for the moment replaced the old system of individual overtime payments. Production was still calculated on a piecework system, though not on an individual basis. We all knew a little more about the dictatorship of the proletariat and what Marx, Engels, and Lenin had said about this stage of socialism. In our little group, not that much had changed, though for a while there was a great deal of tension in those two small rooms. The better workers (the Old Craftsman, Moonface, the Model Worker, and the Little Listener) seemed to form a group in opposition to Bullethead, Earthquake, and Auntie Chatterbox. I tried to stay out of it, partly because I respected the Old Craftsman and he was my friend, and also because I had been chosen to attend classes at the July 21 university program. I didn't want to jeopardize my future career by crossing Bullethead either.

The split in our group wasn't a serious one, but in a sense it was the logical result of a campaign that tried to make us choose between politics and production. You couldn't do that and still produce gears, at least not the way it turned out. Those who tried to push politics had to pay the consequences of lower production. By the fall of 1975 we were down 20 percent in our output and everybody was complaining. It had been twenty months since I had come to the factory, and I had never seen the workers' spirits so low and production so low. The workers were restless and the cadres uneasy. It looked like the campaign wasn't faring too well in our factory or in other Wuhan factories. As more and more enterprises failed to reach their planned production targets, factory directors began to relax their vigilance against bourgeois rights. Soon the factory directors were quietly allowing overtime and piecework on an individual basis, on instructions from higher authorities.

It was about this time, in late 1975, that I visited my uncle in the south, and after some thought I left China in early 1976 at the age of twenty, just when Premier Zhou died. Factory life in Hong Kong is as different from Wuhan as night from day. I wish that China might one day have factories that are as productive as those in Hong Kong. I suppose that's impossible because Hong Kong is a capitalist city, but factories are factories and gears are gears and, who knows, maybe it will happen. When it does I imagine that the Old Craftsman will puff on his pipe and turn to his machine with a wink, a crooked smile, and a fitting proverb.

Flying Kites on White Cloud Mountain

CHINA'S YOUTH has always been in the center of change in the turbulent twentieth century, whether it was the May 4th Movement of 1919, which fueled China's nationalism, or the Cultural Revolution of 1966-1968 and its attack on privilege and bureaucracy. In the 1960s millions of young people joined the Red Guards, and many earnestly thought they could have an impact on policy making, especially in making policy more responsive to mass needs. By and large, most of these "concerned youth" were eased out of politics a couple of years after the first Red Guard demonstrations, and a process of "rebureaucratization" of leadership took place, amid a series of struggles for power at the very top (the purge of Chen Boda, the downfall of Lin Biao, the struggle between the Gang of Four and the moderates). Some of China's youth became increasingly cynical as they watched these struggles for power taking place in the name of the masses, but without their participation.

In Canton a young intellectual named Li Zhengtian had become critical of many aspects of the post-Cultural Revolution system, especially the suppression of opposition opinion and the constant ideological contortions designed to justify the claims to power of those engaged in struggles at the top. Li developed his thoughts in a penetrating analysis of what was needed to change China's politics to provide more democracy within a Marxist-Leninist framework. In 1974 he and his small group, using the name Li Yizhe, began to put up posters in Canton in which they publicly criticized the authorities. One of these posters, later

257

revised, was called "On Socialist Democracy and the Legal System" and appeared in Canton in its revised form in November 1974. I saw and read parts of this poster in December of that year. Later the complete poster was published abroad.

The appearance of the Li Yizhe poster coincided with the events on White Cloud Mountain mentioned in the following story. The demonstration by over 100,000 youths, most of whom were young factory workers committed to the system and not sentdown youth demonstrating to return, was of concern to the local authorities. Li was not immediately arrested and was even permitted to debate his views with Party officials before finally being packed off to prison as a counterrevolutionary.

In early 1979 he was released from prison, a popular move since much of what he and his group said in 1974 has been incorporated into the new Party line. For example, at the 1979 National Peoples Congress, local levels were given greater control over the election of governmental representatives and a new criminal code was published, standardizing sentencing and establishing for the first time a comprehensive legal code based on principles of "socialist legality." Now a new group of young people, more daring than Li, puts up wall posters in Peking protesting current policies, criticizing Chairman Mao, and even lobbying for foreign support of their cause.

The episode on White Cloud Mountain is an interesting link between China's past and present. Chairman Mao portrayed climbing mountains as a revolutionary act, and in the context of Chinese history climbing a mountain symbolizes a major event in one's life. The second half of the annual festivals honoring ancestors usually involved going into the hills to tend their graves. Ironically, the Tiananmen incident in April 1976 in Peking (which led to the second downfall of Deng Xiaoping and those opposing the Gang of Four) occurred on Qing Ming, the first of these two burial festivals. Then, too, a large group, predominantly young people, voiced their protests against the system. Since that time significant changes have taken place producing policies that have become more responsive to the people, promising them a larger role in the ultimate formulation of policies in the future. Thus, the events on White Cloud Mountain, and their association with the Li Yizhe movement in Can-

ton, follow a traditional Chinese pattern in which youth is the
focal point of change.

THEY USED TO SAY that on the ninth day of the ninth lunar month the dragon closes his mouth and no more thunder is heard until the coming of spring. On this day you
should climb the highest hill to see the sun and walk around a bit.
Especially young people, because it brings good luck in the
coming year. In some places they used to make paper kites and let
them fly out as far as they could go. Then they cut the string and
away those kites soared, to Heaven itself. That was also a sign of
good luck. On the ninth day of the ninth month they say you can
appease the gods of fertility. Childless couples climb the highest
peak to offer food and burn incense, so that in the coming year
the spirits will reward them with a son. The main thing we do
on this day is to honor our ancestors by sweeping clean their
graves. You go to the grave sites twice a year—in early April at
Qing Ming and then on the ninth day of the ninth month. Qing
Ming is more important and the bigger of the two holidays. In the
old days if you didn't tend to your ancestors' graves on Qing
Ming, then you and your descendants would never become officials. People used to take whole roast pigs up to the grave sites;
families gathered together to honor their ancestors and sometimes the ceremony took five or more days, especially if a family
had many ancestors.

The ninth day of the ninth month wasn't as important as
Qing Ming. You went to clean up around your ancestors' graves if
you hadn't done so at Qing Ming. Usually it was to tend the grave
of someone who had died since spring. You went up into the hills
because that's where most graves are located, taking along a hoe
or shovel, some incense, food, and maybe a few sheets of paper
money. That's all. You got rid of the weeds, put dirt all around
the grave, left the food, and burned the incense and paper. In the
fall the ground is drier, and that's also the time of year when you
can rebury your ancestors' bones. The flesh is more likely to have
rotted off the bones in October because it's dry then. During the
Cultural Revolution they tried to stop us from celebrating Qing
Ming or 9-9, but that's hard to do because we have strong feelings
toward our ancestors, and people want to be respectful. So we

continued to tend the graves, on a smaller scale. Qing Ming always seemed more solemn an occasion to me than 9-9, at least where I come from. We made 9-9 a happy occasion, a time to wish for good luck and just to have a break after a hard summer's work in the fields. It was a holiday for young people. Even if you had no ancestors, you got together in a group and headed for a nearby hill to climb up for the day, bringing along some food to eat when you got to the top.

When we decided to climb to the top of White Cloud Mountain in 1974, it wasn't because we wanted to make trouble, at least that wasn't my own intention. It was October 23 (by the western calendar), a weekday. We decided to hike the 30 kilometers from the village where we had been living to the outskirts of Canton, to climb White Cloud the next day. There were fifteen of us and we had been to White Cloud before, so we weren't going to make a special protest or anything like that. We had heard rumors that "every young person in southern Guangdong was going to White Cloud Mountain this year," so we were curious. But we never expected to wind up in the middle of over 100,000 people swarming up the mountain, like ants on a rice cake. When we arrived in the outskirts of Canton the night before, we could see that something big was happening. The area was teeming with people, and they had spilled over into the nearby public parks where they were bedding down for the night. Some had come from as far away as Shaoguan in northern Guangdong, hitching rides on trucks and walking for days. There were also a lot of sent-down youth who had decided to "come back" to Canton and climb to the top of White Cloud on this day.

The next morning the crowd got thicker. As we climbed up the mountain, the paths were so choked with people that we were stepping on each other's heels at every turn. The bulk of the crowd turned out to be young factory workers from Canton. They had taken the day off from work without permission. That surprised me because young workers are privileged and rather conservative. You wouldn't expect them to do something like that. Sent-down youth had a grievance against the authorities for having been uprooted from their Canton homes, but workers were privileged. Yet on this day these young factory workers had come to White Cloud in large numbers, and there was a recklessness about them as we all climbed White Cloud together.

White Cloud is a beautiful hill, 1400 feet high. When you get to the top, the view of Canton is spectacular. You really feel, as the local saying goes, that the peak of White Cloud must touch the stars. You can see the Pearl River and the entire delta spread out far below. Along the way there are beautiful villas with sunken ponds, bamboo groves, and elegant gardens. They're reserved for high officials and their guests. We didn't go into them, or into the teahouses and pavilions at the summit. We also carefully threaded our way around the defense installations that bristle all along the sides of White Cloud. No one wanted a confrontation with the soldiers, that's for sure.

By the time we got close to the top I realized that this was going to be a very special day in our lives. The factory workers hadn't taken off from their jobs just because the sun was shining or because they wanted to honor their ancestors. They had come because they were frustrated with their young lives and wanted to express that frustration. That feeling had taken root and grown by itself, without conscious effort. You would talk with people, asking why they had come, and they replied: "We're here because we're fed up with what's going on in Canton. Young workers are unhappy. We've been waiting for the fruits of the Cultural Revolution to ripen, but all we've gathered is a sour harvest. We're fed up with campaigns and with the privileges of the cadres." One youth said: "Maybe they'll listen to the voices of the young factory workers. Aren't we supposed to be the vanguard of the revolution? If we are unhappy, then maybe the leaders should find out what's wrong and change the system." I heard the name Li Yizhe mentioned many times — that this attack on elitism was a good thing; that they were right in saying the masses had no say in their future; that the Cultural Revolution had been fought by the masses to win privileges for a few who had now barricaded themselves in power. A group of factory workers were shouting: "White Cloud Mountain is a symbol of revolution in Canton. We liberated it from the Japanese invaders and made it a symbol of revolution. It was the masses who did this and we have a right to climb it whenever we wish, to show it is ours, even by our revolutionary blood. Down with all the fancy villas and fishponds for the elite that have grown up on this revolutionary monument! Down with the authorities who suppress criticism and don't listen to people like Li Yizhe!"

I was at first taken aback by these open criticisms, although who among us had not felt that way in our hearts for a good part of our lives, especially those of us who had been sent to the countryside or who were unemployed and hiding out in Canton? Arriving at the summit of White Cloud I saw hundreds of kites flying, many of them containing hostile slogans. Some had long streamers on which were written the audacious characters: "Wishing for a successful journey to Hong Kong." Others acclaimed: "Better fifty years in Hong Kong than a hundred years here." Some kites had the Chinese characters for "good luck" and "good fortune" inscribed on them, slogans no longer allowed in China because they're a symbol of feudal times when people wished for money and wealth. Now on White Cloud Mountain one group was sending kites to Heaven so that the spirits might grant their wish to leave China. Some factory workers got angry at these youth, saying: "Leaving China is anti-Chinese. We are here to make things better in China and not to be traitors to the Motherland." Others shouted: "You don't deserve to be Chinese and you are nothing but scum and turtles' eggs!"* There were fist fights and people were hurt. Some people were yelling out such slogans as "Down with those who worship foreign things"; "Reform ourselves"; "We must make foreign things serve China and not the other way around." A few kites went up saying: "Uphold Chairman Mao's Thought" and "Finish the main tasks of Revolution." The crush of people by that time was so bad that bodies were being trampled and people were screaming in pain.

By this time, too, the police had arrived with truckloads of reinforcements, and the bad temper of the crowd began to subside. It was getting late and people began to drift down the mountain. The kites, released from their fliers' hands, had vanished into the Heavens. I headed home with my companions, a bit dazed by it all and wondering what it meant. The next day an editorial in *Nanfang ribao* angrily attacked events on White Cloud as being reactionary and an example of feudal superstitious practice. I also heard from friends in Canton that the authorities were visibly shocked by the size of the demonstration, by the open defiance of authority, and by the massive participation of young factory workers. They tried to get the names of every-

*Common expletive that means "child born out of wedlock."

body who had participated, and the Public Security Offices were kept busy for quite a while with that impossible job. The Canton Revolutionary Committee ordered all citizens to report the names of participants, but few people did so. A week or two later the Guangdong Revolutionary Committee established the Canton Militia to help maintain order and especially to keep an eye on the young people. We were sure this was a direct result of the demonstration.

In November, too, another event occurred in Canton, not officially sanctioned and directly related to what had happened on White Cloud. Li Yizhe finally put up their revised poster, "Concerning Socialist Democracy and the Legal System," on Peking Road in the middle of Canton. Perhaps they were emboldened by what had happened on 9-9 or it was just the natural sequence of events, but the poster went up and sent ripples of excitement through Canton's citizens. Maybe there was hope in the future. Maybe the ancient Chinese proverb had been wrong— the dragon had closed his mouth, but the thunder would continue to roar in the hearts and minds of China's youth.

THE EVENTS *on White Cloud Mountain occurred a half dozen years ago. Since then China has undergone a major change in leadership, attempted to reorganize its economy, introduced a measure of intellectual and political liberalization, and rehabilitated many who had been purged or defined as class enemies. Every one of the top leaders purged during the Cultural Revolution, with the exception of Liu Shaoqi, has been rehabilitated. Even Liu's crimes have been reclassified and made far less serious, and his wife Wang Guangmei has been released from prison. Following the death of Chairman Mao and the quick fall from power of his wife Jiang Qing and the rest of the Gang of Four, even the hitherto sacrosanct Thought of Chairman Mao, as well as many of his policies including the Cultural Revolution itself, has been called into question. Ideology and struggle have been downgraded, and China now emphasizes expertise over redness, material incentives over politics, consumerism and foreign capital investment over self-reliance. There is little left of the so-called Maoist line, other than the May 7 Cadres Schools (which are reportedly about to be phased out) and the policy of sending urban youths to the countryside (which cannot be easily altered for so-*

*cial and economic reasons, but which remains a nagging problem
for China's current leaders).*

    *The China that has emerged at the end of the seventies once
again must confront the problems of elitism and bureaucratism.
Policies designed to increase production through material incentives, in factory or rural team, inevitably lead to greater inequali-
ties. In stressing expertise, production, and modernization, the
new leaders are adopting the very Liuist model that Mao rejected
fifteen years earlier. After a decade of Cultural Revolution,
however, it appears that most Chinese are prepared to risk these
dangers, not only because living standards have perceptibly risen
but, as one respondent said just after the fall of the Gang of Four:
"We need time to relax. The Chinese people are tired. Too many
campaigns. Too much politics all the time. It was exhausting.
We need the rest."*

    *The Chinese Revolution seems to have changed course and is
now more comprehensible to us. China has reduced its isolation
from foreigners, both economically and in the area of culture.
Shakespeare and Coca-Cola can be found in some Peking stores;
foreign experts are busy all over China building new factories;
and large numbers of Chinese are going abroad to learn about
foreign technology and culture. The exact impact of all this ex-
posure to new techniques, values, and cultures is difficult to as-
sess, but it will be profound and extremely complex. If the magic
formula of Western technology fails to provide the solution to
China's "modernization problem," then China could again revert
to cultural isolation and antiforeignism. The problem of China's
relationship with outsiders, as noted in "Return to the Motherland" and "Oil Man," is by no means an easy one to solve. Nor
are several of the other critical problems that have beset China in
the twentieth century. China is still too large, too overpopulated,
and remains a poor peasant society trying for that "big breakthrough" to modernization. With a population over a billion and
growing by twenty million each year, with per capita grain production unchanged since the late fifties despite major improve-
ments in agriculture, one wonders if the Chinese countryside
(where 80 percent of the population lives) can ever support that
big breakthrough. In "A Foot of Mud and a Pile of Shit" we saw
how small changes are taking place in the rural areas. But in*

terms of China's developmental needs, how significant ultimately are these small gains when time is short?

Time is also short for China's youth, especially those waiting to return from exile in the countryside. In "Chairman Mao's Letter to Li" and in several other stories in this book, we are made aware of the dimensions of China's youth problem. In "Flying Kites on White Cloud Mountain" we are reminded of the very real revolutionary potential of some 500 million young people. Not only can young people criticize the authorities and put up wall posters, but they can demonstrate in large cities (as was the case several times in 1978 and 1979) against being sent down to the countryside or demand to return to their home cities. China's young people will have to be treated with extreme care by the current leadership. The youth constitute a volatile group that can easily create major problems in the future, especially if the economy remains sluggish and there are not enough jobs to go around.

Thus, in spite of what appear to be spectacular changes in the past three or four years, the same problems remain. China may have changed leaders, become more open, modified its economic system, and adopted new policies, but it is still a big, overpopulated peasant society conditioned by centuries of tradition and slow to respond to any type of change from above, no matter how dramatic it might appear from the vantage point of policymakers sitting in Peking or those of us looking at China from the outside. This is not to say that China is not changing for the better, or that life has not improved for more Chinese with each succeeding day. Rather it is a recognition of the vast dimension and slow pace of change in a unique country with special needs and problems. The stories in this book, from "Thousand-Dollar Pig" to "Flying Kites on White Cloud Mountain," are just one attempt to broaden our understanding of what China is now and what it might become in the future.

Notes

Introduction

1. See Doak Barnett, *Cadres, Bureaucracy and Political Power in China* (New York: Columbia University Press, 1967); Thomas P. Bernstein, *Up to the Mountains and Down to the Villages: The Transfer of Youth from Urban to Rural China* (New Haven: Yale University Press, 1977); Gordon A. Bennett and Ronald N. Montaperto, *Red Guard: The Political Biography of Dai Hsiao-ai* (New York: Doubleday, 1972); Gordon A. Bennett, *Huadong: The Story of a Chinese People's Commune* (Boulder: Westview, 1978); Michel Oksenberg, assorted articles in *China Quarterly* and elsewhere; William Parish and Martin King Whyte, *Village and Family in Contemporary China* (Chicago: University of Chicago Press, 1978); Richard Solomon, *Mao's Revolution and the Chinese Political Culture* (Berkeley: University of California Press, 1971); Ezra Vogel, *Canton Under Communism* (New York: Harper and Row, 1967); Lynn White, *Careers in Shanghai* (Berkeley: University of California Press, 1978); Martin King Whyte, *Small Groups and Political Rituals in China* (Berkeley: University of California Press, 1974). Other scholars are currently doing work in which refugee interviewing forms an important part—for example, Marc Blecher, John Burns, Victor Falkenheim, Deborah Davis-Friedmann, Richard Madsen, Stanley Rosen, and Susan Shirk.

Thousand-Dollar Pig

1. For more about ghosts in everyday Chinese life, see Maxine Hong Kingston, *The Woman Warrior: Memoirs of a Girlhood Among Ghosts* (New York: Vintage Press, 1975). Old China was full of ghosts: "It rolled over her and landed bodily on her chest. There it sat. It breathed airlessly, pressing her, sapping her. 'Oh no, a Sitting Ghost,' she thought" (p. 81). In new China there are always campaigns against "ghosts, freaks, and monsters," a category of criticism reserved for those who don't easily fall into "normal" political categories. America is full of ghosts because most people are white: "Taxi Ghosts, Bus

Ghosts, Police Ghosts, Fire Ghosts, Meter Reader Ghosts, Tree Trimming Ghosts, Five-and-Dime Ghosts. Once upon a time the world was so thick with ghosts I could hardly breathe; I could hardly walk, limping my way around the White Ghosts and their cars" (p 113).

2. Steamed bread (*mantou*) is commonly consumed by wheat-eating northerners, those who live north of the Yellow River. Those living south of the river traditionally eat rice as their staple food.

3. Estimates of Greater Peking's population in 1971 range from six to seven million and, of the inner city, from three to four million. In 1978 the estimates were eight and five million, respectively. It is apparent that the policy of deconcentration of urban population has not been successful in Peking. Statistics suggest that urban growth has been contained in Shanghai.

4. Some May 7 Schools have a "permanent staff" of peasants who live on the grounds in special housing and are employed by the school to teach the cadres agricultural methods. This was the case in the famous Nanniwan May 7 School located near Yanan, which I visited in 1975.

A Foot of Mud and a Pile of Shit

1. See Jack Chen, *A Year in Upper Felicity: Life in a Chinese Village During the Cultural Revolution* (New York: Macmillan, 1973), pp. 64-65, for a list of the twenty-four Chinese solar terms, nine nine-day cold weather periods, three ten-day hot weather periods, and lunar New Years.

2. In 1971 Lin Biao's introduction to the little Red Book was removed, following his downfall. By 1975, the Red Book no longer was a significant factor in daily life and politics. In 1978, Chinese openly criticized overzealous application of the Red Book's maxims during the Cultural Revolution.

3. Peasants like to drink a small glass of *bai jiu* (grain alcohol) in the evening, when eating supper or while talking with friends. The alcohol is available in the local brigade store. Peasants do not normally make their own alcoholic drinks (unlike their Soviet rural counterparts, who are famous for making *samogon*, or moonshine). Chinese peasants rarely drink to become inebriated, again in contrast with Soviet peasants.

Chairman Mao's Letter to Li

1. Another respondent referred at length to the document but thought it was No. 40. For a good study of this type of central Party document, see Kenneth Leiberthal, with James Tong and Yeung Sai-cheung, *Central Documents and Politburo Politics in China* (Ann Arbor: University of Michigan Center for Chinese Studies, 1978).

2. Refers to the Chinese term for the sending down of youth: *shangshan xiaxiang*, which is translated as "up to the mountains (hills) and down to the villages."

3. The figures are omitted in Li's letter because the respondent didn't remember them, but he thought that Li's son was receiving less than 30 catties of staple food per month, or about a pound of grain per day. This is not enough to sustain an able-bodied young person engaged in farm labor.

4. The campaign to "Let a Hundred Flowers Bloom and Let a Hundred

Schools of Thought Contend" was encouraged by Chairman Mao in 1957. He indicated that it was time to air criticisms of the system, including the Party itself. As a result many people, principally intellectuals, came forth and widely criticized the Party for being arrogant and incompetent. The criticism got out of hand and was soon defined by the Party as "reactionary." Those who had thought they were "planting fragrant flowers of criticism" were now accused of being "poisonous weeds of socialism." See "The One Whose Girlfriend Turned Him In" for more details.

5. "Youth farms" were set up, both within existing communes and as separate agricultural units. See T. Bernstein's excellent study *Up to the Mountains and Down to the Villages: The Transfer of Youth from Urban to Rural China* (New Haven: Yale University Press, 1977), p. 68.

6. It is unclear how widely this policy was applied outside Guangdong or even inside the province.

7. Other respondents later indicated it wasn't that easy to get one's 100 yuan from the commune. "They didn't want to give it to us in one lump sum because they knew we'd take it and run." Yet other youths reported that some communes were happy when they fled back to the city because they were an economic burden on the commune. Commune officials viewed the 100 yuan payment by the provincial authorities as a subsidy from the province to the commune, with the added bonus that it might encourage the youths to leave for the city.

8. In the old days gifts of money were given to children by the older generation and were placed in red envelopes called *hong bao*. This practice has been discouraged by the Communists because it perpetuates "feudal-capitalist consciousness," the worship of wealth and money.

9. These campaigns are discussed more fully in "The Apprentice" and briefly in "Little Brother's Wedding." The "Criticize Confucius, Criticize Lin Biao" campaign appeared to have been a creative attempt to restore political balance after the downfall of Lin. The "Study the Theory of the Dictatorship of the Proletariat" campaign was one of the last attempts by so-called moderates and radicals to settle their differences before the events of 1976, when their fragile alliance was ended with the toppling of the Gang of Four.

Oil Man

1. Yumen is located in Gansu province, northeast of Qaidamu Basin. Yanchang is in Shaanxi province, north of Xian. Both fields produce a relatively negligible amount of oil today.

2. The purpose of "tracking" is to find and map out the exact location of the oil-bearing deposits under the well.

3. For an analysis of China's position as a world oil producer, see *China: Oil Production Prospects,* Central Intelligence Agency, June 1977; Chu-Yuan Cheng, *China's Petroleum Industry: Output Growth and Export Potential* (New York: Praeger, 1976); Wolfgang Bartke, *Oil in the People's Republic of China* (London: C. Hurst & Co., 1977).

4. Lei Feng was China's greatest revolutionary model in the early 1960s. He excelled at helping other people and in setting a good example for the

masses. Wang Jie became a hero in 1965 and the *Diary of Wang Chieh* was read by millions during the Cultural Revolution. For more on Wang Jinxi, China's "iron man," see *New China News Agency,* January 7, 1973.

5. They also began to substitute Chinese-made catalysts for foreign imports that had formerly been used in oil refining.

6. Yu Qiuli is now a member of the Politburo and one of China's top economic planners, a vice-premier in the State Council. He reappeared at the end of 1974. Kang Shien became Minister of Petroleum and later vice-premier in the State Council (March 1978). By the end of 1978, both men had moved to the top rank of government.

7. For an opposite view, see *New China News Agency,* September 29, 1966: "Heroes of the No. 32,111 drilling team said that in the unprecedented, great proletarian cultural revolution, all revolutionary workers and staff members of the team held high the great red banner of Mao Zedong's Thought, kept on with the study and application of Chairman Mao's works in a living way, imprinted Chairman Mao's teachings on their minds, made them part of their blood and carried them out in action. Mao Zedong's Thought is the soul of their lives . . . Just the Thought of Chairman Mao fills us with immense strength. Our results should be attributed to the Party and to Chairman Mao. In the future we will raise the great red banner of Mao Zedong's Thought still higher, promote more fully the revolutionization of our ideology, and win still greater successes in production."

Down with Stinking Intellectuals

1. The *dazibao,* or "big character poster," is a traditional form of Chinese communication and protest. During the Cultural Revolution, however, the *dazibao* acquired new significance because of the scale and intensity of poster-writing activity. Nie Yuanzi symbolically started the Cultural Revolution at Peking University in 1966 when she put up her big character poster denouncing the authorities, and Mao approved her actions. In the fall of 1978, in the post-Mao succession period, big character posters again became prominent, this time on Peking's short-lived Xidan Democracy Wall, advocating more participation in politics by the masses. See also "Kill the Chickens To Scare the Monkeys" for a description of how posters were composed and used during the Cultural Revolution.

2. For more on Ye Fei and his wife, see "Eating Pears in Fuzhou."

3. An old Chinese saying used to criticize people who pretend to be something that is beyond their capacities or position in life.

4. See William Hinton, *Hundred Day War: The Cultural Revolution at Tsinghua University* (New York: Monthly Review, 1972), and Victor Nee, *The Cultural Revolution at Peking University* (New York: Monthly Review, 1969), for accounts of what happened at two other universities at the time.

5. The reference is to Chairman Mao's famous essay, "The Foolish Old Man Who Moved Mountains," in which an old man kept chipping away at a mountain until he and his descendants had removed it. In a similar fashion, argued Mao, China will eventually remove the two mountains of feudalism and imperialism that have oppressed it in the past.

6. In 1975 at Peking University and at Zhongshan University in Canton, officials told me that 20 percent were now being admitted from the urban population, although they insisted that many of these were the sons and daughters of factory workers. In general, universities in China in 1975 were much less "radicalized" than in 1971, at least comparing my visits of 1971 and 1975. The rhetoric was more subdued; the student body again contained a significant number of the sons and daughters of intellectuals and urban cadres; more time was being spent on study and less on "practice."

Little Brother's Wedding

1. Parish and Whyte in their outstanding study of village life in Guangdong province observe: "Dowries are now of negligible value in rural Guangdong; they seem invariably to be much smaller than the cash and gifts delivered to the bride's family by the groom's family" (p. 183). William L. Parish and Martin King Whyte, *Village and Family in Contemporary China* (Chicago: University of Chicago Press, 1978).

Return to the Motherland

1. The term as used by the Chinese means "those who are from outside the country," from outside China. It also is translated as "foreigners," and it is amusing to hear Chinese in North America referring to North Americans as *waiguoren*, foreigners in their own country.

2. Foreigners living in China today can sell their belongings to state purchasing stations, which sometimes pay a surprisingly good price for these used items.

3. Fang Fang, who was deputy director of the Overseas Chinese Affairs Commission, was criticized in May 1967 and did not reappear. Liao Chengzhi, however, is today a member of the Central Committee of the Party and still the head of the Sino-Japanese Friendship Association. He disappeared in July 1967 but reappeared in 1971.

4. The Four Olds were: old ideas, old culture, old customs, old habits.

5. Before the Cultural Revolution, overseas Chinese were encouraged to return to China and even live in their own houses. The state built fancy housing with deluxe facilities in special areas of big cities like Canton, Fuzhou, and Peking. Wealthy overseas Chinese could invest their money in these houses, which they could later pass on to their children. This practice was stopped during the Cultural Revolution. In 1979 it has apparently been resumed.

6. Fang Fang had been third secretary of the Guangdong Provincial Party Committee but in 1952 his power was reduced. In 1953 he confessed to a number of alleged crimes against the masses and disappeared from view (Ezra Vogel, *Canton Under Communism* [New York: Harper and Row, 1971]). Fang reappeared a year later in Peking as an official in the Overseas Chinese Affairs Commission, where he remained until 1967.

7. Zhou Enlai was premier of China; Chen Boda was a leading member of the Cultural Revolution at the time; Kang Sheng was a key supporter of the Cultural Revolution Group and a long-time crony of Mao's; Xie Fuzhi, like Kang Sheng, had built a career in internal police work. Xie was on the rise,

about to take over the entire Peking Party apparatus. He was wounded and died quite unexpectedly in the midst of the Cultural Revolution.

8. Qiao at one time was China's foreign minister and cut a dashing figure in foreign capitals in the mid-seventies. But he was too closely associated with the Gang of Four and in 1977 lost his high position.

9. For more details, see Melvin Gurtov, "The Foreign Ministry and Foreign Affairs in the Chinese Cultural Revolution," in T. Robinson, ed., *The Cultural Revolution in China* (Berkeley: University of California Press, 1971).

10. In the Soviet Union I drank kumiss (fermented mare's milk) in Kazakh-stan, near the Chinese border. The milk is buried in the ground in a leather bag for seven days, and each day some fresh milk is added. The taste is sour and refreshing.

11. Ulanfu managed to survive these criticisms and was rehabilitated in 1973.

Eating Pears in Fuzhou

1. The honey wagons are animal-drawn vehicles which collect the night soil each morning and take their precious burden of human excrement to suburban communes for use as fertilizer. You can tell a honey wagon by its aroma and the oozing trail it often leaves behind.

2. Urban housing rents in China are low, about 5-7 percent of monthly wages, depending on size, location, and type of housing. Average urban housing space, based on approximately eighty respondents' replies, is about 3-3.5 square meters a person, that is, a space about the size of a large western bed.

3. In cities like Peking and Shanghai, large high-rise housing develop-ments were constructed in the fifties. In Shanghai especially, they were called "urban villages," suggesting that the warmth and neighborliness of village life could be duplicated in a city environment.

4. On the scarcity of lighter-flints, see "A Man Who Knew China," *China News Analysis*, May 21, 1971. Flints are in scarce supply throughout China, are easy to smuggle, and are a major item of speculation on the black market.

5. The free market is where certain goods, almost all of them agricultural products, may be sold by individuals at prices above the prices in state stores. The backdoor is a complex arrangement of various favors and trade-offs de-signed to get privileges and goods in short supply. The black market is a system whereby scarce or illegal items (flints, gold, hard currency) are bought or ex-changed for profit to the speculators involved.

6. For the full text see "Chairman Mao's Letter to Li."

7. For more on wage grades and wages see "The Apprentice."

8. Those who are housed and fed in the factories or organizations where they work get their food coupons distributed through their work unit. In gen-eral, some part of every individual's coupons, housing, and other allowances is allocated through the work unit.

9. The five red elements were drawn from the so-called revolutionary classes — workers, poor and lower-middle peasants, revolutionary martyrs, revolutionary cadres, and soldiers. See Gordon Bennett and Ronald Montaperto, *Red Guard* (New York: Doubleday, 1972), p. 3.

10. In the purge of the Gang of Four it was argued that Jiang Qing, Wang

Hongwen, Zhang Chunqiao, and Yao Wenyuan were trying to build a power base for themselves in the urban militia, especially in Shanghai, and they tried to disengage this militia from the army's control. My respondent did not perceive the urban militia as a tool used by one side in an ongoing power struggle, but as one more facet of the whole system of control.

11. This is especially true for top Party officials who get the same privileges as their Soviet counterparts—see Hedrick Smith, *The Russians* (New York: Quadrangle, 1976). For more on privileges, see "Flying Kites on White Cloud Mountain."

12. See "The One Whose Girlfriend Turned Him In" for more on this campaign.

13. For details see Michael Y.M. Kau, ed., *The Lin Piao Affair* (White Plains, N.Y.: International Arts and Sciences Press, 1975).

14. For example, the Fujian military commander, Han Xianqu, was abruptly sent off to Lanzhou, thousands of kilometers away, to head that military region.

Frontier Town

1. The Yellow River periodically bursts its dikes and floods large sections of the surrounding plains, killing hundreds of thousands of peasants and leaving millions homeless; hence the reference to "China's sorrow." Under the Communists these natural disasters have been significantly reduced in scale by massive dike building and irrigation work.

2. This is borne out by my personal observations during a week-long visit to the Xi Shuang Banna Autonomous Region in southern Yunnan province in 1975. It was stated that the native Tai minority group received a number of benefits normally denied to Han Chinese, such as exemption from military service; exemption from birth control regulations; quick advancement for minority group cadres who can speak some Mandarin.

3. Because he only arrived in 1968, the narrator may have missed some of the struggles. Other accounts suggest there were bloody battles in Sichuan, Xinjiang, Tibet, and Lanzhou (all in the surrounding area) in 1967. Here is an account by a British businessman who was in Lanzhou in 1967: "There must have been 50 vehicles. They trundled along about 20 feet apart at about five miles an hour. Across the radiator of each truck was lashed a human being. Some trucks had two people roped across. All had been spreadeagled diagonally and tied down with wire or rope . . . the mob surround[ed] a man and plunged their crude javelins and spears into him, until he fell in a twisting heap of spurting blood." George Watt, *China Spy* (London: Johnson, 1972), pp. 110, 119.

4. Recent maps do not show a railroad running from Xining to Gonghe, although the narator was certain that it was under construction by 1973.

Kill the Chickens To Scare the Monkeys

1. There are twenty-four grades for cadres and a rank of Grade 10 or 11 is very high, replete with many privileges, such as cars, housing, and access to special resorts and travel benefits. See "Ranks and Wages," *China News Analysis*, July 12, 1974, for more details.

2. When a target was struggled he was criticized at special meetings and

asked to make a self-criticism and ultimately a confession of his crimes. This could go on for a long time and could be rather violent. If the target were "set aside," that meant he was not permitted to work (although he continued to receive his full salary while he was being struggled and reeducated).

3. Schools like these were nicknamed Precious Pagoda Schools. The government is now reopening them to accelerate old-style education once more.

4. *Reference News* is more widely distributed than *Reference Research Materials*. The latter is a compendium of all documents pertaining to domestic news. The repondent estimated that ten million Chinese read *Reference News,* but less than a million read *Reference Research Materials.*

5. There are still a few servants in China for such situations as Big Gossip's or to help high-ranking cadres. Sometimes the servant may be a poor relation in need of work and a place to sleep.

6. Most of Peking closed down by 9:00 or 10:00. So staying up to midnight dancing (a foreign *and* bourgeois custom) was considered rather unusual. All dancing for Chinese was abolished by the Cultural Revolution. Now a few Chinese in the capital once again have been permitted to indulge in limited public dancing, even with foreigners.

7. The bride was carried on a sedan chair to her new home. This practice was criticized by the Communists for its feudal nature and was abolished in the mid-sixties. (See "Little Brother's Wedding.")

8. Lei Feng, the great hero of the early sixties, was a model citizen, and all Chinese were encouraged to emulate him.

9. Peng Zhen, the head of the Peking Party organization, was purged in mid-1966, the first major casualty of the Cultural Revolution. Now he has been rehabilitated and is a member of the Politburo.

10. For a good description of a poster campaign in a similar bureau, see Jack Chen, *Inside the Cultural Revolution* (New York: Macmillan, 1975), p. 231: "Poetic exaggeration was a recognized essential of such style. No revisionist ever 'made a mistake,' he 'committed crimes that tower to high heaven.' The reactionaries' actions were invariably *kwang hung lan tsa*[sic], wild and indiscriminate, or some other classical four-character adjective, and in the face of the rebels' criticism they were always *ken teh yao shih, pa teh yao min* [sic] — filled with hatred to the death and fearful for their very existence. It was *de rigueur* for Mao's name to be prefixed with 'great.' It was nothing to 'boil' an unpopular minister 'in oil,' or to 'smash his dog's head.' These last two phrases went out of fashion when it was reported that foreigners were taking them at face value."

11. These texts of Chairman Mao have been published in *Mao Zedong sixiang wansui* (Long Live Mao Zedong Thought; Taipei, 1969), and in Stuart Schram, ed., *Mao Tse-tung Unrehearsed, Talks and Letters: 1956-1971* (Toronto: Penguin, 1974). Chinese readily admit these texts are genuine: they complain only that it wasn't proper to circulate Mao's speeches before they had been "properly edited."

12. Chen appears to argue that 516 was a conspiracy centered on Lin Biao. That was the explanation before the fall of the Gang of Four, but now one can accuse the Gang of Four of being the so-called masterminds behind the affair, the real "monkeys."

The One Whose Girlfriend Turned Him In

1. Hakka or kejia (guest) people were latecomers to Guangdong. They came from the center of China and had a history of being involved in revolutionary ventures (the leader of the Taiping Rebellion was a Hakka) and in traveling abroad to seek a better future. Hakka women wear distinctive clothing and are known as hard workers. Mei county is well known as an area where Hakka have settled.

2. I visited that area in 1975 with a Canadian forestry delegation and saw large areas near the Soviet border that had been reforested in the fifties. In trying to restore the forests, the Chinese have done a good job under difficult circumstances.

3. Gao Gang, Party head in the northeast, and Rao Shushi, another top Party official, were purged in 1955 for attempting to set up "independent kingdoms" of their own in opposition to Chairman Mao.

4. He had to wear a hat that said "rightist" on it during demonstrations and mass meetings when he was the target. Symbolically he had been given a rightist hat because his political status had permanently changed. Even when he didn't physically wear the hat, everyone knew it was there.

5. See Bao Ruo Wang, *Prisoner of Mao* (New York: Coward, McCann, 1973), for a similar description of how a target finally confesses.

6. At that time a large number of rightists were rehabilitated—their hats were taken off.

7. Interestingly enough, a similar plan for the reconstruction of Moscow was put forth by Soviet city planners in the 1920s (and later rejected).

8. The conflict between Mao and Peng Zhen has been traced back to the mid-nineteen-fifties by Roderick MacFarquhar in *The Origins of the Cultural Revolution* (New York: Columbia University Press, 1974).

9. See "Kill the Chickens To Scare the Monkeys," and also Jack Chen, *Inside the Cultural Revolution* (New York: Macmillan, 1975), pp. 310-311.

10. In the late 1960s there was a half-hearted attempt to send large numbers of people out of Peking permanently. According to what I heard from refugee accounts and from direct discussion with Chinese cadres in Peking in 1974-75, this policy was never applied on a large scale and was soon allowed to lapse.

11. An allusion to the view held by most respondents, northerners or southerners, that southern cadres can be more easily corrupted than northern.

12. Bao, *Prisoner of Mao*, p. 279.

Rubber Man

1. For more on Yingde, see "The One Who Loved Dog Meat"; *Political Imprisonment in the Peoples Republic of China* (London: Amnesty International, 1978); and Lai Ying, with Edward Behr and Sydney Liu, *The Thirty Sixth Way* (New York: Doubleday, 1969).

2. For more on the problems of sent-down youth see "Chairman Mao's Letter to Li" and "Flying Kites on White Cloud Mountain"; also T. Bernstein, *Up to the Mountains and Down to the Villages* (New Haven: Yale University Press, 1977).

3. State farms, in which peasants are employees, drawing fixed daily wages from the state, are a small percentage of China's rural economy, estimated at 5-10 percent. State farms are more likely to be established where there is one large staple crop (such as rubber) in a strategic area (such as Hainan, Xinjiang, or Heilongjiang) with a high proportion of sent-down youth and de-mobilized soldiers. Often the army, especially on the northwestern frontier, es-tablishes a military farm and then, when it is functioning successfully, turns it over to the state. In Xinjiang, according to Chen, 35 percent of agricultural production comes from state farms. Jack Chen, *The Sinkiang Story* (New York: Macmillan, 1977), pp. 291, 322-325.

4. Dreyer points out that the Communists used Li hostility to the Chinese Nationalists to help them win Hainan, by establishing a base area there in the forties, helping to weaken the KMT's position on the island. Basic Li hos-tility to the Han was, however, transferred to the Communists by the mid-fifties. June Dreyer, *China's Forty Millions* (Cambridge: Harvard University Press, 1977), pp. 77-79.

5. During interviews, respondents were always asked if they wished re-freshments, and we would break for a drink from time to time. Coca-Cola was the most popular choice and, ironically, the Chinese have just reached agree-ment with the Coca-Cola company to begin limited distribution of this drink in China in 1979.

The One Who Loved Dog Meat

1. The dog is cut up, browned with black beans, mushrooms, and a bit of ginger, and then stewed for three-to-four hours. Many respondents insist that dog meat tastes better than pork, beef, or chicken and that the aroma is deli-cious. North American dogs are not considered tasty, probably because of their diet. Some respondents who are dog-meat connoisseurs report that North American dogs have a fishy smell and a gamey taste.

2. One of the dominant factions during the Cultural Revolution. In "Kill the Chickens To Scare the Monkeys," it is identified with the ultraleftists. See also Jack Chen, *Inside the Cultural Revolution* (New York: Macmillan, 1975), for more on factions, and Hung Yung Lee, *The Politics of the Chinese Cultural Revolution: A Case Study* (Berkeley: University of California Press, 1978).

3. For a vivid portrayal of the meaning of classification, determining one's class status and the effect of this decision, see William Hinton, *Fanshen* (New York: Monthly Review, 1966).

4. For a recent description of conditions in one Peking prison see *New York Times,* May 7, 1979, which contains excerpts from a March 3 Peking poster describing the Qin Cheng prison, in which many high-ranking political prisoners, including Liu Shaoqi's wife, Wang Guangmei, lived for many years.

5. The same point is made by Bao Ruo Wang in *Prisoner of Mao* (New York: Coward, McCann, 1973). He notes that eventually prison officials cut back their rations because if the Chinese people were going hungry, then pris-oners should not be allowed to eat well. That was when they gave the prisoners sawdust and other ersatz materials.

6. This is also what Bao did. He became a model prisoner and eventually was put in charge of political study and struggle sessions.

7. The seven categories of bad or black people were: landlords; rich peasants; capitalists; rightists; bad elements (criminals, petty thieves, former convicts, unemployed loafers); snakes, ghosts, and monsters; and capitalist roaders. See Bennett and Montaperto, *Red Guard* (New York: Doubleday, 1972), p. 3.

8. Doctors were an initial target in the Cultural Revolution and were criticized by Mao for staying in the cities, catering to urban elites when they should have been working with the rural masses. Large numbers of urban doctors were sent down to labor in the countryside. At the same time, the concept of the "barefoot doctor" was developed, as part of a campaign to build up the image of the army. Its paramedical corps became an example of selfless dedication to the masses, of simplifying the delivery of medical services, and of rediscovering traditional Chinese herbs and treatment, such as acupuncture. I visited several army-run rural medical facilities in 1971 when this campaign was at its peak. By 1975 it had significantly declined, and now urban doctors again are in a favorable position.

9. Infanticide is described by Maxine Hong Kingston, *The Woman Warrior* (New York: Vintage Press, 1975), p. 101. The midwife brought along a box of ashes to suffocate an unwanted female baby by pressing its head down in the ashes after birth.

My Neighborhood

1. Black youth are sent-down youth who have returned to the city illegally from the countryside. They do not have a residence permit and cannot legally obtain ration cards or a job. The residents' committees and neighborhood organizations periodically try to round them up and send them back to the countryside because they are a significant source of urban crime and disaffection, but many are resourceful and manage to stay in the cities indefinitely. See Bernstein, *Up to the Mountains and Down to the Villages*, pp. 77, 93, 264, 267-269; also, "Flying Kites on White Cloud Mountain."

2. A phrase used widely in China to denote the equality of women: "man holds up half the sky and woman the other half."

The Apprentice

1. See Yao Wenyuan, "On the Social Base of Lin Biao's Anti-Party Clique," *Renmin ribao*, March 1, 1975; Zhou Si, "The Historical Duty of the Dictatorship of the Proletariat," *Renmin ribao*, February 9, 1975; Liang Xiao, "It Is Necessary To Enforce the Dictatorship of the Proletariat over the Bourgeoisie," *Renmin ribao*, February 10, 1975; and Zhang Chunqiao, "Report on the Revision of the Constitution," *Peking Review*, January 24, 1975.

2. In 1971 when receiving a delegation of Canadian educators at Peking University, Chou Peiyuan, the vice-chairman of the university and one of China's leading academicians, said that the question of reducing wage differentials was on the immediate agenda in China: "Frankly, many people are

impatiently awaiting this decision. During the Cultural Revolution many Red Guards were very concerned about the big differences in wages in our society. So our foreign friends today have correctly focused upon a problem of national concern that is still not resolved. We hope that you will be patient with us—give us more time to finish our revolution. Perhaps you should return in a year or two." B. Michael Frolic, "A Visit to Peking University: What the Cultural Revolution Was All About," *New York Times Magazine,* October 24, 1971.

3. I heard this rumor while living in Peking in 1975. It apparently was taken seriously by a number of Chinese, including officials of the Ministry of Foreign Affairs, one of whom said: "Computers can do almost anything. Maybe they can solve this question for us."